Time Added On

Time Added On

The Autobiography

GEORGE HOOK

PENGUIN
IRELAND

PENGUIN IRELAND

Published by the Penguin Group
Penguin Ireland, 25 St Stephen's Green, Dublin 2, Ireland
(a division of Penguin Books Ltd)
Penguin Books Ltd, 80 Strand, London WC2R ORL, England
Penguin Group (USA) Inc., 375 Hudson Street, New York, New York 10014, USA
Penguin Group (Australia), 250 Camberwell Road,
Camberwell, Victoria 3124, Australia (a division of Pearson Australia Group Pty Ltd)
Penguin Group (Canada), 90 Eglinton Avenue East, Suite 700, Toronto, Ontario, Canada M4P 2Y3
(a division of Pearson Penguin Canada Inc.)
Penguin Books India Pvt Ltd, 11 Community Centre,
Panchsheel Park, New Delhi – 110 017, India
Penguin Group (NZ), cnr Airborne and Rosedale Roads, Albany,
Auckland 1310, New Zealand (a division of Pearson New Zealand Ltd)
Penguin Books (South Africa) (Pty) Ltd, 24 Sturdee Avenue,
Rosebank, Johannesburg 2196, South Africa

Penguin Books Ltd, Registered Offices: 80 Strand, London WC2R ORL, England

www.penguin.com

First published 2005
1

Copyright © George Hook, 2005

The moral right of the author has been asserted

Set in 12/14.75 pt Monotype Bembo
Typeset by Rowland Phototypesetting Ltd, Bury St Edmunds, Suffolk
Printed in Great Britain by Clays Ltd, St Ives plc

A CIP catalogue record for this book is available from the British Library

ISBN-13 978-1-844-88076-8
ISBN-10 1-844-88076-1

This book is dedicated to the memory of my parents George and Anne Hook, who passed on to me the love of language that eventually was the tool that saved my life. I hope they would have been proud of their son.

This story honours Michael Pender and G. K. Boyd, who did not live to see that their confidence in me was not misplaced.

This journey could not have been completed without the late Jack Ormond, a special doctor who never let time or trouble get in the way of his efforts to help me.

Contents

Prologue

The man staring back at you from the cover of this book is a living, breathing miracle.

I don't mean that in a conceited way. He's a miracle because he's alive to tell his story, not from a padded cell in some home for the deranged, not sat under a pile of rags on O'Connell Bridge, but from a house in Foxrock that's paid for, doing a job he was born to do, with a wife and three children who still love him, for all his terrible failings.

That's what makes him a miracle.

The odd thing about this book is that you may already know the ending; the mystery is all in the beginning and the middle.

Everybody knows my media persona — big, gregarious and outspoken — but not many people know me. I was 57 when I got my first big break in television. My life — my *real* life — is like an iceberg. What you see of me is what you know of me, yet there's far more going on beneath the surface.

The story between these covers shouldn't have had a happy ending. The final chapter should have had me behind bars. Or slumped against a wall beside an ATM somewhere, clutching a polystyrene cup. Or dead. The end might have come on a bleak winter's night when I decided to throw myself off Dun Laoghaire pier, convinced as I was that life was never going to get any better than the hell I was living.

For most of my adult years I worked in catering. I was a bad caterer, perhaps the world's worst. I was the man who knocked back McDonald's, certain that the Big Mac was only a flash in the pan. But worse than being a bad businessman, I was also a bad husband, a bad father, a bad son and a bad friend.

I had none of the vices classically associated with lives that go off the rails. I didn't drink, smoke or gamble. If my wife, Ingrid, was left at home on her own every night, it wasn't because I was spending my nights in the flesh-pots of the city. My mistake was choosing the wrong career and, having done so, not knowing when to bail out.

I hated my life. For twenty-five years, I would wake up in the early hours of the morning and say a quiet prayer: 'Dearest Jesus, please don't let the sun come up.'

If it did, it meant I had to face another day riding the cusp of bankruptcy and breakdown. If stress really does shorten your life, then I don't know how I'm alive today. I don't know how I didn't keel over or go round the twist. I always figured, though, when my life eventually ended, it would be a photo finish between my heart and my head.

The main focus of my day, just about every day, was lodging enough money into the bank to meet the cheques I'd written forty-eight hours earlier. I had until three o'clock every day to find the money and I'd wake up in the middle of the night in sheer terror of that deadline. I was like a drug addict who gets up in the morning knowing he needs three or four hundred euros that day, just to keep the horrors at bay. I was like that, except my habit was cheques.

In the movie *Catch Me If You Can* Leonardo DiCaprio plays a conman trying to stay one step ahead of the FBI. There's a scene where a federal agent calls to his home and tells his mother that her boy has got himself into big financial trouble. His mother takes out her chequebook and says she'll cover it.

'How much are we talking about?' she asks.

'One million dollars,' the agent says.

I must have been one of the few people who watched that film and thought, *Yeah, I can understand that.*

It's funny, but most of the mail that passes through my door these days comes from banks and other financial institutions. They write to tell me I've been cleared for loans and overdrafts that I never asked for in the first place. Credit-card companies, who once pursued me across two continents, are pushing their plastic on me.

As far as they're concerned, they're writing to George Hook, the television and radio personality. Sometimes, for fun, I phone them up and ask, 'Do your records not go back more than ten years?'

My friend Kyran McLaughlin used to say he didn't know anyone who got himself into as many fixes as I did, but, equally, anyone who could get himself out of them like I did. I was a Harry Houdini; I should have died so many times. I survived in business as long as I did because people put their jobs on the line for me. I had friends who were bank managers and they lent me money when head office told them not to allow me even to cross the threshold.

The other thing that saved me was rugby, both as a means of escape and as a means of establishing friendships and contacts, the sumps I drew from when times were hard. They gave me money when the kindest thing to do would have been to say no.

For most of my adulthood I continued doing something I was extremely bad at, before a series of random events changed the entire trajectory of my life.

My all-time hero is Winston Churchill. I've had a lifelong fascination with him, ever since my father, on the long walks we used to take after Sunday-morning Mass, told me about El-Alamein and the D-Day landings. In a recent poll by the BBC, he was voted the greatest Briton of all time; greater than Charles Darwin, greater than William Shakespeare, greater than Isaac Newton, Richard III, King Alfred and Isambard Kingdom Brunel.

What appeals to me most about him now, in my later years, is that – oddly, for a man who lived until he was 90 – there were only six years of his life in which he could lay claim to greatness. The rest of it was distinguished only by mediocrity and failure. In that, I see some small reflection of myself. I finally found what I was born to do eight years shy of retirement. It doesn't matter that I'm going to enjoy it for only a few years. The point is that this talent I had, which I subjugated inside myself for all those years, finally found expression.

But what I'm proudest of is that I saved my marriage. I discovered very late in life that love is a give-and-take thing. I was

3

just a taker. I spent most of my married life thinking only about myself.

Ingrid and I were married in 1969, but I'm in year eight of my marriage, not year thirty-six. The first twenty-eight don't count. What makes us such an extraordinary couple is that we're enjoying our marriage back-to-front. Only in the last few years are we enjoying the love that most married couples take for granted at the beginning.

In painting this portrait of myself, I've chosen not to accentuate my good features, or de-emphasize my bad ones. This is a picture of me in all my unexpurgated ugliness. If you manage to get through these pages without thinking at some point, *What a shit!*, then I haven't been hard enough on myself. If, by the time you get to the back cover, I'm still the same person you thought you knew, then it's not the book I wanted it to be.

If this account of my life has a theme at all, it's redemption. I hope people will read it and think, *Yeah, that guy was an unbelievable bastard, but he came good. He's got a wife and three kids who adore him. He's reinvented himself, personally, professionally and financially. He's alive and knows it.*

That's the miracle.

1. Growing up in Jew Town

When you're a child, and you're poor, and you live next to other people who are poor, you never think of yourself as being poor. I lived in a two-up, two-down house with no bathroom or indoor toilet. I also went to the Presentation Brothers' College, the most prestigious fee-paying school in Cork. But I hardly noticed that I was different from the other boys at school. In fact, I never really thought of myself as poor until I was about 12. And when I did, the realization hit me like a pail of cold water.

Pres never produced yearbooks like other schools, but 1954 was different: an extension had been added to the school and, to mark it as a special year, Brother Alphonso, the school principal, decided to publish an annual, the centrepiece of which would be a photograph captioned 'The Sons of Pres Men'. Every kid in the school whose father had gone to Pres went out into the schoolyard. I persuaded myself that my father had gone to Pres too. He hadn't. He had attended St Joseph's National School, a hundred yards up the Mardyke, though it might as well have been a hundred miles for what it meant in social terms. But I still turned up in the yard to have my picture taken.

We were marched out on to the rugby pitch at the back of the school. As he was lining us up, Alphonso noticed me and as delicately as he could he tried to tell me that I couldn't be in the photograph because my father wasn't a Pres boy.

'He was,' I said.

'George,' he said, 'I'm very sorry, but your father didn't go to this school.'

I was distraught. Even now, fifty years later, I can remember how I wanted to be the son of a Pres man. Sobbing uncontrollably, I pleaded with Alphonso. 'He did, he did, he did.'

Seeing my distress, Alphonso did the Christian thing and decided that one boy wouldn't make much difference to the photograph. But now the dilemma was where to put me. I was so poorly dressed that he didn't want me standing somewhere prominent. As we were assigned our places for the picture, and one by one the better-dressed boys were put in position, I was gripped by a quiet terror of being the last one picked. And I was: a battalion of boys was whittled down until I was standing alone next to the principal. Finally, I was placed in the least conspicuous spot. My gratitude to Alphonso was tempered by the knowledge that we both knew I should not be there.

Our simple terraced house was number 79 Albert Road, close enough to the Cork City Hall for me to hear the tolling of the clock every night before I fell asleep. Cork had a small but thriving Jewish community, most of whom had settled in Albert Road earlier in the century. Many had migrated from Limerick, where the local Redemptorist Fathers had stirred up anti-Semitism. Thus in the patois of the city Albert Road was called 'Jew Town', although when I was growing up there, only three Jewish families remained. They were wonderful characters who added colour to so many of my childhood memories. Fanny Goldwater, the rabbi's widow, was a good friend of my mother's; they seemed to spend half their waking lives on one another's doorsteps, chatting. Mrs Levin's husband was a travelling salesman. On Friday nights I'd call to her house and she'd give me a penny for lighting her gas because she couldn't do it herself: observant Jews have this rule about not igniting a flame on the Sabbath.

My old man led a sort of double life. By day he was a clerk for CIÉ. By night he was a drummer in a dance band, Billy Brown and His Music. He'd work at the train station in Cork from 9.15 a.m. until 5.15 p.m., come home and grab a couple of hours' sleep, then at 8 p.m. he'd be gone again to provide the percussion in the local dance halls. As the band's fame grew, they went on the road and did gigs all over the south, which meant my father oftentimes rarely slept between finishing the day job, driving to a dance and then getting home. The extra money was absolutely vital to the Hook family budget.

I have an early memory of kissing him goodnight and watching him disappear up Albert Road with a bass drum on one hip, a side drum on the other and a pair of hi-hat cymbals under his arm. I would stand at the door until he turned the corner at the top of the street. How he managed to walk the couple of miles under that load, to the Arcadia, Cork's finest dance hall of the era, I will never know.

The Musicians' Union was strong in those days. If a British band wanted to play in Ireland, they had to use a local band as the support, so often I would wake up in the morning and find my autograph book full of the signatures of Joe Loss, Geraldo, Oscar Rabin and others of the British big bands.

The old man was regarded as a white- rather than blue-collar worker, though the only real distinction in his case was that he was paid fortnightly rather than weekly. Every two weeks he'd come home with cash in a brown envelope, which he would pass, unopened, to my mother. She would hand him back money for cigarettes and beer and, with what was left, she would perform the most impossible financial gymnastics to make sure there was food on the table, that my school fees were paid and that we had a holiday by the sea every summer.

My parents were married for seven and a half years before I came along, which was a long time in those days, so they had more freedom than most couples their age. They were keen cyclists and owned a tandem that they used to take all over the country. They'd cycle to Galway or to Dublin or to the Meeting of the Waters in Wicklow, putting their heads down at night in guest houses and B&Bs. When I arrived, they hitched a sidecar to the tandem and took me with them. One day my father was cycling up Carr's Hill, near Douglas, with me in the sidecar – no mean feat, propelling a bicycle made for three on his own. Whatever happened, he had to swerve to avoid a truck; the bike tipped over

7

and he was thrown over the handlebars into a ditch. A few seconds later this little bundle – six-month-old George – dropped into his lap.

This was to be the first of many childhood brushes with death. I cannot have been much more than four when I fell into the Lough, the large pond in Cork's southern suburbs. Then, as now, people strolled around its perimeter, fed the ducks or watched the coarse anglers fishing for carp. Somehow I toppled into the water. Luckily my mother happened to be looking in the right direction and saw me falling in. She ran over, reached in and pulled me out. Although I can't have been in the water for more than ten or fifteen seconds, that moment of terror – lying on my back with the foaming water overhead, thrashing about, unable to breathe – is my earliest memory in life.

When I was seven I was in the kitchen in Albert Road with my cousin, Shaun Pugh, who was a couple of years older than me. We were playing barbers. He had a scissors and he was pretending to cut my hair. Then he said he was going to cut it for real and we started tussling. I pushed him away, fell, and somehow ended up with the scissors buried between two of my ribs. An ambulance was called and it cleared the road to the South Infirmary. The scissors had missed all the vital organs. The doctor pulled it out, a nurse cleaned me up and I lived to face another day.

I was born on 19 May 1941. I was a breech baby. My mother had an incredibly difficult birth, in labour for thirty-six hours and lucky to survive, but I entered the world big and healthy. Obstetrics were poor enough in those days and it was clear there weren't going to be any more babies.

When I was five, she took me on a trip to England. We got the Innisfallen ferry from Cork to Fishguard and then the train to London. We ended up at this big old grey building. I remember standing facing a little boy wearing round, National Health glasses. He was called Arthur and he was four.

Arthur was screaming blue murder. My mother asked the nun what was wrong with him and she said he was pining for his sister.

'But don't worry,' she said. 'You're getting a lovely little boy. We'll find a home for his sister.'

But my mother couldn't have taken him and left his sister behind. So suddenly I was standing facing a little girl. Her name was Frances and she was three.

In one fell swoop, I had a brother and a sister.

My mother phoned my old man from a public phone box to tell him she was coming home with not one, but two, new children. There was an interminable wait before the operator managed to connect her with the CIÉ office in Cork to break the news. How he took it, I don't know. I presume he just accepted it. My mother ruled the roost.

Frances and Arthur were her sister Molly's children. Nobody talked much about Auntie Molly and all I ever knew about her was that one day, having survived the Blitz, she collapsed in a London street and no longer knew her own name. She was declared mentally ill and placed in a hospital.

What happened next is shrouded in mystery, but seems to have been a classic case of an Irish reaction to illegitimacy. Molly had three children – Anne, Arthur and Frances – who had been born out of wedlock. Nobody appeared to know who was the father. Years later I found out that her brother Tommy was aware of her situation and, given the kind of person he was, must have been giving her money to help support them. Maybe my mother knew too; our family was so adept at keeping secrets it wouldn't surprise me. To this day I do not know the truth. Molly, Tommy and finally my mother went to their graves without telling all.

Social work was still a thing of the future. Would-be adoptive parents did not go through a vetting process, they just came and collected. And that's what happened to Molly's children. My mother took Arthur and Frances out of the convent orphanage and her youngest sister, Elizabeth – 'Lil' – who lived in Harrow, took Anne.

My mother never figured out what to tell Arthur and Frances about how they came to be adopted. There was no advice in those days. There was no counselling. Illegitimacy was an awful disgrace even for those peripherally involved. Though my mother was happy to adopt her sister's children, she felt it was best never to reveal the skeleton in the closet: that they had been born out of wedlock. She didn't know how to talk about something so shameful. So Arthur and Frances were kept in the dark about where they'd come from and it was never spoken about.

Because my mother never talked about it, it's hard even at this remove to separate truth from fiction. Arthur and Frances grew up apparently unaware that Auntie Lil's Anne was their sister and Cousin Anne didn't seem to know that her Auntie Anne's Arthur and Frances were her brother and sister. On top of that, the three of us always knew we weren't really siblings, even though, after a lot of trying – you could even call it brainwashing – my mother finally got them to call her 'Mammy'. If anybody asked me if I had brothers or sisters, I always said I had one brother and one sister. (I still do.) Until I had left school, and my Uncle Tommy had a few drinks on him one night and revealed their origins, I didn't really know exactly who they were. They were just Arthur and Frances. You didn't ask questions in those days. It was a shambles, it was unfair and it hurt everybody involved. Tragically, Anne never recovered from the trauma and ultimately ended her own life, leaving a husband and children.

Eventually Molly was brought home to Cork and placed in St Patrick's mental asylum. Every Wednesday and Sunday afternoon my mother and grandmother, who lived behind us in number 88, would set off, laden down with bags, to catch the two buses to the asylum. Mental healthcare then was not far advanced from the horrors of Bedlam. The heavy bags contained food to supplement the meagre hospital diet and often the two women would see the ravages that experimental electric-shock treatment had wrought on Molly. The toll was particularly heavy on my grandmother, by then widowed and into her seventies. Neither Arthur and Frances nor I made any connection between the visits to the hospital and their existence.

★

After Arthur and Frances arrived in Albert Road, my parents, a couple that couldn't really afford one child, found themselves with three. The financial pressure may well have been at the root of the difficulties of the following years. My mother – a woman of unbelievable generosity, who, if there were Victoria Crosses awarded for running a home, would have a row of ribbons strung across her chest – made a complete and utter mess of things.

If there was a textbook somewhere on how to handle an adoption badly, my mother was following it step by step and to the letter. The fundamental problem was that she couldn't escape the fact that I was her child and Frances and Arthur were not. I can still see her trying to divide a cake into three pieces and unable to do it fairly. Invariably the biggest slice would end up on my plate. I think she felt that she had robbed me of my birthright in some way. But instead of making it up to me, she was going the right way about fostering resentment in my brother and sister. How they felt, I do not know. We didn't talk. Seeing how close my children are, I realize now how much better it could have been for all of us if circumstances had been different.

Though there were five mouths to feed instead of three we were never deprived. I was an adult before I ever had turkey for Christmas dinner. (My first real Christmas dinner was in 1968, when, following my engagement to Ingrid, I spent the holiday with her family in Manchester.) Similarly, I never had a Christmas tree until after I was married. Yet my memories are of amazing mornings after the arrival of Santa when books filled the pillowcase that doubled as a Christmas stocking. In the early years it was *Rupert the Bear* and then the great boys' annuals like *Champion* and *Tiger*. We got everything that other kids got because of the unbelievable financial plate-spinning act my mother was engaged in. A choice between a turkey and presents for the children was no choice at all.

She'd squirrel away money throughout the year and in the summer we would rent a cottage just thirty yards from the beach at Crosshaven, thirteen miles from Cork City. Not for two weeks, or a month, but for the entire summer, from the end of May when the schools broke up until the beginning of September, when we went back.

Crosshaven was where the well heeled – the 'Merchant Princes' – holidayed in Cork. How my mother afforded it I have no idea. But I have many wondrous memories of endless, sun-kissed summers learning to swim, climbing rocks and fishing for mackerel.

The boys and girls I played with were the children of the well-to-do, usually in the legal or medical world. There was Jackie O'Sullivan, whose father was a doctor, and Angela Powell, whose father was Mickey Powell, the Sheriff of Cork and later an Irish rugby selector. Angela gave me my first kiss and is now a Mother Superior in a convent; I hope the two aren't connected.

My mother never went to Mass on Sundays, which was unusual for a Catholic woman in the Ireland of the 1940s and 1950s. I never really thought about it but I suspect it was because she didn't have anything good to wear. My mother had one dress during my entire childhood. Whatever money she had passed straight through her hands to put us through school – myself and Arthur to Pres, and Frances to the Presentation South Convent. Whatever errors she made, we all had an equal educational chance.

I went to church with my old man. Every Sunday without fail we went to 11.15 Mass at St Augustine's on Washington Street. Through those mornings we formed the most incredibly strong father–son bond. An hour spent talking to my dad was a remarkable education. His proudest boast was that he'd never read a work of fiction in his life. But this man who left school at fourteen devoured books about war and politics and biographies of the great world leaders. There was nothing he didn't seem to know.

We'd arrive just about on time for Mass and the back of the church would be thick with men who stood for the duration. My father had this belief that the Mass was the Offertory, the Consecration and the Priest's Communion. We'd leave the church the very minute the Communion was over and he'd take me for a long walk. He didn't buy me an ice cream or a bar of chocolate like other dads because he didn't have a dime. Instead, we'd just walk and talk and he taught me all about the world. He taught me the facts of life – the actual mechanics involved in the act of intercourse. He taught me about a thing called colour prejudice. He taught me about different political systems, about democracy, communism, Nazism.

Remember, the Second World War wasn't that long over. Even the Easter Rising was still in the relatively recent past. There were truckloads of people walking around the streets in Cork who'd been involved in the War of Independence and were still fighting the Civil War in their heads. It was all just yesterday. He explained Republican politics to me but not because he had any IRA sympathies. His own father was English and married an O'Sullivan from Cork, so he settled in Ireland after retirement from the British Army at the end of the First World War. My old man was the first man in the family for about four generations not to serve in the British Army. He had been born blind and did not see for some years, but he was also a teenage Irishman during the War of Independence and that, rather than poor eyesight, made following in his father's footsteps unlikely.

Although he was a committed trade unionist, he didn't have any strong political leanings, unlike my mother, who was a rabid Fine Gael supporter. To her Michael Collins belonged up there in the communion of saints. Beal na Bláth was still recent enough to be considered current affairs rather than history and she was convinced that Éamon de Valera masterminded the assassination. It was always brought up around election time, when she would tell the old man exactly how to vote. He did as he was told, though he didn't care one way or the other. He just had an insatiable appetite for knowledge and he wanted me to have it too.

We were probably the only poor family in Cork to own a copy of Hitler's *Mein Kampf*. Nobody knew for sure at the time whether Hitler was dead or not. Half of the world believed he escaped the bunker in Berlin while the Russians were hammering on the doors of the chancellery upstairs. Remember, Rudolph Hess, Albert Speer and the Führer's successor, Admiral Dönitz, were still in Spandau Prison in Berlin. Dad talked of the birth of fascism, the landings at Normandy and the post-war annexation of eastern Europe by Russia. It was terribly exciting. The fighting was over but the war was still very much alive in people's imaginations, especially mine.

He encouraged debate. He always taught me to think for myself and loved it when I argued back. I remember once, when I was 11 or 12, walking down Washington Street debating whether Churchill should have gone to Yalta or not. And I prefaced some point or other with the words, 'I'm sorry, but . . .' and the old man just stopped walking. 'Don't ever say you're sorry in an argument, son. Hold your ground.'

My father was a fine public speaker. Being involved with the Irish Transport and Salaried Staff Union, he was asked to make presentations from time to time and he would deliver great speeches, which he wrote himself. I only heard him once, when I was working in his old office at Ceannt station during school holidays and he spoke at someone's retirement party. He had impressive opening and closing lines, a technique that I copy to this day.

He also wrote poetry. Doggerel we'd call it nowadays, I suppose, but they were still wonderful. When I joined the Boy Scouts he bought me my first-ever sheath knife. Fixed to it was a little card with a few lines from him that I can still recall: 'And if you fail in word or trust, the blade will dull, the edge will rust.'

I really thought my father was the bee's knees and I idolized him. The great Hollywood star of the forties was Clark Gable and he was a dead ringer for him, from the lantern jaw to the slicked back pompadour to the trim pencil moustache. He had a free CIÉ travel pass and we got public transport everywhere. I loved getting on the bus with him. As you walked down the centre aisle, you'd hear this whispering behind you: 'Isn't he just like Clark Gable?' I'll never forget the thrill of that.

The awful sadness of this story is that while I was bonding with my father in this wonderful way, I neither knew nor cared where Arthur and Frances were or what they were doing. There was I having my eyes opened to the world by my father — following

14

Marco Polo to the court of Kublai Khan or in a trench in the Somme in the First World War or jumping out of an aeroplane over Arnhem – and I never wondered where my brother and sister were. They are merely peripheral figures in my childhood memories, and I'm saddened and shamed by that.

They'll find it painful, I'm sure, to read these pages, but I can't put my life into proper context unless I explain this enormous event that had such a formative influence on my life. I've asked myself the hard questions and still do to this day. I recently read Dirk Bogarde's autobiography, in which he said that as a child he felt terrible resentment towards his little brother when he arrived. Similarly, I've asked myself whether, having been an only child for the first five years of my life, I was on some level jealous of Arthur and Frances for diverting my parents' attention from me. I don't think that was the case. Like most only children, I wanted siblings; sadly, when it happened it was not in the fairy-tale way I had imagined, and that was compounded by my mother's ham-fisted handling of the adoption. We had nothing in common except that we lived under the same roof. I can't recall a happy memory or even a single important conversation we shared. I just wish it could have been different and even now, late and all as it is, that I could make up for the hurt they were caused.

For all her faults, my mother was the rock of the house, a woman of the most extraordinary courage and nerve. She had this ability to tough out seemingly impossible situations, which is interesting in the context of my later life as a failed businessman. When I came to play metaphorical poker with bankers and clients, staking my family's future on one busted flush after the next, I discovered that I had absorbed so many lessons from my mother.

The Second World War ended in 1945 but the rationing that had become a way of life in Britain continued until well into the 1950s. My mother used to take me on covert missions over to Lil in Harrow with a couple of suitcases full of foodstuffs that she'd somehow smuggle on and off the ferry. In those days, there were customs points at both Cork and Fishguard. There were no red, green and blue channels, either. Every single case was opened and then marked with a piece of chalk to show it had been checked. She always seemed to know someone on the Irish side of the water who was prepared to turn a blind eye.

Once we got to Wales, money changed hands and we would be taken round the back of a hangar by a bent porter who'd help lift our contraband off the boat. Failing that she'd stomp right up to the customs desk, slam the cases down and say, 'I have nothing in here,' just daring them to open them, and they'd let her through. What she was doing could probably have landed her in jail, but she was never caught. To this day if you ask my cousin Shaun about his auntie Anne, he'll come straight back to you with the words 'Chipolata sausages'.

Most of my childhood memories of my mother involve demonstrations of her great physical strength. One day I was wading with a few friends in a stream that ran through the playing fields near the Ford factory – locally known as 'the boggy road'. I stood on a broken bottle and ended up with this deep, crescent-shaped cut in the sole of my foot. It bled quite heavily. Someone raced home to get my mother, who promptly threw me over her shoulder and carried me – I remember looking down at her long, purposeful strides – all the way to the South Infirmary.

It wasn't long after that that she took me by the hand and marched me up to Presentation College. I was terrified. I remember cowering behind her skirts and looking up at a bald-headed giant of a man in a habit who turned out to be Brother Alphonso. When I think about that day I think of her as a lioness with her cub. 'I want my son to have the best education in Cork,' she said. Alphonso replied that this was not a problem. 'But I can't pay you,' she added. 'That might well be a problem,' said the brother. 'What I mean is, I can't pay you up front,' she said. 'My husband gets paid every fortnight and what I'll do is I'll pay you in instalments over the year.'

And that's how I ended up at the most prestigious boys' school in Cork. On the never-never!

★

My memories of Cork are all in technicolour. In the forties and fifties the two biggest employers in the city were Ford and Dunlop, where, if you were fortunate enough to get in, you had a job for life. They were big paternalistic organizations in which brothers worked alongside brothers and fathers worked alongside sons. Every evening at five o'clock the factories would disgorge thousands and thousands of men and they'd move as one towards the city centre. It was an astonishing sight, like Pamplona during the Running of the Bulls.

Men who didn't get into Ford or Dunlop invariably had to emigrate. During the war years conscription had robbed Britain of most of its male workforce and the British industrial machine was crying out for bodies to go and work in its factories. Tens of thousands emigrated from Cork – or sort of emigrated. What always fascinated me was the blind optimism of the male émigrés that working in England was only a temporary inconvenience. They left their families in Cork and always assumed they were coming back, even if they were away twenty years, sending money back in remittances and returning home twice a year to wives and children who recognized them less and less as time wore on. Cork was one of the few cities in the world where adults had a mating season: children were conceived on one of two occasions in the year – during the big August holiday or at Christmas.

My mother's family was typical of many in Cork. Her four siblings, Tommy, Eddie, Lil and Molly White, all emigrated to England. The women went to London, where Lil married Dick, a major in Montgomery's 8th Army. The men went to Coventry, where they survived the fire-bombing of the city. Tommy was a bachelor but Eddie had a wife and family back home in Gurranabraher – or 'Grawn', as it was known.

These aunts and uncles played a big part in my early life. Tommy and Eddie would return home in the summer and at Christmas, packed like battery hens among the thousands on the Innisfallen. We'd stand on the dockside and watch the ferry arrive with all these men hanging off it. They'd usually been up all night drinking, celebrating this all-too-brief hiatus from the daily grind of the assembly line or labouring in the building trade.

A large number of Irish were employed at the giant Ford plant in Dagenham and the ease with which they picked up the Essex accent was a source of amusement. They became known as the Dagenham Yanks, first because they spoke English in this strange dialect and second because they all dressed identically in blue double-breasted suits with twenty-four-inch trouser bottoms and brown shoes. But by the standards of an industrially backward Cork they were millionaires.

I'll never forget the thrill of excitement I got in my stomach waiting for the boat to dock. Eddie always had his family there waiting for him and Tommy had me, Arthur and Frances, who were his three surrogate children for the holidays. If it was Christmas week he'd take us to visit every Santa in Cork. We'd see Santa in Cash's and Santa in Roches. We'd visit Santa's igloo and Santa's cave and Santa's waterhole. It was the rare occasion when we three were like real brothers and sister.

To me, Tommy was a giant: six feet tall with shoulders you could land a plane on. I'd watch from the front door and see him walking up Albert Road with his big, broad chest and his hands dug deep into the pockets of his long black coat that looked like a cloak, and I'd think, *I wish I had shoulders like that.*

He was as hard as tempered steel. He worked on the Underground, digging the tunnel for some new line or other using a drill that you held in your hands. When it came to St Patrick's Day the foremen would say to him, 'Paddy, you're working tomorrow.' Tommy's reply was, 'No, I'm fucking not.'

Eddie, by contrast, was a big softie. He was a great storyteller, too. I'd sit and listen to him describe this living purgatory that the Irish navvies endured in these English cities they were helping to rebuild after the Blitz. He'd talk about these hard, unfeeling landladies who'd order the men out of the house at 7 a.m. and wouldn't allow them back in again until bedtime. They wouldn't even cook them a meal. So life for the Irish in cities like Coventry and London and Manchester began to centre more and more around pubs. It was standing around in pubs comparing atrocity stories about these women who were making their lives hell that turned them into such renowned drunkards.

Eddie was a huge boxing fan. In Cork, he'd trained amateur fighters at Sunnyside Boxing Club and while he was working in Leamington Spa in Warwickshire, he started helping out at the local gym. One young kid of mixed race who had a couple of nuclear warheads for fists especially impressed him. His father was an immigrant from British Guyana and reputedly the first black man ever to live in Leamington Spa. He died young, leaving his wife to raise their five children. Eddie found himself training the youngest of them and, though he never claimed for himself any great part in the story, the boy grew up to be Randolph Turpin, who beat the great Sugar Ray Robinson and was middleweight champion of the world for all of sixty-four days.

L140,358/384.54092.

I never felt deprived as a child, not in the sense that I was ever hungry. It was just that every now and then, there was something – like the school photograph – to remind you that you were poor.

Every classroom in Pres had an altar. Every day in May and June – May being the month of Mary, June the month of Jesus – each boy took it in turns to bring in a flower for the altar. We didn't have a garden at home. We had a yard and you couldn't pick a daisy from it. So I was the only boy in the class who didn't bring in a flower.

Aware as I was that I was different from the rest of the boys, I can't think of a single time when it was thrown in my face.

My years at Pres were an incredible experience that changed my entire perception of the world. The quality of teaching there was extraordinary. The standard textbook for mathematics in Irish schools for donkey's years was written by two teachers from Pres – Freddie Holland and 'Fox' Madden. Freddie was a magnificent teacher. Fifty years on, I can still recall his lessons. Nowadays, every article I write in the *Sunday Independent* is a testament to Madden, who taught me English. I had Danny Duggan for Latin. He was in his sixties but he'd come through the classroom door like a tornado. Under Danny the magic of Latin opened up for me like the dawn. I remember him telling us, 'Latin will teach you English. Remember, *obitus* is death. That's where we get "obituary" notices from,' and I thought, if I listen to this guy I'm going to be able to do crossword puzzles, though for some reason I never could and still can't. But I did learn about Caesar's Gallic Wars and Virgil and other things I've never forgotten. There are people of my era in Cork who still talk about Danny with tears in their eyes.

Then there was Denis 'Pug' Buckley for Irish. He used to walk at an angle of forty-five degrees, carrying a big pile of copybooks on top of his case, the fascination for us being how the copybooks never fell off. 'Irish is the simplest language in the world,' he'd say. 'And why is it so simple? Irish has just ten irregular verbs, unlike German which has hundreds.' And because of him, we didn't fear the language like so many schoolchildren do today. We even learnt Aesop's Fables in Irish. He told us that it's not a difficult language once you're grammatically correct, then made a big show of holding up the grammar book that was on the course and dumping it in the bin. 'I'll give it to you,' he said. And he did. He had his own grammar book and he dictated bits to us every day until we had it all down. It says something that I still had it thirty years later and I taught my eldest daughter Irish using Pug's Irish grammar notebook. (I'm not sure when I found the time because a model father who oversaw homework, I was not.)

At a very early age my father took me to the lending library on the South Mall. I remember he was very keen for me to read *Gulliver's Travels* by Jonathan Swift. I picked it up, took it home and told him that I loved it. The truth is I never got further than the first few pages because I thought it was rubbish. But soon we were making weekly visits to the library and I discovered books that I did like. In successive weeks, I found *Just William* by Richmal Crompton and Frank Richards' Billy Bunter books about public schools in England that were a world removed from my own experiences but no less thrilling.

Our visits to the library became another ritual in my relationship with my old man. We'd step in through the door, I'd turn left into the children's section, he'd turn right into the adult section and we'd eventually meet up again, maybe an hour later, at the far end of the building. For that hour I slipped into my own private little world.

I consumed books. I discovered G. A. Henty and his books about the Spanish Main. I even read *The Silent Three at St Kitt's*, which was about a public school for girls, the kind that never existed except in fiction.

My old man would select my mother's books. My memories of my mother being out of doors are few and far between, for reasons I've explained, so in her spare time she read – fiction. She read Georgette Heyer, a great romantic novelist who wrote stories set in Georgian England. The old man would have chosen Edmund Hillary's *How I Conquered Everest*, or the Juan Manuel Fangio story, or a biography of Winston Churchill.

Most of our reading was done in the kitchen in Albert Road, a small, poky room. (The other room downstairs was a living room, which contained the few fancy bits of furniture we had, but we rarely ever went in there.) My mother would sit over the two-bar electric fire and my father would be sunk deep into the comfortable armchair on the other side of it. I'd be sat at the table. The room would be silent save for the rustle of the turning pages. My brother and sister did not read with the same appetite and I have to confess I am vague as to what they did. Homework, I suppose, or playing in the street, which was a safe activity then.

Through reading, my vocabulary grew and grew. I discovered new words with the wonder of a baby exploring new textures and found ways to engineer them into my English compositions in school. When I was in second year, I used the word 'topography' in an essay with a proud sense that I was the only 13-year-old in Cork who knew what it meant. I remember the teacher telling me to stand up in front of the class and asking me, 'Where did you get that?' like I'd stolen it.

As well as books and comics, I loved movies. When I was small my father took me to the pictures. Invariably, it was to see one of the great musicals. I can remember the first time I saw *Singin' in the Rain*. It was in the Lee Cinema in Cork and I could nearly tell you the seat. I remember the curtain going up and the old man turning to me and saying, 'Here he comes – this is Kelly.' He always thought that Gene Kelly was better than Fred Astaire. I think I only ever went to the cinema with my mother about three times.

From age 12 onwards, on a Wednesday and a Saturday afternoon, me and my mates would go on our own, usually to see westerns – Hopalong Cassidy, Lash La Rue, the hard-fighting, fast-riding Durango Kid, and all kinds of cowboys massacring Indians in the most gloriously un-PC way. I was blown away by *Northwest Passage*, in which Spencer Tracy and Robert Young played two Colonial rangers who wiped out an entire Indian village. It was great stuff. Cinema had the added attraction that you might enjoy a quiet smoke in the back row or get to hold a girl's hand.

The other thing I loved was radio. Early on we were one of only three or four families on Albert Road with a radio and the neighbours would call in just to listen to it. It was a great big black contraption that was powered by a wet battery, like a car battery, that you had to have recharged every couple of weeks.

A sensitive hand could tune it to the BBC and with one ear clamped to the speaker you could hear *The Goon Show* and *Hancock's Half Hour*. Even now, fifty years on, when I'm broadcasting I have all these phantoms from my childhood in my head. I can hear Raymond Glendenning, the boxing commentator. I remember getting up at five o'clock in the morning to hear Joe Louis beat Billy Conn and Jersey Joe Walcott and then later, in his ill-starred comeback, lose to Ezzard Charles and Rocky Marciano. I got up in the middle of the night to hear Rex Alston and Harold Abrahams, the hero of *Chariots of Fire*, do the commentary on Ronnie Delany's victory in the 1,500 metres at the Melbourne Olympics in 1956. The following Sunday, the actor Joe Lynch, who had a show called *Living with Lynch*, sang a song that he'd written about the race.

On short wave you could pick up jazz from the likes of Benny Goodman, the Dorseys, Nat 'King' Cole, Dean Martin and Frank

Sinatra on AFN – Armed Forces Network – that broadcast for the American GIs based in Germany after the war. Another twist of the dial led you to Radio Moscow. I remember listening to it one night when I was 12 and hearing the news that Stalin had died of a brain haemorrhage. I always felt a slight frisson of danger listening to Radio Moscow. In Holy Catholic Ireland of the fifties it was like receiving messages from Satan himself and I felt like I might have to tell the priest in confession. Like most things that require absolution, it was very exciting.

I also loved Radio Luxemburg. Every night at fifteen minutes to seven, it was, 'Dan Dare, Pilot of the Future – Sponsored by Horlicks, the drink that puts you to sleep.' For fifteen minutes I was glued to it. Every episode had a cliff-hanging ending, followed by an advertisement: 'To get your Dan Dare, Pilot of the Future, Interplanetary Badge, send a postal order together with three lids from a jar of Horlicks to this address.' I had my mother buying Horlicks, which I detested. When she wasn't around, I'd tip it down the sink and tell her we needed a new jar, just to avail myself of all the special offers.

The John Arlotts and the Raymond Glendennings and the Rex Alstons were as much my heroes as the players they brought to life on the radio. My father took me to the Mardyke, the UCC sports ground, every second Sunday to watch Cork Athletic in the League of Ireland soccer. On Saturdays we went to the same ground to watch Munster play in the inter-provincial championship. I would sit in the old wooden stand holding a stick with an empty Heinz baked beans can on the end of it performing my own private commentary. It caused great mirth, especially when on a supposed radio commentary I pointed flamboyantly to the left and announced that 'the wind is blowing that way'. That should have sown the seeds of an interest in a career in broadcasting, but I never had the confidence to write to Radio Éireann – boys from Jew Town did not appear on the radio.

I was very catholic in my sporting tastes, trying everything and anything. I played cricket well enough to represent Munster

Schools. I also played handball, Gaelic football, hurling and soccer, and I especially loved track and field.

In 1954, when I was 14, Roger Bannister broke the four-minute barrier for the mile. Two years later Ronnie Delany won the 1,500 metres in Melbourne. Middle-distance running grabbed my imagination in a big way. For most of my time in secondary school, I sat beside a boy called Mick O'Connell, who was equally fanatical about it. We'd cock a deaf ear to our lessons to debate where Bannister and Delany and John Landy stood in relation to each other. At one point I could name every winner of an Olympic track and field medal from 1896 onwards. In some cases, like the 1,500 final in Melbourne, I could give you all twelve finalists and the order they finished in. We joined Hilltown Athletic Club, where Mick became a very good miler and I discovered that my talents were best used on the infield, throwing the discus and putting the shot. I represented Pres at both, but cricket was my real love. (Our neglect of our lessons clearly did Mick no harm; he went on to set up the Irish arm of Adidas.)

Rugby didn't make much of an impression on me. My father took me to Lansdowne Road twice, both times to watch Ireland against Wales. I remember seeing the great Jackie Kyle drop a goal with his left foot. But I can't claim any great lifelong love affair with rugby. Perhaps the reason for my passion for it now is that I never went through the burn-out experienced by a lot of successful schools players.

The reason I'd no great love for rugby then was that I wasn't very good at it. The only real assets I had as a rugby player were good hand–eye co-ordination, honed from years of playing cricket, and two feet I could kick with, my payback for endless hours spent practising against the wall of the ESB station near our house. Every night I was out there, like a metronome, kicking ball after ball – left foot, right foot, left foot, right foot – and I became that rarest of things, a forward who could kick with both feet.

What I lacked was confidence. I was a physical coward. Having a vivid imagination was my undoing. There's a scene in the Joseph Conrad novel, *Lord Jim*, where pirates capture the book's eponymous hero. The pirate leader, Brown, tells him that people crack under torture, not because of the pain they're made to endure, but because of their imagination of how bad the pain is going to get. I think of Lord Jim when I throw my mind back over my rugby career. To put your head into a ruck, to tackle a seventeen-stone prop forward, requires a suspension of imagination like that needed to go over the top in warfare. You have to assume you won't get hurt. I thought too deeply to ever believe that.

The coach of both the junior and senior rugby teams at Pres at that time was an extraordinary man called Pat Barry. He was one of the many thousands employed by Dunlop and he worked the night shift just so he could coach rugby at the school. On Monday and Wednesday afternoons he took the juniors. On Tuesday and Thursday afternoons he took the seniors. Afterwards he'd throw his leg over his bicycle and head for work.

Pat was a brilliant coach but the wrong kind of coach for me. His way was to show you a brick wall and tell you to run through it. If it didn't work the first time, you should try to run through it again. He was quite old fashioned in that sense – a macho coach for macho boys – and didn't understand that a young person going through all these hormonal changes might lack self-belief.

I didn't have a huge physical presence. I was quite a scrawny teenager, which didn't matter much when I was a junior, as puberty hadn't yet determined which of us were going to be scrum halves and which of us were going to be prop forwards: we were all small. Despite my lack of both girth and confidence, I managed to pass myself off as a hooker.

At 14 I had high hopes of making the Junior Cup team but didn't. Despite my disappointment I was still eligible the following year and thought I had a good shot at it. I contracted jaundice during the summer and was confined to bed for two weeks, but by the time September came round I was fine. I went back to school and made the junior team for a couple of friendlies, the second of which was against Mungret College in Limerick. We absolutely annihilated them. I was certain I would be in the Cup team.

On the bus on the way back to Cork, I started to feel ill. Then I puked everywhere. I knew what was coming: I got home, charged up the stairs and looked at my face in the mirror. The whites of my eyes were yellow.

A relapse of jaundice is very serious because it can cause irreversible liver damage. My mother took my to see a doctor, F. X. O'Connor, whose son, Rex, was, by a perverse twist, my opposite number as hooker on the Christian Brothers team, our great rivals.

After a quick examination he turned to my mother and said, 'Take this boy home, feed him fluids and don't let him out of bed until I tell you.'

That was in September. I got out of bed just before Christmas and, to my everlasting regret, I never reclaimed my place on the team or got to play for my beloved Pres. The following March, Pres won the Munster Junior Cup with a guy called Liam Cogan as hooker and I knew in my heart and soul that I was a better player than he was. I remember standing in Musgrave Park, where all the schools cup games were played, watching him collect his medal, thinking that it really belonged to me.

Jaundice is a horribly debilitating illness. My recovery coincided with a sudden and dramatic surge in my physical development and I grew six inches in the months I spent on my back: I was five feet nine when I went to bed and six feet three when I got up again. But the growth was all upwards. My weight stayed the same but now what little cargo I was carrying was stretched over a bigger frame and I was little more than skin and bone.

One day Brother Athanasious said that I could possibly make the Senior Cup team if I gained some weight. I had read somewhere that drinking two pints of milk a day was good for adding bulk. So, using basic arithmetic, I figured that if two pints of milk a day was good, then eight pints was four times better. A gallon of milk a day was quite difficult to drink until I discovered Jacobs Chocolate Goldgrain biscuits, striking up a love affair that lasts to this day. To cater for my new regime, once more my mother had to stretch the budget. Eight pints of milk a day leaves you constipated like you have never known constipation and for the month or two that this experiment lasted I spent about half of my day straining on the toilet.

My father was worried enough about my appearance to take me to see Len Bernabo, a trumpet player he knew who was into bodybuilding and built like a Panzer. The old man asked him to look after me. Len was years ahead of his time in his scientific knowledge about bodybuilding. Weight training in those days was regarded as being like witchcraft. It was juju stuff. It went on, but you did it in secret.

Len's gym was just off Patrick's Hill, at the end of a sinister-looking laneway in what looked like a lock-up garage. To avoid detection I used to walk past the entrance to the laneway, look slyly around, then double back when I was happy that no one was about before slipping down there and in through the door.

After a few months of training I started to add some poundage to my wiry frame, but I never made the senior rugby team. My heart wasn't in it any more. When you go to one of the macho rugby schools, such as Pres in Cork or Blackrock College in Dublin, you can be a very decent rugby player and find yourself on the fourths team. If you were in Conleth's or Pres. Bray, you'd be good enough to make the firsts. When you're put in a position where you start to think of yourself as a fourths player, your interest slides.

After that, the only battle of any consequence I was involved in was a fight with the boys from Christians at a cup match in Musgrave Park. They had a mascot called Percy, which was a mannequin dressed in the CBC colours and held up on a stick. At some point in the match it was decided to raid the Christians end of the ground and take Percy prisoner. Emboldened by my father's stories about the Light Brigade at Balaclava, I led the charge. The Christian boys put up a ferocious fight. We captured Percy but our losses were considerable. My good tweed coat was torn. I couldn't lie to my mother about how it happened because the *Cork Examiner* carried a photograph of the mêlée, with me in the centre of the frame, one hand around Percy's neck, the other jabbing one of his guardians. I was hauled before the headmaster to be told I'd heaped shame on the school, but somehow I escaped expulsion.

What weight training gave me more than anything as I grew out of my adolescence was some semblance of self-esteem that I'd always been lacking. It arrived not a minute too soon because by that point I had discovered girls. When I was in third year, I lied about my age so I could date a girl in fifth year in St Aloysius called Bernadette. She was my first girlfriend and the only one of the many girls I was crazy about at the time who I actually had the courage to date. Essentially I was shy, lacking in confidence and increasingly conscious of my position on the social ladder.

When I was 14, my father had been offered a promotion which involved a transfer to Dublin. My mother hadn't wanted him to go but I think it suited him. He liked his space, being footloose and fancy-free. (It's one of the aspects of my father's personality I think I might have inherited.) The rest of the family had stayed in Cork because he wanted me to do my Leaving Cert in Pres. The new job had come with a pay increase but we weren't any better off because of having to run two homes. After he moved to Dublin he would come home on the train every Friday night and I'd walk to Ceannt Station and meet him stepping off the last train at 9.30 p.m. On Sunday night I'd walk him back to the station to wave him off.

The old man's digs were on Dangan Avenue off Kimmage Road West. During the summer holidays I'd spend weeks on end living with him and suddenly this whole new world opened up for me, a world in which nobody knew my background. I played cricket in the field behind the house with other boys from the area and Jew Town was a distant memory.

It was during one of those glorious summers that I met Frances Smyth. I think I was 15. I was mad about her. I had a new confidence about me because she knew nothing about how poor we were. Cork was 160 miles away. I might as well have come from New York. Frances became my girlfriend.

We exchanged Christmas and birthday cards for the next couple of years and then one Saturday morning when I was back in Cork there was a knock at the front door. I pulled my bedroom window open, stuck my head out and saw Frances and her parents on the doorstep. I went downstairs and opened the door. I was still in my pyjamas and although I had a sweater over them I felt utterly naked because now she was seeing where I lived and who I really was.

I couldn't offer them a cup of coffee because I didn't think we had any. Anyway, we might have had three cups, but only two saucers. I ushered them into the front room, and we sat there on our bits of good furniture and had this horrible, awkward conversation. Half an hour of stilted awfulness. I met them in the city centre later that day but when they got the train back to Dublin I knew I was saying goodbye to Frances.

I had bad acne as a teenager and had heard a rumour that fruit juice was good for the skin. I told my mother and, spoiled like I was, she made sure there was a glass of orange juice for me on the breakfast table every morning. Only the very rich could afford orange juice at the time. My old man used to bring cans of it on the train from Dublin. The word got about Albert Road that young George Hook was getting ideas above himself: bad enough that he's staying on to do the Leaving Cert; now he's drinking orange juice.

When I think about stories from my childhood, they all come accompanied by a stink of body odour. There were no deodorants or after-shaves or perfumes in those days; certainly none that people like us could afford. We had no hot running water, so a bath wasn't something you had every day. As I grew through my teenage years, and joined Dolphin rugby club as a schoolboy member, I was at least able to shower regularly.

I remember when we got our first washing machine. It was just a washer – you still had to hang the clothes out in the yard to dry. I didn't have a lot of clothes – when one shirt was in the wash, I'd nothing to change into – but there was a great shirt-maker called

29

Van Heusen. The fantastic thing about Van Heusen shirts was that they had detachable collars, and you got two, which meant you could wear a shirt for a week. You'd wear it on Monday and then on Tuesday you'd turn the collar round. On Wednesday you'd put on the second collar, flip it over on Thursday and then on Friday, Monday's collar was out of the wash. The cuffs would get dirty but Van Heusen had thought of that, too; their shirts had double cuffs, which meant you could turn them back.

The big social thing for teenagers in Cork in those days was 'doing Pana', which meant walking up and down Patrick's Street, checking out girls you fancied. At four o'clock the schools in the city spilled out hundreds of boys and girls who spent the next two hours traipsing back and forth between Roches Stores at one end of the street and Woolworth's at the other. You had all these matchmakers fixing people up: a girl who knew a girl who fancied you. It was all very innocent.

The music that reached our ears in our mid-teens was unswervingly middle-of-the-road – Frankie Laine and Doris Day and Rosemary Clooney singing saccharine love ballads. It's hard to fathom now, but Lita Roza got to number one singing 'How Much is that Doggy in the Window?' Then in 1955 came *The Blackboard Jungle*, a film about a school in an American slum starring Sidney Poitier. The film itself was forgettable enough but its soundtrack featured Bill Haley's 'Rock Around the Clock'. It came out of nowhere like a thunderclap. Boom! Rock 'n' roll. It was one of the seminal moments in the twentieth century and it changed the world. In Cork, like everywhere else, priests denounced rock 'n' roll from the pulpit as the devil's music, which made it even sexier in our eyes. It wasn't just the music that was exciting. The attitude informed the collective unconscious of our new 'teenage' generation.

In fifth year I started dating girls from St Angela's, a big fee-paying school for girls. Coming, as I did, from Jew Town, they were way out of my league in social terms, but all they knew about me was that I was a Pres boy. I was ashamed that I lived on Albert Road and I kept it a secret from all the girls I went out with.

When I was finished doing Pana, I'd catch the number 1 bus, which passed close to my house. The thing about the number 1 was the further it travelled away from the city centre, the better the quality of the houses, until it finally arrived in swanky Black-rock, where a lot of the girls from St Angela's lived. The handiest place for me to get off the bus was at the Sextant pub, but if I got off there everyone on the bus would know I was headed for Albert Road. So I'd stay on for one or two more stops until the bus reached the beginning of the more acceptable drop off at Victoria Road. Then I'd hop off, loiter until the bus moved off and then, when it was out of sight, turn round and walk back – usually in teeming rain, as I remember it – to Jew Town.

I was a smart kid in school thanks to my voracious appetite for books. Pres had quite an enlightened attitude towards education and even back in the fifties it had a transition year between the Inter Cert and Leaving Cert courses. Fourth year was a doss year in which you essentially repeated the Inter Cert, an exam you'd already sat. I had started school late and was one of six boys in the class who were older than everyone else. So it had been decided that the six of us would skip transition year and go straight into fifth year.

But they made a terrible mistake with me. In those politically incorrect days, boys were divided up according to intelligence. There was an A class for smart kids and a B class for dumb kids. Though I had missed half a year of school I had still achieved honours in every subject in my Inter Cert. In fact, for the three months I was laid up with jaundice, I hadn't opened a book. I spent that October, November and December with my ear glued to the radio, listening to *Woman's Hour* and *Letter from America* and the afternoon play and the new pop music stations that were playing Elvis Presley and Bill Haley and Johnnie Ray. Despite that, I still got the best Inter Cert results of anyone in my class. But because we were younger than the rest of the fifth years we were dumped into the B class.

It was one of those small, seemingly inconsequential events that can change the current of your life. I swanned my way through the last two years of school under no pressure at all, did a very ordinary Leaving Cert and left Pres with a lack of direction that would cause me to make an utter calamity of my life.

2. Reinventing George Hook

After you sat the Leaving Cert back in the fifties, there were generally three paths you could go down, if paying the fees for university was not an option: the priesthood, the civil service or the bank.

One night, not long before I left school, I was discussing what I was going to do with my life with my mother. She asked me if I wanted to go to college. I said no, which was a lie. I desperately wanted to go but I just couldn't ask my parents for the money. It would have meant another four years of scrimping and saving for them. I thought it was time I became a contributor.

During the summer between fifth and sixth years, I had worked as a temporary clerk in my father's old office in Ceannt station. With that experience I had the option of a job with CIÉ, so as soon as I finished school, I went back. I worked without much enthusiasm. Becoming a temporary clerk in the railway station held out little promise for me but I was still waiting for the thunderbolt of inspiration that would tell me where I was heading in life.

As the months rolled by insurance looked a good alternative to the bank, which took the elite of non-university boys. I applied to the Shield Insurance Company and was called for interview. It was going really well until I was asked, apropos of absolutely nothing, what books I liked to read. I should have mentioned Richmal Crompton, Frank Richards and G. A. Henty. I could have talked about those guys for ever. I thought the interviewer would consider them too lowbrow so I told him that I'd just finished *A Tale of Two Cities*. He nodded. Then he said, 'Who is the hero of *A Tale of Two Cities*?'

Of course I hadn't a clue. There was no third interview.

It was probably for the best. My father was long settled in Dublin and the plan was for the family to move up and join him as soon as it was practical. I started to write to various financial institutions in the capital and was eventually called for an interview by Sun Life of Canada on Suffolk Street. This time, there were no lies and after two interviews I was sent to a small room to complete an IQ test. I had never seen one before but I had what the test meant to find and apparently passed with flying colours.

The manager for Ireland was a larger-than-life figure called Colonel F. C. Jackson, ex-Indian Army Medical Corps. 'Mr Hook,' he said, as he perused my results, 'we cannot pay you the six pounds a week we promised.' I was so happy to get the job that I just nodded dumbly. 'No,' he said, 'we will pay you *eight* pounds a week.' It was about three pounds a week more than the average recruit was earning in banking, the Mecca for school-leavers. I ran all the way to my father's office in O'Connell Street with the good news.

I left Cork for Dublin in April 1960. Moving allowed me to reinvent myself. I took to all the things I'd failed at in Cork with the enthusiasm of a sailor on furlough – rugby, debating and girls. Nobody knew I hadn't the courage to throw my head and shoulders into a ruck. Nobody knew that I hadn't the confidence to stand up and talk in front of a crowd. When I asked a girl to dance she didn't know that I'd grown up in a two-up, two-down house with no indoor toilet on a road they called Jew Town. I dreamt myself anew.

One of the first things I did when I arrived in Dublin was to join Pembroke Cricket Club in Sydney Parade. George Mullan, with whom I had played on the Munster Schools cricket team, was living in Dublin and suggested I join. I went out to Sydney Parade for midweek nets. They took a look at me, liked what they saw and named me in the third XI for a cup match against Civil Service in the Phoenix Park the following weekend. I was to be picked up by a guy called Jerry Liston outside the Ballast Office on Westmoreland Street at one o'clock. That Saturday, when Jerry turned up – half an hour late – as I hopped into the car so did another guy who had also been standing around waiting, rather more patiently than me. I was introduced to Simon O'Leary, who was pursuing a classics scholarship in Gonzaga. We opened the batting together that day and later became close friends, a friendship that has endured for more than forty years, through times thick and thin.

On Saturday nights in the summer Pembroke hosted the best dance in town. It was *the* place to be. Because the dances in Sydney Parade were so good, when the cricket season ended I joined Monkstown Rugby Club, which shared the same premises. Monkstown then as now were not one of Dublin's premier clubs, but with my rugby pedigree it hardly mattered. It was full of nice people, the dances continued to be great and my rugby confidence was boosted by the lack of real competition for places. In the space of four weeks I went from the fifth team to the first team. My debut in senior rugby was against Wanderers, whose back row consisted of Paddy, Gene and Ronnie Kavanagh. Between them they had represented Ireland at rugby, boxing and water polo and ran onto the pitch like 18-year-old recruits leaving the landing craft on Utah Beach. Confidence, as any performer knows, is a flimsy thing and my newfound bravado had me relegated to the second string where I saw out the season.

Dancing mattered more to me than rugby. Suddenly I had this exciting social life opening up before me. In the space of two weeks I danced with the daughters of the American and German ambassadors. Celtic Tiger or no, the 1960s were the best of times for Dublin as a social and sporting city. For me every day was a living dream in which class distinction was a memory, my failings were unknown and my social acceptance total. And I had money in my pocket to boot.

By now my parents had rented a house on the Harold's Cross Road near Kenilworth Square and every Saturday night I'd walk home with Simon from Sydney Parade, stopping off for a two-hour pit stop at his house on Palmerston Road. We'd sit in the comfortable study surrounded by his father's legions of books, drinking pints of milk, devouring Goldgrain biscuits of the non-chocolate variety and talking about girls we'd danced with or just chatted up. Dawn was usually announcing itself by the time I finally reached my home on a Sunday morning. That period cemented our friendship and remains one of the most important parts of my life.

Ryle Nugent, my colleague in RTÉ, recently showed me an old black and white photograph of his mother, Barbara, standing next to a guy in a dinner jacket. The photograph was taken at one of the dress dances that filled Dublin's hotels in those years. I'm the guy in the dinner jacket.

I fell for Barbara like no one ever before. She was small and petite and had this wonderful red hair that she kept in a plait. The word was that she was a distant cousin of Dusty Springfield, which made her even more glamorous in my eyes.

My great rival for Barbara's affection at the time was John D. O'Brien, who, forty years later, by a funny twist of fate, would be my boss as a producer of television sport in RTÉ. John had the jump on me in that his sister played tennis with Barbara and they were great pals. But I still beat him to the punch. I dated her for the best part of a year and was absolutely crazy about her.

But then, in September 1961, I was offered a transfer to Sun Life's head office in London. Much as I hated to leave behind my new life in Dublin, the job was a promotion and the prospect of living in a big, bad city like London excited me. Barbara and I had this big sobbing farewell at the airport that was like something from a Bogart movie. We swore to one another that we'd be true, as you do when you're young. Three months later it was over and, tearful and depressed, I stopped off at W. H. Smith's bookshop in the Strand for some reading to while away the lonely hours. I picked up a biography of Brigitte Bardot and Barbara was a ringer for the picture on the inside cover. I think I kept the book for about five years.

If Dublin was where my reinvention began, then London was where the process was completed. It embarrasses me now to think how innocent I was when I stepped off the train at Euston station with all I owned in the world packed into a small suitcase. Aunt Lil had agreed to put me up for a few months while I got my bearings.

Sun Life of Canada's London offices were on Cockspur Street, which took up all of one side of Trafalgar Square. When I walked in there for the first time, I was like a child in a toffee factory. There were 1,500 people working there and 1,200 of them were women. It was all short skirts and bouffant hairstyles and a miasma of perfume seemed to hang over the place. It was a big shock to the system for a 20-year-old Catholic virgin who had become such an avid masturbator that he was checking his eyesight on a daily basis to make sure he wasn't going blind. My job was in the accounts department: four men, forty women. I liked the odds. I thought I'd just rolled up in heaven.

The work ethic at Sun Life was still quite Dickensian. The day started at a quarter to nine and when you arrived, you signed your name into a ledger. At exactly 8.45 a.m., as certain as clockwork, George Morley, the chief clerk, would take a red pen and a ruler and draw a line under the last name. If you arrived late, you signed below the line. When you reached a certain number of lates, you were called in for a dressing down.

The office was open plan. Geoff Bryan was the supervisor of the accounts department and he sat in a glass office at the top of the room, overseeing the serried ranks of paper pushers outside. The pecking order was reflected in the floor plan – the farther you were away from the supervisor's office, the lower down the food chain you were. Your whole raison d'être, in the forty-five years or so between joining the company and retirement, was to move, year-by-year, in slow increments, closer to Geoff's office and then – if you were very lucky – into it.

I was a bottom feeder in this great bureaucratic food chain. My job was mind-numbingly dull. To get an insurance policy, you had to be sent for a medical examination. Doctors were paid two guineas for each medical and Sun Life paid them by cheque. My job, eight hours a day, five days a week, was to file the returned paid cheques in numerical sequence in a shoebox.

37

For excitement, once a month, I had my reconciliation to do. Adding machines were still a plan on a drawing board somewhere. Everything was done by pen and ink and if you didn't balance, all hell broke loose. When the reconciliation was on, the world stopped spinning on its axis. The fear of not balancing was the only thing that stopped me from dying of boredom in the first few monotonous months at Sun Life.

One day I decided I couldn't go on. In the Dublin office, I'd been cut a lot of slack, as much as I wanted really. It was a much smaller office, just me, the office manager and twenty women, and I enjoyed a lot more independence. Now I was a small cog in a big and complex machine.

I knocked on Geoff's door and told him that I needed a word. I told him that I had a reasonably good education. I reminded him that I came to him from Dublin, where I was something of a shining star. I said that I didn't consider putting cheques into numerical sequence to be an appropriate use of my many talents.

Geoff sat forward in his chair. 'George,' he said, 'I think you're going to do well here. In a few years, you might even be sitting where I am now, in this very chair.'

'Thank you,' I said.

'But if you are, George, how are you going to understand the problems of the person sitting at the far end of the office filing cheques in numerical sequence if you've never done it yourself?'

And I went back to work happy.

Geoff taught me two valuable lessons: firstly, you can't supervise people unless you appreciate what it is they do; secondly, you should always make people feel that their job is important.

I remember this period of my life in a sort of dull monotone. Mick Jagger is still at the London School of Economics. The Beatles are singing backing vocals to 'My Bonnie Lies Over The Ocean' in a poky little club in Liverpool. It might be 1961 but it still feels like the fifties.

I catch the Tube every morning along with the faceless multitudes. Everyone has a briefcase, an umbrella and a bowler hat.

There's nothing in the briefcases except maybe a sandwich and an apple but it's part of the uniform. Everyone stands at exactly the same point on the platform every day. If you stand at the third light standard down, you know that that's where the middle door on the fourth carriage will stop. You sit in the same seat every morning and you read the *Daily Telegraph*.

These were grey, repressed times.

Rugby made life that bit more bearable for me during those first months in London. Folded up in my pocket when I got on the plane was a piece of paper with a number for a Dave Craig, who was involved with London Irish. I phoned him on a Tuesday night, the day after I started work, and told him that I had played rugby the previous year, mostly for Monkstown's seconds, which didn't cut a lot of ice with him. He said they'd already picked the team for the weekend, so he couldn't guarantee me anything, but he'd get back to me and he asked for a number.

Even as I'm giving him the number for Sun Life, I know I'm creating a problem for myself, because we're not supposed to take personal calls at work. On Thursday, Dave rings and is put straight through to Geoff Bryan. Geoff comes out of his office with a face like thunder and he calls my name. I have to walk to the far end of the office with every pair of eyes in the place on me. I go in and pick up the phone.

'Listen,' Dave says. 'You're playing for the As next Saturday against Catford Bridge. It's away. We're on the 2.30 train from Waterloo. Platform six. You'll see the rest of the lads there.'

The As are the London Irish third team. *From little acorns*, I think.

On Saturday I arrive at Waterloo. On platform six I pick out the guys straight away. They're all Irish or Anglo-Irish.

We tog out to play Catford Bridge. Fifteen minutes into the match, something happens that has an everlasting effect on the way I think about myself. We win a penalty. Our captain, Matt Moran, realizes there's no one to kick it. Our out-half has two left feet. Our full-back has never kicked a penalty in his life. The seasonal nature of the employment that most of the ex-pats were

39

involved in made London Irish a transient club. Moran himself was an architect who had played with De La Salle Palmerston. With all the comings and goings, it wasn't difficult to imagine going out to play a match with no specialist penalty kicker. I'd always fancied myself as a goal kicker, ever since all those afternoons and evenings spent kicking balls up against the ESB wall back in Jew Town. I'd never had the opportunity or the confidence to do it in a match before. But suddenly up pipes the new number 8.

'I'll take it,' I say.

The old Gilbert ball was like a block of granite when it was wet. You kicked it toe-end-on. You didn't go around the corner and visualize your shot while standing in the attitude of a golf swing. You counted your steps backwards, and then you charged straight at the ball and launched it like a Scud off the end of your reinforced toecaps.

So that's what I do. I take this kick and I slot it over. My first deposit on the 150 points I kicked for London Irish that year. Another notch on the Hook confidence meter.

A couple of weeks later, the under-21s were without a goal-kicker. They discovered that I was still young enough to be eligible to play. I was called up. It felt wonderful to be wanted. No one cared that I never played for the Senior Cup team back in Pres and because, for the first time in my life, I had confidence, I discovered that I wasn't actually a bad player.

They asked me to captain the under-21s. Now I was a leader and beginning to think about myself in slightly heroic terms. To this day, the London Irish fixtures book lists every honours scarf awarded, season-by-season, all the way back to the club's formation. And if you look at the 1961–62 season, you'll see George Hook, awarded in recognition of his performances for the under-21s.

When I joined London Irish I gained a whole new set of friends. And, just like when I moved to Dublin, I had no history with them. I could be anyone I wanted to be. I hoped there'd be a social dividend in being a star for London Irish. There were parties every Saturday night. In the expectation that I'd soon be bringing home gaggles of women, I moved out of Lil's place and into a flat in 106 Haverstock Hill in Hampstead, with four English public-school types who were studying chartered accountancy and playing rugby for Richmond.

Among the four were Tim Scarborough, an Old Harrovian whose parents lived in Jersey, and Mike Nicholls, a giant second row who seemed to embody everything I wanted to be. We became special friends as he joined Sun Life as an auditor shortly after we met and the weekends spent with Mike and his family in Buckinghamshire were a wonderful antidote to a flat-sharing existence in central London.

That year in Hampstead was another milestone and very much part of developing the Hook persona. Cork was finally beginning to leave my consciousness and I never saw myself going back to that life. I was associating with four non-Catholics, which was a big deal to a wet-behind-the-ears, 20-year-old Catholic boy brought up to think that Communion on a Sunday was the centrepiece of the week. And though my flatmates were only a couple of years older than me, they were infinitely more experienced in matters pertaining to the opposite sex.

Since I had arrived in London I had been trying to cast off my virginity, which hung around my neck like a leper's bell. I was having a lot of urges but no luck in doing anything about them. I was ridiculously innocent for a man of my age. It had a lot to do with the times. Despite the arrival of Bill Haley, Elvis Presley and Jerry Lee Lewis, the love they sang about in rock 'n' roll songs tended to be of the puppy variety, which didn't correspond to the desires I was having. According to Eddie Cochran, there were three steps to heaven, which involved finding a girl you loved, having her fall in love with you, then kissing and holding her tightly. It sure didn't sound like heaven to my hormone-crazed body.

My only sexual experiences had been fumbling and fondling of a very innocent nature. The idea of *doing it* terrified me, as I'm sure it did most Presentation Brothers-educated young men. But at least now, I thought, I was in London, where the women were

Protestants, and there was a hell of a lot more of *it* about the place.

My desperation must have been pretty clear. Geoff Bryan called me into his office one day, sat me down and told me he had some advice.

'George, there are a lot of women in here,' he said, his hand sweeping the office. He was right: there were hundreds of them. I was going testosterone crazy.

'There are *hundreds* of women in here,' Geoff said, 'but there are *millions* of women out there,' and I followed his finger to the window. 'Take my advice, look for girls outside of here. If you meet someone at work and you have a problem, then you're reminded about it every day when you step through that door at twenty to nine.'

It was advice I took to heart and never dated anyone I worked with, either in London then or anywhere else afterwards.

This, though, was still the era of dancing. The dance halls invariably had foreign-sounding names, like the Lyceum or the Palais. There was a Palais in Hammersmith and a Lyceum on the Strand. They were unlike any dance hall I'd ever experienced before. In Ireland, if you asked a girl to dance, she'd say yes, even if you had one eye, cauliflower ears and were too drunk to stand. In London, if they didn't like the look of you, they just said no. It was new to me. You'd get more rejections in one night in London than in five years in Dublin.

Shortly before my move to Hampstead I get what the English call 'lucky'. I am in the Lyceum on the Strand. Distance is obviously a problem. She is from somewhere in Essex and I am still at Auntie Lil's in Middlesex. There is simply no way that I can take her home to Essex on the Tube and get back to Lil's. Staying at her place simply doesn't cross my mind. However, she is well ahead of me and proceeds to guide me behind one of the many theatres on the Strand and push me up against the emergency exit, which is set into a discreet alcove.

All I know about sex are the mechanics of the act, which my father had explained, and the moral baggage that the Presentation

Brothers have encumbered me with. Like thousands of others my age, I am going through the agonies of the damned about sexuality, never realizing that the men who taught us are a bigger emotional mess than we are.

We start kissing each other. In the darkness, I feel her hand move towards a part of my anatomy where only my hand has been before. Suddenly I'm terrified. I feel her hand slip down the front of my trousers and between my legs.

I push her away. She looks at me, offended. I mutter something feeble about having to catch the last train. I take off, leaving her there in the alcove. I run through Trafalgar Square and all the way to Piccadilly Circus, where I know there's a late-night chemist. I buy a family-size bottle of Dettol and then catch the Bakerloo Line train back to Harrow. Everyone is in bed when I arrive home. I fill the bath with scalding hot water and I pour in the entire contents of the bottle. Then I lower myself down into it until my privates are submerged and sit there in the burning water silently praying that I don't get VD. All I get, as it happens, is second-degree burns.

During the summer of 1962 I returned to Dublin for a fortnight's holiday. The first weekend I was home, I went to a dance in Bective Rangers rugby club and fell head over heels for a girl called Mary Pat McLoughlin. She was there with Mickey Butler, who'd been the scrum-half on the Rockwell Senior Cup Team. She was gorgeous. I presumed they were a couple but it turned out they were just friends. Their families had holiday homes next to each other in Donabate.

I asked her to dance. We talked all night. She was very conservative and deeply Catholic – but weren't they all? I had it bad for her. I must have seen her every day for the fortnight I was home. Once again a trip to London began with me pledging my troth. Falling in love was never my problem; staying in love was.

I was miserable for the next few weeks without Mary Pat. I couldn't settle back into work in London. On an impulse I decided to come home. I handed in my notice, left London Irish, said goodbye to my friends from Haverstock Hill and flew home.

The cover story was that I was returning to go to college and my parents seemed happy enough with that. The real reason was to see Mary Pat. But by then, she'd cooled on me. She broke my heart. Broke it like nobody before or since. And that was the end of that.

I probably should have applied to study in Dublin. There was no points requirement for UCD in those days and, having saved some money while I was away, I probably could have afforded it. In London, I'd enrolled to study corporate and certified accountancy by night, but with work and rugby, I never found the time to go to the lectures. I still thought I wanted to be an accountant. The College of Commerce in Rathmines ran a two-year course in business studies. It covered the first two of the five professional examinations you had to sit to become an account-ant, so when you graduated from Rathmines, you were 40 per cent of the way there. My plan was to get my qualification and then take a job somewhere while studying at night for the remaining two years.

I loved Rathmines. We did economics, law, accounting, and the standard of teaching was extraordinary. It came easily to me. It helped that I was 21, while most of my classmates were 18. I was that bit more mature; I knew what I was there for.

I got a lot more than a diploma in business studies from my two years in Rathmines. My personality developed. The slight undertow of insecurity that I felt all my life disappeared, probably from being, as I saw it, a grown man in a class full of teenagers.

During my first week in Rathmines we had an election for class captain. Because of my age, the rest of the class pushed me forward. A couple of weeks later the college's vice-principal came into the class looking for volunteers to speak in a debate in the town hall the following night. I stuck my hand up. I had no idea why. I had never debated because I never had the confidence to speak in front of a roomful of people. When I was at Pres the star debater was a guy who was two years younger than me, Eoghan Harris. He had such incredible confidence. He'd stand up and spout out all this Republican twaddle about burning Union Jacks and driving the

Brits out of the Six Counties. Fifty years on I can still remember the last line of one of his speeches: 'The men who watched the tricolour flutter over the GPO will not rest until this is solved.' I know I wasn't the only one thinking, 'Who is this guy? He's fucking brilliant.'

The motion for the debate at which I was going to speak was that Ireland should rejoin the Commonwealth. I was to speak against. I went to the debate the following night without a note prepared. I walked from Harold's Cross to Rathmines and ordered all my arguments in my head on the way. I surprised nobody more than myself by speaking really well.

One of the great features of social life in Dublin in the 1960s was Switzer's coffee shop, where anyone who was anyone went to sup coffee and watch the world go by. One Saturday morning, soon after I had returned to Dublin, I ran into my old friend Mickey Butler there. Mickey had played in the Rockwell team that beat Pres in the Munster Senior Cup final, though since he had also introduced me to Mary Pat I didn't hold it against him.

'Are you playing any rugby?' he said.

'I was with London Irish, but I'm back with Monkstown now.' In other words, no.

'You can do better than that, George,' he said. 'I've just joined Mary's. Why don't you come down to the club one night?'

I went along the following Tuesday, sought out the club secretary, Hacker Roche, and explained who I was and where I was coming from. 'There's a game on Saturday,' he said. 'It's a bit beneath you, actually. The third Bs.'

I figured it was as good a place to start as any. After the game Mattie Jones, the captain of the thirds, asked me to play for them the following day, as they were short a player. I was clambering up the rungs at breakneck speed. The following week I was asked to play for the seconds in Carlow and clearly impressed someone, as a week later I was promoted to the firsts, a team that included the future Lions prop forward, Sean Lynch, Sean Cooke, Ned Carmody and Denis and Tony Hickie.

After a couple of first-team games as a late call-up when someone was injured, I received another Friday-night telephone message to report as number 8 for a match against Wanderers on the morrow. In the dressing room I was, as usual, paralysed by nerves, compounded by the fact that Wanderers had a second row called Jack McGowan, who, although little older than me, always terrified me. In business Jack was a lovely man but in rugby he was a Martin Johnson-type character who exuded aggression. Not the kind of guy someone of my less than Lion-hearted disposition would have chosen as an opponent. I had an urge to run out the gate.

Wanderers had a young out-half making his debut that afternoon called Mike Gibson. My most vivid memory of that game was watching him run rings around us like a skywriter. Even in those eighty minutes, you could see that he was destined to become an international. I clearly wasn't, but I played reasonably well, without imposing myself on the game, and was bullish about my chances of holding on to my place.

The following day I was due to play as originally scheduled, for the second team against University College Dublin in Belfield. Midway through the first half of that game, I was tackled by two defenders. My leg was twisted when I hit the turf with the full force of my body weight. I heard a sickening crack and felt a degree of pain I never knew was possible. I looked down to see my kneecap sticking out of my leg at a grotesque angle.

Many of the UCD team were medical students. One of them knocked my knee back into place and I was chair-lifted off the field, put into a car and driven to St Vincent's hospital, which was then behind Hartigan's pub on Leeson Street. It was teatime on a Sunday and the hospital wasn't exactly swimming with doctors. I sat there for a couple of hours in a lot of pain and was eventually seen by Ray Carroll, who, as it happened, had been the out-half for UCD that afternoon. He sent me to have my leg X-rayed. Ray studied the acetates and shook his head solemnly. 'I'm not an expert,' he said, 'but I think you're in a very bad way.'

'Will I ever play rugby again?' I asked him.

'I doubt it. But I'm just the registrar. The real expert is Joe

Gallagher. Come in and see him at the orthopaedic clinic in the morning. Be there at about 10 a.m.'

As I hobbled away on crutches, he said, 'Oh, and George, it may be a long wait. Bring *War and Peace*.'

I arrived back at St Vincent's the next morning and the queue to see Gallagher was like a bread line in wartime London. I sat on a hard plastic chair and waited for hours. The guy beside me was reading the *Irish Press* and on the back page was a photograph of me tackling the great Mike Gibson. It looked like a requiem for my rugby career.

Eventually I was called in to see the great man. My leg was swollen from knee to ankle and to get into my fashionable drain-pipe trousers I had to slit them up the side like a bar hostess in Bangkok.

Patients tended to be terrified of Gallagher, who had a brusque manner that implied he was far too busy to engage in small talk. 'There's a lot of ligament damage in your knee but your ankle's in even worse shape,' he said to me. 'Still, you're not going to die. Come back in six weeks.'

I lost it. 'What do you mean, come back in six weeks? The doctor last night said it was so bad that I'd never play rugby again. You're saying come back in six weeks. What the hell is going on?'

He smiled then, a rare enough occurrence I later found out. I suspected that patients didn't talk to him like that every day. 'Look, you're going to be fine. Go home and don't get out of bed for a fortnight until the swelling on that leg comes down. Then come back and see me in six weeks.'

During my recovery I was selected, along with Maria Regan, who was doing secretarial studies, to represent the College of Commerce in the Irish Times Trophy, an intervarsity debating competition. It was black-tie affair, held in the boardroom of the Pharmaceutical Society on Shrewsbury Road. My knee and ankle were still in bad shape and I could walk only with the aid of a stick. The stick, I found, was a great prop for emphasizing points. Maria and I won and qualified for the second round. It was a huge deal because Rathmines had no great history of debating.

Unfortunately for us the next round took place in UCC in Cork. To this day, all my failed speeches have been in Cork. Then as now, I felt a crippling anxiety about going back and seeing this phalanx of old faces that I knew in the tiered seating of the lecture hall. I was too determined to impress.

The motion that night, as I remember it, was, 'That nationalism is the last refuge of a scoundrel.' Maria was excellent. I was appalling. I got it all wrong. We came last and I returned to Dublin utterly depressed.

All winter I was laid up with my knee, unable to train with Mary's. I sat out November, December, January and most of February, presuming, like the time I contracted jaundice before the Junior Cup at school, that my place on the team was now someone else's. One night towards the end of February, Sean Cooke called to my door. Sean was an extraordinary captain who led by example. 'How's the knee?' he asked.

I hadn't subjected it to anything more vigorous than some gentle running. 'I'm not sure,' I said.

'We want you for the cup, George.'

My heart was off and running like a moped. It was like being asked to play in the European Cup; the Leinster Senior Cup was the biggest competition there was at that time.

'Can you train?' he said.

'I'll try.'

I trained on Tuesday and Thursday night and the knee held up well. I eased myself back in with an anonymous enough performance the following Saturday and went straight into the team for the first round match in the cup. It was a local derby against Terenure, which added to the tension for me. I was as nervous as a kitten, not just because I'd played only one match in four months, but also because my opposite number was Mick Hipwell, who was the Irish number 8 in the Five Nations Championship.

Before the match, I psyched myself up to a frightening degree, virtually hypnotizing myself into believing that no one was going to pass me. I had a great match against Hipwell, who, it turned out, was the nicest kind of gentleman. I caught him several times in the lineout when the ball was nowhere near and, though he would have been well within his rights to cuff me round the ear, he was so good that he didn't need to do it. I wasn't in his class but there was one moment in the match when I managed to upstage him. That season the laws had changed and the number 8 was allowed to pick the ball up at the base of the scrum. Early in the second half, we put in, the scrum half-wheeled and I found the ball at my feet. Instinctively, I picked it up and took off. My greatest sporting memory bar none was hearing the Ireland number 8 say, 'Oh shit!' as I left him marooned in my wash, making forty yards before I was tackled. Paul McWeeney of the *Irish Times*, the doyen of rugby writers, was very complimentary about my performance on the Monday and I felt that I had arrived.

We drew with Terenure and, although we won the replay, my lack of match fitness claimed its forfeit. I had a very ordinary game and was dropped for the semi-final against Bective Rangers. The humiliating thing for me was that I didn't know I had been dropped until I turned up at the next training session. Sean Cooke had made three changes, scrum-half Mickey Butler and wing Noel Kenny had also been dropped, but they'd had prior warning. The protocol was that the captain phoned you to tell you, but 'Cookie' hadn't been able to get in touch with me because we still didn't have a phone at home. Those were the days of a five-year wait for a phone line.

As it turned out, another player, Ned Carmody, had to cry off and I got to play after all. We took two bites at beating Bective and I did well enough in the two matches to be picked for the final against UCD in place of a still-unfit Ned. Despite losing in the final it was the best year I had yet had in rugby.

In 1963, without any consideration for my social life, my parents bought a house in Beaumont on the north side of the city. My entire life – college, cricket, rugby, dancing – took place on the south side. Now, if I went to a dance in Sydney Parade, I had the choice of leaving at 11 p.m. to catch the last number 3 bus home or staying until the end and making the one-and-a-half-hour trek across the city on foot. As a student, taxis were not an option and Simon's father read the dials to check any unnecessary mileage.

It was one and a half hours on a good night. But then there was the additional hazard of dogs. I was – and am to this day – terrified of them. Walking home in the early hours, I'd hear a bark in the distance and take a twenty-minute detour to avoid it.

In my second year in college I got very friendly with Pat Campbell, whose parents ran a number of budget hotels around the Gardiner Street area of Dublin. I was elected president of the students' union in Rathmines and he was my opposite number in the College of Catering, Cathal Brugha Street, where he was studying hotel management. I found Pat wonderful company. He was a visionary; full of innovative ideas not only for student activities but for the hotel business he expected to inherit. A few years later, that friendship was to change my life.

The library facilities in Rathmines were rudimentary at that time so I started using the reading room in the National Library on Kildare Street to study for my finals that summer. There were a few UCD guys I knew through rugby who used it as well and we formed a little coterie. Every few hours we'd take a coffee-and-fag break in a little café beside the Freemason's Hall across the road on Molesworth Street.

One day one of the guys tips me and tells me they're heading out. 'Follow us out,' he says, 'and tell Slammer.'

Five rows behind me is a guy with his head buried in a book. I tiptoe down to him and I say, 'Are you going for a cup of coffee?' and, without looking up, he says, 'Fuck off.'

That was my introduction to Kyran McLaughlin, a man without whose friendship I'm reasonably certain I wouldn't be alive today.

'Slammer', so called because of the resemblance of his golf swing to 'Slamming' Sam Snead, clearly took his studies seriously but over time, and a lot of coffee breaks, we started to hit it off. Kyran was shy socially, while I was great at chatting up dames, if nothing else. I also owned a dress suit and Kyran didn't. So I became his social fixer, lending him my tux and introducing him to girls to take to dinner-dances.

He and Simon and I became firm friends. Years later I'd think back to the early years of our friendship together and smile. There I was in 1963, the one with the dress suit who knew all the right things to say to the ladies and could stand up in front of a room full of people and talk. Twenty years later, I was bankrupt and a gibbering wreck, while Kyran and Simon were thriving in their careers.

And we've remained the firmest friends to this day. They bailed me out, financially and emotionally, more times than I could ever hang a number on. In the bad days, when *Stubbs Gazette* were thinking of bringing out a weekly supplement dedicated to my bad debts, it must have been an embarrassment to be a friend of George Hook. And though I tested our friendship again and again, they never, ever turned their backs on me.

At the end of two years in Rathmines, I sat the exams and took first place in the class. Later that summer I was playing cricket in the Pembroke and was opening the batting with my friend Jerry Liston. During the tea interval, Jerry told me about a pal of his who had joined an American company called Burroughs Machines Limited and was pulling in a fortune as a salesman. I was very impressed. Shortly after I graduated I presented myself at the company's offices on Nassau Street and walked out half an hour later with a job as a salesman.

Burroughs manufactured adding machines. The all-steel forerunner of the calculator weighed a ton and portability was not exactly a selling point. The non-electric version was operated by pulling a handle for every transaction. It was still the early 1960s; there was no such thing as the microchip and the idea of the pocket calculator belonged in the space age. The Burroughs machine was capable of adding (subtracting was available at an extra charge!), but that was all it did – basic arithmetic. If you wanted to multiply 27 by 18, you keyed in 27 plus 27 plus 27 and so on until your finger went numb.

Each machine cost £100 – a small fortune. You could buy a house for £1,000. A Burroughs counting machine wasn't exactly an impulse buy, though I was working on the basis that it was. I was selling them on the knocker.

My first patch was Capel Street. Over the space of a couple of weeks I worked the length of the street on both sides, cold-calling from one shop to the next, with the dead weight of my demonstration machine almost pulling my shoulder from its socket. Shopkeepers would look at me and say, 'Sorry, I must have misheard you. I thought you said £100.'

I didn't go into it totally green. The company sent me to London for a training course in the art of selling. I came back to Dublin thinking I was Phineas T. Barnum.

So the first day I'm working Capel Street, I walk into a shop and there's a guy up a ladder counting boxes on a shelf. I hoist this machine up onto the counter and launch into my spiel. 'This machine is going to change your life,' I say, but the guy's not minding me at all. He continues counting.

I say, 'This machine will save you money. This machine will keep a permanent record of your purchases. It will keep a permanent record of your creditors. It will ensure that all of your –'

I'm in mid-sentence when he looks down at me for the first time and says, 'Will you ever fuck off?'

But my patter improved and so did sales. I managed to sell quite a number before the end of my six-month apprenticeship and I was given my own territory, which was all of Dublin city centre. I had been a fully salaried salesman for only a few weeks when I got a call from head office asking me go to England for an interview. It wasn't an interview, it turned out, so much as a job offer. They wanted me to go on the 'Dem Van' – the demonstration unit – which meant driving a Land Rover hitched to a 22-foot caravan, up and down the highways and byways of Britain, performing demonstrations for big companies interested in buying Burroughs machines. There was no selling involved. My boss in Dublin had already tipped me off that I was likely to be offered the job and he told me I should take it.

There was a problem: I could barely drive. I was the proud possessor of my first car – a green mini, registration number KZH

728. Happily, an Irish driving licence could be procured by the simple expedient of filling in a form to confirm that the applicant was neither blind nor deaf. Even better, it allowed the licence holder to drive every class of vehicle, bar a Dublin bus.

I was now qualified to take a 30-foot long articulated vehicle around Britain without let or hindrance. The early weeks were positively scary as my progress around the island resembled *Carry on Trucking*. Yet I survived, and even became rather adept, especially at reversing, which is quite an art as every caravanner knows.

For the next eighteen months, life was a breeze. I was earning a fortune; I was in charge of the National Demonstration Unit; I *was* the National Demonstration Unit. There was no one else in the company doing what I was doing so there was no benchmark for my expenses. Burroughs was picking up the tab for hotels, meals, drinks, everything. Nothing was ever queried.

I learned all the creases and invented one or two of my own. I discovered what an extraordinarily hospitable people the English are. I'd roll into town and meet my contact, who'd usually insist that I had dinner with his family that night and stay over in his house. So I'd save myself a night's board. I was already up on the deal. Hotels didn't have computers like they do today and receipts were filled out by hand. I had a mountain of blank receipts from hotels in every major town and city in England, Scotland and Wales.

It cost fourteen pounds to clean and wash the caravan. I'd get a scrubbing brush and do it myself and then charge Burroughs the fourteen quid. I had all kinds of scams going. At the end of each week, I'd spend three hours filling in my expenses. They were among the greatest works of fiction of the twentieth century. My annual salary was £750 but I never touched it. I lived like a lord off my expenses and banked my wages every week.

Rarely in my life have I been as happy as I was then. The hours were long. Often I worked seven days a week. I might finish Liverpool on a Friday night and be expected bright and early in Glasgow on Monday morning, which meant setting off on Saturday and driving over the weekend to get there in time. But it was the perfect job for a single man with wanderlust. I liked meeting strangers and I liked my own company. I liked having to organize myself.

More importantly, for the first time in my life I was doing something for which I had a natural flair – I was performing in front of an audience and I was brilliant at it. My reputation started to precede me. A guy I'd just performed a demonstration for would phone the branch in the next town and say, 'There's this Irish guy on the way to you in the Dem Van. A great character.'

One day I was in Perth, doing a demonstration for the Scottish Co-Operative Movement. Perth was *real* Scotland and the secretary of the Co-Op was a rabid Scots nationalist. He was a tough cookie. Our opposition was NCR, one of Scotland's biggest employers, whose machines were made at a huge plant in Dundee. There was a lot of patriotic buying in Scotland and the Co-Op had batteries of NCR machines. My guy had never bought a Burroughs machine in his life. What I had in the Dem Van was the new Burroughs E2000, the first machine capable of multiplication and division. It was partly electronic, but it was also the size of a single bed and the mechanical parts still chug-chug-chugged away while performing calculations. It cost £30,000, which, in 1964, was a jackpot divided on the football pools.

People were easily impressed by technology in those days. The E2000 had one of the early golf-ball printers. Before I did a demonstration, I would key in: 'The Burroughs E2000 welcomes [the client's name] to this demonstration of its incredible capability.' I would switch the machine on first, then put the plug in the wall, leaving the three pins loose in the socket so that there was no connection. Then I'd launch into my script. 'The E2000 – can you believe it – holds 2,000 digits of information . . .' and then, unseen, I would kick the plug and the machine would spring into life, without any apparent human contact, and greet the client by name. The potential client would nearly wet himself at the thought that this computer actually knew his name.

However, the secretary of the Scottish Co-Operative Movement wasn't easily impressed. I was introduced to him, as I often was, as 'the Irish guy I was telling you about', and he looked at me with ill-disguised contempt and said, 'Och, you Irish, you don't even speak your own language.'

'Well,' I said, keen to placate him, 'would you like me to do the demonstration in Gaelic?'

His face lit up. 'You can do that?' he said.

'Well, I'm not sure if there is a Gaelic translation for "ferrite core memory", but I'll do my best.'

I ended up doing what all the politicians do today. I spoke the first five sentences in Irish and then returned to the script. But he was fierce impressed. He was looking at me differently, almost reverently.

A few months later I got a call from one of the Burroughs reps: 'George, we did it! We cracked the Co-Op!'

It was around that time that I almost died again. As was my wont for long journeys, I was driving on Sunday afternoon between Sheffield and Middlesbrough when I jack-knifed on the A1(M) just before Boroughbridge. Had the accident happened a few miles earlier on the M1, I would not have survived because the motorway had a concrete central barrier. Luckily for me the road I was on had a grass reservation dividing the carriageways.

For no apparent reason I lost control of the Land Rover and caravan while driving on the inside lane. My vehicle took off backwards across the three lanes of traffic, led by the caravan with me in the cab behind. We crashed through the central reservation, crossed another three lanes of fast-moving traffic and came to a juddering halt in the hard shoulder on the other side. The entire exercise was accomplished without hitting anything. It was 64-carat miracle. I got out of the cab in deep shock.

An Esso tanker pulled in behind me. The driver stuck his head out the window. 'You OK?' he said.

'I just need to catch my breath,' I replied.

Then, recognizing a fellow knight of the road, he said, 'Are you going to be in the shit with your boss? Because I'll swear blind I saw you hit a patch of oil.'

I think that was the first time I joined up the dots between all my brushes with death. I started to develop this unshakeable belief in my own indestructibility. I don't go around telling people that I'm invulnerable, but I've cheated death so many times that I think there must be some almost karmic reason I've been spared.

Early in 1965, the sixties in England were well and truly swinging. Though there was just a sliver of water separating us on the map, Britain was twenty years more advanced in terms of sexual liberation. This was obvious when Ireland rugby fans came to Twickenham. After the match, you'd see them in Soho, wobbling – wide-eyed and pasty faced – out of red-lit doorways. I wonder how many bottles of Dettol were sold on those weekends.

I was chasing sexual gratification as eagerly and as fruitlessly as ever, though my desperate air had been replaced by a cocksure self-belief that had grown from my success with the E2000.

Now, I even had a sales pitch for myself. Up and down the country, I was chatting up secretaries and receptionists, taking them out to lunch. I was having the time of my life with my unlimited expense account. I had no responsibilities, no worries, and no fetters – except the embarrassment of being a 24-year-old virgin with a terror of the unknown.

I arrive one day in Northampton, the centre of the British shoemaking industry. I'm meeting with one of our local reps, who has just sold a machine to one of the biggest manufacturers in the region. He has to call to the office to collect something or other and while I'm waiting I get talking to a woman. She's blonde and more than a few years older than me. She embodies all my fantasies. Geoff Bryan's advice about the incompatibility of business and pleasure comes to mind, but this woman is worth breaking the rules for.

I'm staying the weekend in Northampton so the following day I phone the company and ask to be put through to the accounting department. She comes on the phone and I give her the unforgivably cheesy, 'How would you like to cheer up a lonely Irishman in Northampton?'

But she agrees to go out with me. We arrange to meet outside

56

1. My parents, George and Anne Hook. I'm not sure exactly when this picture was taken, but it was well before I came along. They married in 1933 and I was born in 1941.

2. A recent photograph of our old house, 79 Albert Road, in the heart of Cork city. (*Provision, Cork*)

3. With my father in Patrick's Street in 1946. I am five-and-a-half. The high arched doorway in the background is the entrance to the *Cork Examiner*.

4. Spruced up in my Pres uniform on my confirmation day in 1953. My classmate is Donal O'Sullivan.

5. A First Communicant in 1948: I'm in the back row, fifth from the left.

6. One of my first loves: Brigitte Bardot lookalike, Barbara Ryle. Decades later I worked with Barbara's son, Ryle Nugent, in RTÉ.

7. With Pat Campbell on his wedding day, 1965. I was his best man. Sadly our friendship did not survive the difficulties of working together in Campbell Catering.

8. Ingrid Palm pictured in Lytham St Anne's a few weeks after we met on St Patrick's Day 1967. This remains one of my favourite images of Ingrid.

developed sophisticated tastes. I had got used to living in hotels, eating in expensive restaurants and tipping extravagantly. It affected me for the rest of my life. Even later in the story, when I haven't a dime, I'm still eating three-course meals in restaurants.

When I returned from England, Burroughs gave me my own territory, but now I was a sales rep again, living off commission instead of a generous expense account. One day Malachy Sherlock, my sales manager, took me aside and asked me, 'How many suits have you got?'

'One,' I said.

'And when do you wear it?'

'On a Sunday,' I said. 'For Mass.'

And he nodded like he knew the answer already. 'Mass doesn't earn you any money,' he said. 'You wear your best clothes to work.'

In 1965, this kind of talk was heresy. But Malachy was years ahead of his time. He took me to see a tailor friend of his who had a first-floor shop at the bottom of Grafton Street. Frank Gormley was what was known as a 'bespoke' tailor, an old English word meaning 'ridiculously expensive'.

'This is George,' Malachy said. 'He's working with me now. Fit him out.'

I'd never had a suit made for me before. The one I wore to Mass was bought off the peg. Frank took out a big swatch of fabrics and made a few suggestions. Then he measured the vital areas. The suit he made me was a sober blue three-piece. It cost forty-seven pounds at a time when the average industrial wage was fifteen a week. But I looked the business in it. Malachy agreed.

'But,' he said, 'there's no point paying almost fifty pounds for a suit you're going to wear every day. It'll be worn out in six months. You need three suits.'

So we went back to Frank Gormley, he whipped out the scissors and chalk again and then I was the proud owner of three suits costing forty-seven pounds each – my blue one, a grey one and a brown one. Next, Malachy walked me off to buy shoes – three pairs of shoes. I had just spent 50 per cent of my annual basic salary.

'Forget your salary,' he said to me while I was trying on a pair. 'It's a mere bagatelle compared to what you'll make on commission.'

And he was right. He understood the politics of dressing twenty years before power suits were ever invented. Years later, people I'd crossed paths with on my business travels would say to me, 'We always assumed by the way you dressed that you were probably very good and did not need the money. It was natural to go with the guy who seemed to be the best.' It is a psychology that is often forgotten by modern-day salesmen.

Malachy was extraordinary. He saw selling as a profession at a time when it was often looked down on, as something akin to sharp practice. He saw clothing, time-management and training as crucial to success. Forty years later, I still find myself copying many of his ideas. One time we're doing some business in Cork and we check into Jury's Hotel. We have a few demonstrations to do so we're going to be staying there a week. We're sitting in the lobby and Malachy calls over the porter and orders tea. The porter returns with two pots of tea and Malachy tips him a ten-shilling note. I'm not averse to tipping but I tended to tip when I was leaving places and only if the service had been good. 'We've hardly checked into the hotel,' I say, 'and you're giving him ten bob already.'

'George,' he says, 'what is the point of tipping people when you're leaving an establishment? You're gone. Tip them first and you'll get the service you want.'

I follow that advice to this day.

Malachy had an enormous influence over me. He taught me how to manage territory as a salesman, how to beat the competition, the ideal times to call on customers, how to deal with difficult people. When I do management talks for big companies today, it's amazing how many of Malachy's lessons come pouring from my mouth.

It might have been Malachy's influence or it might have been the suit, but soon after I returned to Dublin I pulled off the deal of a lifetime. The *Irish Press* newspaper had its offices at the corner of O'Connell Street and Abbey Street. They had fifteen machines at the time and they were all made by NCR bar one, less than efficient, Burroughs machine, which had more downtime than the other fifteen combined.

However, one of Malachy Sherlock's dictums held good. He drilled into me over and over that people in the front line are often more important than the management to a salesman. The mechanical failures never reached the ears of the management because the machine operatives covered my arse. When the bosses were in, the girls in the accounts department would stand over my machine with a sheet of paper in their hands and a preoccupied look on their faces, to give the impression that this machine was changing their lives.

Noel Dalton was my service man and he would often go into the *Press* at night and work unpaid overtime fixing the machine. Noel was a married man with children and I'd look after him by giving him the Christmas hampers and other bits and pieces I got as bonuses. It was Sherlock dictum number two – 'sleep with your serviceman'. Salesmen were vastly overpaid compared with the service guys, but without working as a team you had no chance.

The *Irish Press* decided to replace all their machines in one fell swoop. It was a massive order. Thanks principally to Noel's skill with a spanner they gave me the contract. Two weeks after they signed the deal the NCR salesman arrived, confident that he had the business in the bag. It was too late; he had rarely visited the *Press* in the intervening years. After all, why should he? The machines worked and there was little need to call. I hope he learned the lesson Malachy had taught me.

Then the *Irish Independent* further up on Middle Abbey Street also decided to expand the mechanization of the accounting department. Within weeks of the good news at the *Press* I had another order from their rival publisher. At the end of the month I got a commission cheque for £3,700, net of tax. Gerry Boyd thought I was Howard Hughes. I was living on Easy Street. Life was a bowl of cherries.

All that remained was for me to screw it up.

3. A disastrous decision

I met Ingrid Palm on St Patrick's Day in 1967. Tom Windridge, who ran the Preston branch of Burroughs, invited me over to England for the holiday weekend. Tom had repeatedly tried to get me to move to his branch rather than return to Ireland when I finished my stint on the Dem Van. I had stayed in his home during my visits to Preston and, although I decided on Dublin, we remained great friends. He also had been an international rugby referee and a keen member of Fylde rugby club, which I used to play for whenever I was in Lancashire.

The Friday night I arrived, there was a dance in the squash club and I went along with some of the lads from the rugby club. I was only just in the door when I saw this woman across the hall. I thought she was incredible. Dark, was my first impression. Dark features. Dark hair. She was wearing a green woollen sleeveless dress and I couldn't stop looking at her. I walked up to her with my lonely-Irishman routine.

'Would you like to dance with an Irishman on St Patrick's weekend?'

'No,' she said, giving me only a cursory look.

I retreated in confusion and disarray. She was with another girl at the dance and I decided she might be my way back. A few dances later, with a bit more humility this time, I asked her friend to dance and she said yes. It was perfectly obvious, as we perambulated around the floor, that I was making progress. All I was interested in, though, was finding out more about her friend, the dark-haired beauty who had repulsed my advances.

It turned out her friend's name was Ingrid. She was a pharmacist and they shared an apartment in Lytham St Anne's. My next trick was to extract a phone number.

When I called the next day I asked for Ingrid. She came to the phone. I told her that my friend Tom was having a drinks party that night after the match and I asked would she come with me.

'No,' she said.

'Oh.'

'I'm washing my hair.'

'That's very original.'

In the background I could hear her friend from last night urging her to go. She hummed and hawed. Then she gave me a far from convinced yes.

Tom lent me his Hillman Imp and I picked her up at seven o'clock and brought her back to the party. I watched her as she chatted to everyone. I don't know if she was aware I was watching. She blew me away.

She had to be up early the following morning to go to London, where she had an interview on Monday with Roche Pharmaceuticals for a job in Switzerland. I ran her home in Tom's car and, ever the gentleman, made a lunge for her before she got out the door and got the palm of her hand in my face.

I knew she had a reservation at the Russell Hotel in Russell Square in London. Early, on Sunday morning I phoned Interflora and arranged for a bouquet of flowers to be there for her when she arrived, with a card wishing her all the best with the interview, and my address – 8 Elm Mount Avenue, Dublin 9 – appended.

A week later a letter dropped through the door. It was from Ingrid. She said she was absolutely astonished to get the flowers and thanked me. Then she said the interview went well but she had decided not to take the job and was working instead as a pharmacist at the Preston Royal Hospital. There was a PS tagged on: 'I must come to Ireland some day.'

Impulsive as ever, I wrote back that day, saying, 'Why not come next weekend? Please find enclosed an return air ticket.'

Ingrid, I discovered later, was in two minds as to whether I was a serial killer or a simple oddball. Her friend said, 'If he's that big an idiot, you should just go and have a good time.'

The following Saturday morning Ingrid arrived and I had an itinerary mapped out to knock her socks off. I checked her into the Lansdowne Hotel, where Don Horgan, the manager and a good friend of mine, gave her the best room in the house. I, of course, was going to be staying at home with my parents. That afternoon, I took her to the races at Leopardstown, despite my lack of affection for the gee-gees. Afterwards we went to the grill bar in the Royal Hibernian Hotel on Dawson Street for a meal and then dancing in Blackrock rugby club.

We went back to the room and nothing happened, except that I mentioned, by the by, that I thought I was falling in love with her and that I might want to marry her one day in the not too distant future. It didn't exactly send her weak at the knees.

'I don't want any of your Irish bullshit,' she said.

Ingrid was right. I was full of bullshit. What I wasn't aware of then – and only became conscious of when I'd made a mess of almost three decades of my marriage – was my absolute inability to give of myself in an emotional sense. Right through my teens and early twenties I was a tireless chaser after women. Energetic but spectacularly unsuccessful. There were many first dates, few seconds. I loved women, but never really *loved* anyone. Many times I asked myself whether I was one of those rare people who are incapable of feeling the emotion. Clearly, I was a romantic. The guy who thinks to send flowers to the Russell Hotel plainly has something of the dreamy idealist about him. But it was all surface romanticism. It was gestures. I was missing the core bits.

I have a newspaper cutting about the Taurus man. I think astrology is twaddle, but whoever wrote the article has managed to distil my personality perfectly into three or four short paragraphs. The Taurus man, it says, is attracted to dominant women. To me the biggest turn-off was a woman who went along with what I wanted just to placate me. Now here was a woman who was prepared to say, 'Yes, I want to go to the cinema. But no, I don't want to see *The Ten Commandments*.'

That strength, that independence of spirit, was incredibly attractive. It was clear from the moment of Ingrid's very first brush-off that I was dealing with someone who would not be cowed by me.

Freud, no doubt, has a theory to explain it, but looking back now I think that when I looked at Ingrid, on some unconscious level, I saw my mother. It wasn't that I had a mother fixation but our parents are the strongest role models we have and my mother was the dominant personality in our household. Though I could see all her terrible weaknesses and failings – like the damage she did to Arthur and Frances by mishandling their adoption – it was her strength and courage that defined her in my eyes. It was the same with Ingrid. Unfortunately it took me nearly thirty years to appreciate what I saw after two dates.

After our weekend in Dublin, Ingrid went back to England and I wrote to her every day of the next two years. That's how we conducted our courtship, through the mail and the very occasional weekends we shared in Dublin or Lytham or Manchester. Two years almost to the day after we met we got married in Manchester.

The wedding was on a Monday so that it would not get in the way of a match I had to play for St Mary's the preceding Saturday – a perfect indication of where my head was. Ingrid's mother made all the arrangements. Like her daughter, she was a great bit of stuff. Because Ingrid was an only child, there was an extraordinary closeness between them. I don't know what she thought of me but I suspect she wasn't overly impressed with Ingrid's so-called catch. In that she was entirely justified.

The night before the wedding, she hosted a drinks party in her home for my parents and me, as well as neighbours and friends and the handful of guests I had brought from Ireland. Halfway through the night I slipped out to have dinner with an old Burroughs buddy and his wife who were staying at a nearby hotel. I left Ingrid behind with everyone asking where her intended was. She was not pleased. When I got back to the house the temperature was arctic.

Kyran McLaughlin was my best man. After the drinks party we went back to the room we were sharing in the hotel where the reception was taking place. Maybe my behaviour earlier that evening was a manifestation of it but I suddenly found myself riven by doubt. Kyran and I sat up until the early hours talking it over.

I said, 'I can't get married. You saw what she was like to me in the house. I can't deal with this woman.'

'Everybody feels like this the night before their wedding,' Kyran said.

At the meal after the wedding my mother was seated next to Ingrid and subjected her to her Irish-Mammy-from-Hell act: 'Now, George likes his eggs lightly boiled, so three minutes is all you give them. And what I usually do as well is that before he gets dressed I hold his underpants close to the fire to make sure they're warm when he puts them on . . .' Ingrid, to her credit, endured it stoically.

We had five days in which to cram in the wedding and some kind of honeymoon before the Mary's game the following Saturday. After the reception we got in a car and drove up the M6, nothing happening by way of conversation. She's looking at the man whom she's sworn before God she'll love, honour and obey, and he's entered into the commitment like he's just signed up for Mary's for the new season. If someone you love is upset, your natural instinct should be to make them happy. I didn't know how. I didn't know this woman. I was about to get into bed with a stranger.

We spent a few nights in a lovely little five-star hotel in the Lake District. Miserable. The honeymoon is a blank, apart from the ugly tension that hung over us like a leaden cloud. The only nice thing we did was take a walk through a wood and I dallied ten yards behind her, feeling sorry for myself and wondering if I had made a mistake.

She was not to blame. She understood the commitment, I did not. All we had going for us was that she genuinely loved me. She had to love me to stand by me while I spent the next twenty-five or more years slow-walking her through hell. The wedding set the tone for the future. The good days ahead would be precious few.

Elsewhere I had already laid the foundations for a very unhappy life. Having clinched the *Press* and *Independent* deals and squirrelled the money away in the bank, I began to believe in the myth of my own invulnerability. And then I made what was the worst decision in a lifetime of bad decisions: I went into business with my old friend Pat Campbell.

Pat's parents had a number of guest houses on Gardiner Street and Middle Abbey Street. They were little more than simple low-budget bed-and-breakfasts, but Ireland was a desperately poor country and there was a fortune to be made in two-star accommodation. When the sixties arrived there was a lot more money splashing around and people were prepared to pay for better. The Campbells largely handed over the business to their children. Each of them – two sons, two daughters – was given a property to run.

Pat's was the Ulster Arms in Gardiner Place. But Pat's calling wasn't to be a simple hotelier. He was a visionary. The B&B business was quiet in the winter and his mind turned to other ways of developing his business, including catering. In 1967, at the age of 24, he set up Campbell Catering Ltd and landed the contract to feed 35,000 primary school children under the Dublin Corporation school meals scheme.

The Corporation's name for the scheme was something of an exaggeration. What the children actually got was sandwiches: on Monday a cheese sandwich; on Tuesday a meat sandwich, usually corned beef; on Wednesday a currant bun; on Thursday a meat sandwich again; and on Friday a jam sandwich. Every day they got a bottle of milk. Pat was preparing all these lunches in the basement of the Ulster Arms, an area that, until two weeks before he got the contract, had been stuffed to the gills with old bicycles and antique furniture.

And this is the point at which I joined him. As I was leafing through the *Irish Times* one day a recruitment ad for Campbell Catering caught my eye. Clearly my old friend from my days in student politics was doing well. I padded across town to Pat's office in Gardiner Place to congratulate him. And I walked out an hour later as the Marketing Manager of Campbell Catering.

This was *the* seminal moment in my life, when I sallied off down a long, awful road that almost cost me my marriage and drove me to the verge of taking my own life. What possessed me to go into catering – a business about which I knew nothing – I do not know. Why didn't I at least try to find out about the industry? Hubris, maybe. I had just lodged a £3,750 commission cheque in the bank and I had a girl I was crazy about. I thought I was invincible.

For the first couple of weeks all I saw were thousands of sandwiches going out the front door every day and five Volkswagen vans criss-crossing the city to get them to the schools. I was so taken with the glamour of being in on the ground floor that I did not concern myself with the finer points of how a new business – particularly one that operated on such tight margins – was going to succeed. After a couple of weeks I realized that there was no easy money to be made in catering. Every penny had to be watched and worked for. Catering was a high-turnover business but the overheads were colossal. The vans were all leased. There was the butcher to pay. The dairy. The bread suppliers. There was insurance. Labour. Though organizationally Campbell Catering was able to fulfil its commitments, it was a real juggling act for a young and inexperienced management to maintain financial control.

Pat had managed to win the schools contract from Lawlors of Naas, which had had it for years. He had approached the Corporation with a good business plan and won the tender based on low overheads and low staff costs. But Lawlors had been heavily unionized and as soon as he won the contract, the Irish Transport and General Workers Union appeared on the scene. The ITGWU was ridiculously powerful at the time. The words Number Four Branch were enough to strike fear into the heart of anyone who ever worked in catering management. The head of the branch was a guy called Mickey Mullen and when he walked into a hotel, it was as if Jesus Christ had just climbed down off the cross: everything stopped. He could shut down a hotel with the snap of his fingers.

Number Four Branch decreed that former Lawlor employees had to have first refusal on jobs in Campbell Catering. It was absurd, but Pat had no choice but to accept it. However, he had bought not only Lawlors' large workforce, but their service records, their business practices and everything else. Right from the start, the budget was blown out the window.

Pat had the most extraordinary imagination of anyone I ever met in business. One day he decided there was an untapped market for sandwiches in pubs and that, rather than publicans doing their own cutting and slicing, Campbell Catering would deliver them, ready-made and wrapped in plastic. He was years ahead of his time. We won the contract to do the catering for the Galway Races. In those days it was a three-day meet, taking place over a Tuesday, Wednesday and Thursday in August, and the turnover from the catering was enormous. Pat had the idea of having all the sandwiches made in Dublin, then frozen and driven to Galway. He had some brilliant ideas, but because we were running on such a tight budget it was sometimes hell trying to juggle all our commitments to make them work.

Typically, when Pat heard about a new invention called the microwave oven that used electromagnetic waves to heat food thoroughly in a couple of minutes, he imported a consignment of them to sell to food outlets. He had no fear of innovation, but then he was young and professionally trained. We discovered that publicans and restaurant owners were a more conservative bunch and it was hard work for the salesmen to persuade them that this appliance could heat a plate of stew in sixty seconds without cooking the livers in their bodies.

One year for the Galway Races Pat was in Galway while I was supervising the operation from the Dublin end. The vans were due to leave at seven o'clock in the morning but when I arrived at Gardiner Place there was a picket on the door. Number Four Branch objected to us using local labour in Galway because, under some arcane rule that was unfathomable to me, Galway was considered a Dublin meet. They wanted us to bus in all the staff – bar workers, waiting staff – from Dublin. I spent the guts of five hours trying to persuade the truck drivers to pass the picket, and at twelve o'clock on the day of the first meet they finally trundled out of Dublin. Meanwhile, Pat was waiting on the other side of the country with three microwave ovens and, now, a serious union problem on his hands.

When our creditors sensed that we were finding the going tough, they did what creditors do: they crowded Pat. There was a time when every second letter seemed to be the worrying kind – registered mail. But regardless of the tough times we were going through, when we could hardly stop to breathe in case the money ran out, I decided that I was sticking with Campbell Catering. Instead of realizing that I was stressed because I was a square peg in a round hole, I came to the conclusion that it was because of the challenge of being part of a tough start-up. Business moguls always had war stories about the tough early days, so as far as I was concerned, I was clearly on the right career path. I was convinced that we could steer the ship through this patch of fiscal turbulence and that one day soon we'd be up on deck, sipping mango daiquiris under the sun and basking in our multimillionaire status.

At some stage in every single one of those difficult days, I found a quiet space to sit down and write Ingrid a letter. It was the thought of her that helped me maintain my mental equilibrium. Then we got married and I brought her back to the house I had bought in Dublin, one of the few sensible things I'd managed to do in the previous year. When I was debating with the Junior Chamber of Commerce, a group of us used to meet in the front room of a house in Foxrock that belonged to a solicitor called Tim Ryan. One night in 1968 he mentioned that he was selling the house. I'd only ever seen the sitting room, and I had once put my head around the kitchen door, but I said I'd buy it. I still had money in the bank from the *Irish Press* and *Independent* deals. In fact, in just over a month I had earned the money to pay for 80 per cent of what has been my home ever since: I bought 52 Foxrock Park for £5,000. Apart from marrying Ingrid, it was to be the only smart thing I did in thirty years.

I also brought Ingrid back to the ground-zero disaster area that I was making of my life. She didn't know anyone in Ireland. She couldn't do the job she loved because there were no reciprocal arrangements for pharmacy qualifications between Ireland and the UK. She took a job as an assistant in the central pharmacy in St James's hospital, where drugs were issued and dispatched to all the other hospitals around the city. She was working using her talents but being paid a fraction of what she was worth. She had no car, so she was reliant on me to go anywhere. Life must have been miserable for her.

I was busy, meanwhile, making it ten times worse. The Catholic Church grants annulments on the grounds that one or both of the parties involved in the marriage was psychologically unprepared for the vows involved. Ingrid could have claimed that in my case with absolute certainty. When we got married, we had spent a total of about sixty days together. I think if she had lived in Dublin for even a few weeks before she married me there would never have been a wedding: the more she would have seen of me, the less attractive I would have been to her. Instead she found herself discovering the awful truth about me after she had made her commitment. On top of that, my mother was hostile towards her. She thought the sun shone from her boy's derriere. If I'd brought home the Virgin Mary, she'd have said her family wasn't good enough.

My old man had a relatively free rein in life because my old dear did all the worrying. He had his band and he had his tennis and he sauntered through life without a care. I repeated the sins of the father. When I got married, I made no adjustment to my life whatsoever. I found someone who was hewn from the same rock as my mother to be my support, and then I took to gadding about the place just like my old man. There's an old Burt Lancaster movie I love called *Apache*. Lancaster plays an Indian chief and the romantic interest is an Apache woman who worships the ground he walks on. But Lancaster doesn't give a shit about her. He's got his battles against the white man to think about. But she follows him everywhere and she does everything for him. For most of our life together Ingrid played Jean Peters to my Burt Lancaster. It's indicative of how seriously Ingrid took her vows that every evening, throughout the years of hell that I put her through, there was a cooked dinner on the table for me. She did her absolute best as a wife while I carried on like marriage was bed and breakfast with privileges.

I continued playing rugby for Mary's. That was a two-night-a-week commitment in itself. But worse was to come. In the summer, I continued playing cricket. I was a decent batsman and a decent fielder but I was a slow mover between the wickets and must have been run out more times than any player in Pembroke's history. My great nemesis was a fielder called Tony Obernik, who played for Carlisle, the Jewish club on the Kimmage Road West. He also played rugby for Carlisle in the winter. I met him in the street one day and he said he'd just been appointed captain of the club but was worried because they weren't up to much. He asked me if I'd lend a hand coaching the team.

My marriage could go hang: I had found my calling. Many starting coaches quit after a short time because of the difficulties of coaching one's peers or the show-us-your-medals kind of resentment at clubs. At Carlisle, no one cared what school I'd gone to, how many Schools Cup medals I'd won or how many Ireland trials I'd had. They wanted me and that fired my confidence. Rugby is often called civilized man's warfare and I'd spent years reading about the great wars – from Napoleon's victories right through to Arnhem – and was fascinated by battlefield strategy. I'd always fancied myself as an armchair general, so I threw myself fervently into coaching. I started to learn about back play. Should they be deep or shallow? Close together or wide? How do you defend? I picked the brains of every backs' coach I knew; read every book I could lay my hands on; and in time I became better at coaching backs than forwards.

Carlisle had a squad of seventeen players from which to pick fifteen, but soon we started winning matches. I offered myself to them as a first-team coach. Being a Jewish club, they played their games on Sundays instead of Saturdays, which meant I could continue playing for Mary's. Like most clubs, Carlisle trained on Tuesday and Thursday nights. I told them that if they switched to Mondays and Wednesdays, I'd be prepared to become their full-time coach. This was in 1970. I was married barely a year and now I was out of the house on Monday, Tuesday, Wednesday and Thursday nights, and Saturday and Sunday afternoons.

The joke in Mary's was that I only coached Carlisle to get 10 per cent off my jewellery purchases. But I just loved the feeling – a feeling I no longer enjoyed in my working life – that what I was doing made a difference. Players improved right in front of my eyes. A year later, I quit Mary's and became player-coach to Carlisle. We pulled off some extraordinary results. We were the equivalent of a fourth team of a senior club but capable of punching far above our weight. We beat teams two divisions above us in the Spencer Cup and no one could quite believe it. In three years, we made it to three cup finals.

I was never home, but never happier. I was slowly worrying at the threads holding our marriage together. The inscription on our wedding rings reads: '17th March 1967 – won. 3rd March 1969 – one.' It was indicative of my commitment to the marriage that I didn't wear mine. It stayed on for a couple of weeks, then I took it off on the flimsiest of pretexts: I was docked marks in a Junior Chamber of Commerce debating competition for fiddling with it, so off it came. I couldn't even wear a small band of gold that signified this commitment I'd made.

What I put Ingrid through was a form of spousal abuse. I never drank. I was never violent. I wasn't in Zhivago's nightclub four nights a week. I never put our mortgage repayments on the 3.30 at Chepstow. But it was abuse by neglect. Even when I was home on a Saturday night, I was watching *Match of the Day* followed by the late-night western. The guy who wrote to his girlfriend every single day for two years couldn't talk to her as his wife.

Darkness was descending fast on my life. My home situation wasn't good and I was miserable in my work. Whatever friendship Pat and I had had withered and died in the intense heat of our business relationship. It had taken me only a short time to realize that getting along well as students wasn't going to turn us into captains of industry. Being friends in college was easy, but we soon saw sides to one another that we didn't like. Though it was entirely my own doing, I blamed Pat for letting me leave Burroughs to enter an industry I didn't understand: it was a classic example of not taking responsibility for my own choices. He blamed me for not performing and he was right. But, though I couldn't see it at the time, we were coming from different places. He had found his natural métier, and no matter how hard it was in these early days, he was energized by doing something he was gifted at. I was in the opposite situation. I was in an industry for which I had no natural aptitude nor understanding and the normal struggles and challenges that came with getting a business off the ground left me feeling demoralized.

Our rows took on a sharper edge. After one exchange of views over the amount of time I was – or wasn't – spending in the office, Pat sent me a memo, at the back of which was a pen-and-ink drawing that he said summed up our situation. (He was a fantastic artist.) The picture was of the two of us on board the Good Ship *Campbell Catering*. The boat was shipping water and he was rowing like a madman trying to get us to dry land. I was standing up in the middle of the boat, saying, 'I can save the boat! But I'm not prepared to paddle or plug the holes!' I felt very hurt. I thought I doing my best to meet my responsibilities. But I guess he was getting at my lack of enthusiasm.

The weekends were balm to my bruised soul. I had forty-eight hours in which no one could get at me. I remember one Sunday afternoon driving Ingrid down to Tipperary. She was studying for her Masters at UCD. Her dissertation was on peppermint and a pharmaceutical company in Roscrea had given her a small square of land to grow plants. Every weekend for four months we drove down together. Ingrid watered the plants, took measurements and carried out tests while I did the legwork, filling containers and digging holes. I remember this one particular Sunday, which came at the end of a week of hell at work, looking at cows in a field and thinking, 'Wouldn't it be great to be a cow?' But the next day it was back to work for more of the same.

★

At the end of five years together Pat and I reached the endgame. We were like a couple trapped in a loveless marriage: we were breathing the same air but that was all we had in common. I hated the business so much I couldn't rouse myself to get out of bed and go to work in the mornings.

There was a rumour that Aer Lingus, which now had a catering arm, was going to tender for the schools contract. Pat picked up the phone, rang Aer Lingus and asked baldly if it was true. It wasn't. Then Mrs Lawlor died and the family business closed. She was a giant in the industry and ran the company from bed in her declining years. Her children seemed less interested in many of the contracts like the sandwiches and racecourse catering. Suddenly, there was no competition and Campbell Catering could start to breathe.

The extra money steadied the ship. I think that's when Pat had time to think about his team and realized he could live without me. I was a pain in the arse. All I was contributing was negativity. So he set up a board meeting and he sacked me.

It took a court case to part the two of us. We settled in camera. We horse-traded. Pat would forget this if I forgot that. I'd write off something if Pat would write off something else. I gave him back the 25 per cent of the business he had given me and I walked away full of sadness and bitterness.

Not long afterwards Pat landed the catering contract for an oil-drilling operation off the south coast. Then – his genius again – he bought Bewley's when it was effectively bankrupt and nobody wanted it. He turned the coffee shops around. The wholesalers became a goldmine. The 25 per cent of the company that I threw back at Pat in a fit of pique was worth millions a few years later.

Pat and I never spoke again. For a long time I harboured a sense of grievance and believed that he wouldn't have become such a success story were it not for me. Had I made a success of business, I could say that I was right and Pat was wrong. However, the fact is that he and some of his other associates became some of the country's most successful businessmen. Gerry Houlihan, who, in the early days of Campbell Catering, quit his job as a barman to become Pat's chief sandwich salesman, now owns Clontarf Castle and DID Electric. Paddy Kelly, his builder cousin, is one of the biggest property developers on this island. I remember sitting in my office in my forty-seven-pound suit thinking none of them had a clue. I don't even have the consolation of being able to say that the experience made me wiser.

4. Building a world on quicksand

It shames me that I know that my first child's birth coincided with Leinster losing 8–3 to the All Blacks at Lansdowne Road on 16 November 1972. I slipped out to the match while Ingrid was counting the intervals between contractions. I got back to the labour ward in the Rotunda with hours to spare and I saw Michelle pulled into the world at about 2 a.m. the following morning. But the fact that rugby entered my thoughts at all is damning.

I was thrilled when this little bundle was presented to me. Throughout Ingrid's pregnancy I kept thinking of the baby as a boy who would grow up and play Schools Senior Cup rugby and achieve everything that I had never done. But when I found out I had a daughter, I was overwhelmed by a tide of emotion. Ingrid was sleeping. I sat there staring at Michelle in her crib for hours and hours, thinking, *How did I achieve this? How come I didn't balls this up like I do everything else?*

I think Ingrid hoped that becoming a father might change me. And when Michelle was a baby, I gave a very good outward impression of a caring, sharing dad. I changed nappies and I went to watch rugby matches with her strapped to my back. But I was still emotionally retarded. Still gadding about the place a boulevardier, footloose and fancy-free. I wanted to be a father but hadn't the first notion how to do it and no real interest in finding out.

Meanwhile, I was making an unutterable mess of the economics of our lives. When Pat Campbell and I parted company, I should have taken a time-out. I was too emotional for my next step to be rational. My ill feelings towards him clouded my judgement. The experience of the previous five years should have told me, at a decibel level that was deafening, that I was in the wrong line of work, but in a fit of petulance I decided to stay in catering. My pride was hurt, my manhood affronted, and now I was going to show Pat what kind of man I was.

I took his catering manager from under his nose. Matt Dowling was a lovely man, a huge guy with a big red beard. He wasn't happy working for Pat and I needed someone: I couldn't make a sandwich. So when I left, Matt hitched his wagon to mine. In 1973 I started Dowling and Associates (I always thought Hook was an unfortunate name for anyone involved in business, appropriate as it was for me). We set up a factory in the kitchen in Ardmore Studios in Bray and later moved to Brown and Nolan's in Clonskeagh. We piggybacked on the spare capacity in their kitchens to make the sandwiches for Dublin Corporation.

Now you had this ludicrous situation of two men – Pat and me – who hated each other, and the focus of their hatred was sandwiches: the six million sandwiches a year needed to feed the schoolchildren of Dublin. We allowed ourselves to be sucked into a self-destructive tendering war, where each would undercut the other with the object of winning the contract from the Corporation. Back and forth it travelled between us, the overheads so high and the tender so low that we were the only two caterers in Dublin interested in it. All that mattered to me was that Pat didn't have it. Maybe he felt the same way.

Despite being blinded by bitterness, I made some sound business decisions at the time. In my own company I sorted out some of the labour problems that were endemic to catering. I mechanized the sandwich-making operation: there were no more production lines of people spreading jam on bread. And I brought costs right down to the floor and the business became profitable again.

But then I got delusions of grandeur. Instead of simply taking the profit and earning a reasonable living. I thought about being a big businessman. Ireland's racecourses had large catering needs and I went after them. Galway was the first big one I attempted and, thanks to Matt, we made a success of it. Lord Killanin, who was chairman of the Galway Race Committee, was a big fan of our work and used his influence to gain an entrée for me to other courses. He picked up the phone and sang my praises to Frank O'Reilly, the Irish Distillers boss who was chairman of Punchestown. We took over at Punchestown, followed quickly by the Curragh and, soon after that, Leopardstown.

This apparent success was the worst thing that could have happened to someone developing notions about himself as a businessman. There's an economic theory called Gresham's Law, often expressed as 'Bad money drives out good': you chase turnover instead of profit. That's the trap into which I gaily stepped. There wasn't really any good money to be made from racecourse catering, but you were fooled into believing you were rich because the turnover – the bad money – was so enormous. You might close up at the end of a race day in Leopardstown with ten grand stuffing the tills. You might owe nine grand of it. But your suppliers didn't have to be paid for ninety days so you used that money for something else, usually to settle other debts. Then you had three months to find the money to pay for the food and drink you sold at Leopardstown. But in the meantime there'd be another race meeting, maybe Punchestown, and now you'd have the money you owed. Now you had ninety days to worry about how you would pay for the supplies for Punchestown.

It was just like having a huge overdraft; one you could mantain only with an ever-escalating turnover. You were always teeming and lading. Robbing Peter, paying Paul.

Because I was such a good salesman, more and more work fell my way. Dowling and Associates ran canteens in some of Ireland's major companies. The *Irish Times*, the *Independent* and Smurfit Group all quickly became part of the growing empire.

One of my early forays into film-location catering was during the Campbell era. An accountant friend of mine, Jim Barry, was managing Ardmore Studios. He rang me and enquired about the possibility of us doing the catering. Our first movie was *Zardoz*, John Boorman's futuristic fantasy, set in the year 2293, when the earth had become a wasteland ruled by the Exterminators.

Typically Matt launched in to the unknown and made an

outstanding success of the job. He was an extraordinary caterer and in different circumstances might have been one of the shining lights of the industry. With the contract in our pocket we did not have the equipment necessary to do the job, but Matt spotted an old Calor Gas mobile demonstration kitchen on a car dealer's lot and had it up and running for the film within a few days.

On *Zardoz*, without knowing the first thing about location catering, Matt delivered a tour de force which enabled us to dominate the industry in Ireland for years. In fact, Matt created the industry. Before *Zardoz* location catering in Ireland was dominated by British firms who were brought over by film makers who despaired of finding an indigenous Irish operator. Rarely, if ever, since *Zardoz* has a non-Irish caterer been used in a film in Ireland.

The star, Sean Connery, used *Zardoz* to break out of the typecasting that was James Bond. He had discovered golf on *Goldfinger* and I think Ireland's courses may have been used as a lure by Boorman. Connery never played the Hollywood card. He'd stand in the food queue with the chippies and the sparks, then he'd say in that wonderfully sibilant way of his, 'Hello, chef, fantashtic day. I shee you have shome bacon and shoshage. That'll do nishely.'

The pity was that they weren't all like him.

Sometime in the mid-1970s Rex Harrison did a commercial for General Motors that was filmed in Ireland. If you read any of the biographies of his life, it's pretty clear that Harrison was a nasty piece of work. In my view, the man was touched by madness. Dowling and Associates catered on the set and had to bring all his meals to him in his caravan. I'd send one of our girls over with his dinner and you'd hear him roar, 'You call this fucking steak? You stupid fucking bitch,' and he'd throw it at her. The next day you'd have to send someone else.

What always amazed me was that people in movies saw these flashes of rage as signs of arrogance. To me, it was crippling insecurity, a flaw I recognized in myself. These people live in a world of uncertainty, where one minute you're hot and the next you're not. They crave approval. Applause is their oxygen. Their way of getting it, like the stars of Hollywood's golden age, is to be difficult.

I remember Joan Collins threw a hissy fit one morning on the set of *The Big Sleep*, Michael Winner's dreadful 1977 remake of the Bogart and Bacall classic. It was shot in England and I got the contract to cater on the set. They were shooting a scene on London Bridge. It was 6 a.m. The breakfast had been cooked and served and we heard the fateful words, 'OK, it's a wrap.'

Matt and the crew wondered how could it be a wrap at six o'clock in the morning. The production manager, Bernie Williams, said, 'No China tea. Joan's walked off.'

'China tea?' Matt said, in shock. 'I could get some.'

'It's not your fault,' he said. 'You weren't told. That's a day's shooting lost. Same time tomorrow.'

It was an unreal world.

I found Pierce Brosnan difficult to like, but then he was in understandably foul form when our paths crossed. The producer Cubby Broccoli had asked him to replace Roger Moore as James Bond but the Mary Tyler Moore Studios decided to make three final episodes of the decommissioned TV series *Remington Steele*, in which he starred, and he could not get out of his contract. So Timothy Dalton became the new Bond and Brosnan continued to get peanuts for making the joyless *Remington Steele*.

One of the three episodes was shot around Malahide Castle in Dublin. He complained about everything. His kid had a birthday during shooting and I had a cake made. I got no thanks from Brosnan. Everything was wrong. Eventually he said he wasn't going on until the caterers were thrown off the set. The producer told him to wise up, but only because it would have been impossible to get another firm in at such short notice.

In 1979, I'm asked to do the catering on another Boorman film, *Excalibur*, his retelling of the legend of King Arthur and Merlin. I'm convinced I'm on the up and up now, so I splash out on a deluxe, state-of-the-art catering truck that I have built to specification. It's my pride and joy. A shining symbol of where I'm headed in life. However, typical of Ireland in the 1970s, the truck isn't quite finished when shooting is due to start. The kitchen equipment isn't fitted, so instead I've got freestanding catering equipment in the back.

Filming is in Wicklow against the stunning backdrop of the Sally Gap, the Sugar Loaf, Childer's Wood and Powerscourt Waterfall. Almost all of the shooting is done at night. Work starts at 6 p.m. and finishes at 6 a.m. Most of the sets are in Ardmore Studios. I have the truck parked in a field at the back of the studios. It's been raining non-stop for the six weeks it's been there. So now the location switches ten miles away to Lough Tay, where they're shooting the seminal scene in which King Arthur throws the sword into the lake. Everyone packs up and leaves. I climb into the truck, turn the key, put my foot on the accelerator and the wheels just spin in the ground. I'm stuck. It's 4 a.m. I'm expected in Wicklow to have breakfast prepared for the cast and crew in two and a half hours.

I manage to find a local farmer with a tractor and persuade him to get out of bed to drag me out of what is effectively a swamp. It's going to involve a lot of bumping and jouncing so I get into the back to make sure the water boilers don't topple over. We connect the towrope and he fires up the tractor. The truck starts to move. I'm standing in the back, in the pitch black, with my arms outstretched, trying to hold two boilers full of water, still hot from the previous evening's endeavours, back against the walls while also trying to keep my balance as I'm dragged 250 yards backwards through the mud towards the road. I arrive in Wicklow a gibbering lunatic.

Location catering was lucrative: movie moguls know, like Napoleon, that the army marches on its stomach and tend not to count the cost of the catering. But it was another profitable business that was to get lost in the maw of my failed enterprise.

I was receiving hundreds of thousands of pounds in turnover every year, employing almost a thousand people in some capacity or other, and losing money hand over fist. It seems ludicrous now, looking back on it at this remove, to believe that someone could exist for twenty-five years in business without ever making a shilling. Let's just say my survival instincts were good.

I had all the old tricks that businessmen fall back on in times of recession. I didn't render unto Caesar that which was Caesar's: I didn't pay my VAT; I didn't pay the PAYE; I didn't pay my creditors, or paid them late, or paid them half of what they were owed.

As well as that, one of my great talents was an ability to borrow money. I was brilliant at it. Sane men with unimpeachable business qualifications handed me thousands and thousands of pounds across counters, believing they were going to see it again. I borrowed from Guinness and Mahon, Ulster Bank, two branches of Allied Irish Bank, and three branches of Bank of Ireland. Anywhere that money was being handed out, I was there with my palm upturned.

Looking back, it was during this period of my life that I started to undergo some form of personality change. I was telling fibs all day. I fibbed to creditors. I fibbed to clients. I fibbed to suppliers. I fibbed to banks. It was a small step then to start fibbing to Ingrid.

Pretty early in our marriage Ingrid had discovered that I was dysfunctional financially as well as emotionally and she took control of the household finances. All she asked of me was that I made sure to pay the phone bill on time and that I gave her a cheque for an agreed amount on the 14th of every month as my contribution to the running of our home. I couldn't even get that right. Sometimes I was late; sometimes the cheque would bounce; sometimes there would be no cheque at all. The phone was cut off an average of six times a year.

Dowling and Associates had the appearance and attitude of a thriving business, but Ingrid knew I had money troubles. She'd answer the phone at seven o'clock at night and a voice would say, 'Where's your bloody husband? He owes me five hundred quid for bread.' But never once did I tell Ingrid that our entire lives were built on quicksand. I could always explain away the calls.

I told so many lies that I lost my moral compass. I didn't now know where fiction ended and fact began. I was engaged in the same battle that my mother fought, smuggling her two suitcases of chipolata sausages into England, except instead of dealing with customs men it was my creditors I had to outwit. But there wasn't a problem I couldn't brazen out.

Cash flow was always a problem so I started doing what we bad businessmen know as kiting cheques. You could hide so many sins in the days before banks were computerized. Every branch was to all intents and purposes independent. If you lodged a cheque in AIB in Ballsbridge on a Tuesday, it went to central clearing on Wednesday and it arrived in the bank you'd written it on, say Bank of Ireland, Baggot Street, on Thursday. So it was in limbo for two days. If you wrote a cheque out to yourself for two grand, for forty-eight hours the bank thought that you had two grand. Then you had two days to get money into the first bank to make sure it was honoured. That limbo period helped keep me in business for twenty-five years.

I was kiting cheques all over town. I had a dozen bank accounts. I'd write a cheque and walk out of one bank with ten grand in cash to pay some debt or other. Then I'd dream up some way of getting ten grand into the account it was drawn on to make sure it didn't bounce.

If I couldn't come up with the money, I'd write another cheque to cover it, drawn on another bank. I had a huge circle of banks involved. I went from Bank of Ireland on Baggot Street, to Ulster Banks in Ballsbridge and Tallaght, to Guinness and Mahon on Dame Street and many more institutions that happily I have forgotten. Except you couldn't lodge a round figure because the bank would get wise to what you were doing. So if I was going to bounce for £10,000, I'd have to make sure to lodge £10,345 or £11,666, some random amount that made it look less calculated. So the amounts I needed to honour these cheques were getting bigger and bigger: what started off as ten grand quickly became fifteen or twenty.

All of these banks thought I was worth tens of thousands of pounds but the cheques were a fiction. I was buying myself time – forty-eight hours at a go – until a race meeting came up and I could lay my hands on some real money. I'd drive home from

Punchestown or Galway with ten or twenty grand in notes and coins in the back of the car, with the boot lid tied down and the exhaust kissing the road, and I'd lodge the cash to stop the cycle. But then I needed £10,000 to settle another debt and it all kicked off again.

Gerry Boyd saved my hide more times than I could ever thank him for. In normal circumstances cheques took forty-eight hours to clear. The bank that the cheque was drawn on had to send it back if there were no funds to cover it. There was a system, though, where it could be held for an extra day. Gerry did that for me. It bought me seventy-two hours instead of forty-eight.

Keeping account of how much money had to be lodged into which account to honour which cheque started to consume all of my energy and attention. There were days of gut-wrenching terror. I'd spend the morning and afternoon staring into the abyss and pull myself back from the precipice by making the appropriate deposit a minute before the banks closed.

One year I'm doing the Christmas meeting at Leopardstown and I have no float for the tills. I'd ordered £10,000 in cash from the Bank of Ireland but Gerry, who's long since discovered I'm not the alchemist he thought I was, had rung to say he couldn't approve it with the state my finances were in. I couldn't blame him.

But now it's Christmas Eve. The meeting starts on St Stephen's Day and I need to raise ten grand in the few hours left before the banks shut for Christmas. If I don't, there'll be no bars or restaurants on the busiest day of the Leopardstown year and I'll quite likely never work in this town again.

I phone Mick Pender in Guinness and Mahon. I can't reach him. I manage to get hold of his secretary, Joan, who reminds me that it's Christmas Eve. He's having drinks. Bankers do that.

'Joan,' I say, 'I'm out at Leopardstown Racecourse on the 26th. I need ten grand.'

'He'll be back around half-eleven,' she says. 'He'll be here for about half an hour, then he has to shoot off again. Why don't I get him to ring you then?'

I look at my watch. It's getting late in the morning. What if he forgets to call me? What if he rings and I'm on another call? The coin centre is closing for the day at lunchtime. I've no choice. I jump into the car and point it in the direction of the city centre. Mobile phones haven't been invented, so during the half an hour it takes me to reach town I'm incommunicado. My heart is thumping. I'm looking at my watch all the way in.

The Christmas Eve traffic is horrendous. Grafton Street hasn't been pedestrianized yet, and it's impassable. The cars are locked solid, nose to rear, right the way down the street. I look at my watch again. I have five minutes to get to the end of the street and up to Mick's office on Dame Street. I turn the wheel left and mount the pavement. A switch has tripped. I'm a man possessed now. It's like a scene from *The French Connection*. I've got one wheel on the pavement and one wheel on the road and I'm sending shoppers scattering. Halfway down the street, outside Bewley's, there's a young Garda. His jaw drops when he sees me. He steps in front of the car and I slam my foot on the brake.

'What the hell are you at?' he says.

'Guard,' I say, 'there's a fella at the end of the street having a heart attack and if I don't get there he's dead.'

I'm the fella having the heart attack but he takes it that I'm a doctor and he tells me to follow him. He races in front of the car and starts shouting at people, ordering them to clear a path, and gives me an escort to the bottom of Grafton Street, where I turn left into Suffolk Street, right at O'Neill's pub and abandon the car outside Guinness and Mahon on Dame Street. I take the steps up to Mick's office two at a time and Joan tells me to go in. Mick is full of the holiday spirit, which I am about to spoil. 'Merry Christmas,' he says.

'Mick,' I say, 'I have to have ten grand.'

There's not a flicker from him. 'When will I get it back?' he says. I feel like kissing him.

'On the fifth day of Leopardstown, I'll have the ten grand for you,' I tell him.

'Fine,' he says and he phones one of the cashiers and he says, 'Have a draft ready for Mister Hook for £10,000.'

So I collect it from the cashier, jump back into the car and spin around to Foster Place. I arrive at the coin centre five minutes before it's due to close for Christmas, looking for ten grand in cash. Not surprisingly, the guys working there don't extend me any Christmas goodwill. They wheel the coins to my car on two trolleys and I load it into the boot. The belly of the car is barely above the ground. I drive home and leave it parked outside the house all night, too exhausted to take the bounty out of the boot.

Then I remember that I haven't got anyone to do security for me at the racecourse over Christmas. The shelves have been stocked with bottles. There's enough food to feed 5,000 people. So I end up spending Christmas night on my own in the racecourse bar. I read a book, drink endless cups of tea and catnap, at no point pausing to ask what the hell I am doing this for.

The penny was a long time dropping.

It was around this time that I had another of my dalliances with death. Ingrid had a blue Mini that I loved driving and occasionally borrowed. For years I'd been promising to replace the tyres, which, by then, had worn down to almost a smooth finish. One night I was on the way home from Dublin and doing sixty miles per hour in the wet on the Rock Road. I hit the brakes approaching the lights opposite the Punch Bowl pub and aquaplaned. I was no longer in control of the car. It flew across the road and crossed to the other side into the path of oncoming traffic. All I saw were all these sets of headlights rushing towards me. Somehow the car skidded between two oncoming cars, like a stunt from a Harold Lloyd movie. But I wasn't safe yet. The car continued skidding sideways across the rain-slicked road and the driver's side was about to mount the pavement and smash into a wall. In my mind, I said, 'This is it, George. You're a dead man.' The car hit the kerb side-on and all four wheels left the road. But then it landed again, safely on the footpath. I was sitting there saying, 'Holy Jesus!' over and over again.

★

Work was an endless series of endless hassles. I was in bed one Saturday morning when the phone rang. It was the secretary of Leopardstown Racecourse. 'There's a picket outside,' he said. 'The staff won't pass it. Even the jockeys won't go in.'

'What's that got to do with me?' I asked.

'It's a woman – one woman – carrying a placard, saying you won't employ her.'

I couldn't remember ever meeting the woman he described. I didn't remember her applying for a job. All Leopardstown cared about was making her go away.

'I don't care what she does,' he said, 'and I don't care what it costs, just give her a job.'

'No,' I said, 'I'm not doing it. Next week, there will be ten of her friends out there.'

The head of Number Four Branch at the time was Tommy White, who lived in a little cottage in Ringsend. I got out of bed, got dressed, drove to his home and rousted him from his bed.

'She's nothing to do with us,' he said.

'Well, will you come up to Leopardstown with me and tell her that unless she moves off, she'll never work in catering in this town again?'

Which is exactly what Tommy did.

It was one of the very few occasions in my life when I could be accused of taking definitive action. I was – and remain to this day – the prince of procrastinators.

The decision to take the wrong job in the wrong industry had a catastrophic effect on my life. Anyone who has spent a long time unemployed, or anyone who has been a failure in a particular line of work, will understand how it erodes your self-esteem. Every time someone called to my home looking for money was a reminder of my uselessness. I lived in fear of those knocks. I started spending less and less time at home.

Every day I set an alarm for half-six to be out of the house before anyone could cold-call me. I picked up an *Irish Times* and a *Daily Telegraph* and ate my breakfast in a hotel somewhere, before turning my mind to finding the money to honour the cheques I'd written.

My visits to the office were few and fleeting. I was in and out again without stopping to hear the ever-lengthening list of people who were after my blood. Had I stayed in the office and supervised the running of the company, I might have manoeuvred my way out of trouble, but I was too scared to face people. I hid like the moral coward I was. Because I wasn't in work, I lost contact with my client base.

I dumped everything on Matt. What he needed more than anything was supportive management and I wasn't there. But even if I had been there, I would have been no use. Catering was clearly the wrong line of work for me. My instincts for it were awful.

I remember getting a call from a businessman who wanted to know if I was interested in putting together the first-ever McDonald's fast-food operation in Dublin. The franchise could be mine if I wanted it. I said I thought it was a ridiculous idea. I couldn't conceive of Irish people buying takeaway food and, worse still, eating hamburgers. I thought the Irish palate was far too sophisticated for Ireland ever to become another outpost of the Golden Arches empire. To me it was simply absurd. I said no thank you.

It was around that time that I decided to enter the property market, another field in which I fancied myself as an expert. I was in the middle of one of my rare and short-lived spells of prosperity and had a few thousand pounds to invest. I bought 83 Waterloo Road in Donnybrook for £11,000. It was a substantial Victorian three-storey building that had been split into flats.

The plan was to renovate the building from top to bottom, converting it into a block of luxury apartments which I would either rent out or sell on. The problem was that the flats contained a few sitting tenants – three old dears – who weren't quite in keeping with the upmarket character I had planned for the place.

My idea was to put rats into the building to get them out. Then I was going to invite some travellers to set up camp on the front lawn.

I paid them a visit – there were two elderly sisters in the ground-floor flat and another elderly lady on the top floor – and discovered very quickly that I wasn't cut out to be a Peter Rachman. They were three lovely old ladies. I started calling in regularly for a cup of tea and a chat. Soon they had me doing their shopping and mowing their grass. And it looked like they were going to live for ever.

I sold the building a few years later to buy myself some breathing space with the banks. It fetched £18,000. Today, it must be worth millions.

Like I said – clueless.

I tried to get out from under the Sword of Damocles. In 1978, I applied for a job as director of rugby with the IRFU. Amateurism was on its last legs and this was the first professional appointment the union had ever made. I sent in my CV, if only as a way of drawing a line under my life as a failed businessman.

I was called for an interview in front of Ronnie Dawson and the interview committee. Beforehand, I went for a cup of coffee in Jury's with Gerry Boyd, who still had far too much faith in me than was good for either of us. I told him I'd applied for a nine-to-five with the IRFU.

'That's all very well,' he said. 'You'll support yourself on a PAYE salary. But you'll never be able to do anything about all the debt you have out there. Forget about the milkman and breadman, George. You owe the banks a fortune and you're personally responsible for that. You'll never make a dent in it.'

'What are you suggesting?' I asked.

'Look, you still have ability as a businessman,' he said. 'You can dig yourself out of this hole.'

Like I said, Gerry had far too much faith in me. I did a terrible interview for the IRFU job, then I slipped back into the old routine: borrowing; kiting cheques; telling lies; staying one step ahead of the posse.

To escape my troubles, I threw myself into rugby. It became my refuge in a literal sense because it had got so that I couldn't go home in the evenings: my creditors were there, parked across the driveway, waiting for me.

I agreed to coach the Junior Cup team at St Mary's College, Rathmines. For a couple of hours every afternoon I was on the rugby pitch in Kenilworth Square and completely incommunicado. I'd finish with them at five o'clock, grab a sandwich, get into my car and drive to Old Belvedere to coach the under-19s. On Wednesday nights I coached the Leinster under-19s and eventually the Leinster under-20s.

All of this was to avoid going home to face the music, but it also salvaged some of my battered ego. Doing something I was good at gave me a rare sense of satisfaction, the feeling that I wasn't completely useless.

I started to act strangely. When I finished rugby training, I generally ate dinner in a hotel somewhere, filled my tank with petrol and spent three or four hours driving around the city, venturing home only when I thought it was safe to. From 8 p.m., until after midnight sometimes, I'd just drive around the city, a hundred miles and more a night, watching the needle on the fuel gauge nudging slowly downwards, going nowhere.

I must have put 25,000 miles a year on the clock just avoiding going home. It was crazy behaviour. There was no question that I was riding the cusp of a nervous breakdown.

There were times when I couldn't hide any more and something would hit my conscience like a bolt of lightning to remind me what a despicable human being I could be. I leased an industrial-sized meat-slicer from Denis Hickie (the uncle of the current Ireland international of the same name). Denis worked for Murray's, a car rental company, which had expanded its business into leasing equipment. We were good friends. We made our debuts together for St Mary's and played in the back row together in a Leinster Senior Cup final. I'd gotten in trouble with Donal O'Sullivan, the man who supplied my meat. He was owed a fortune and wouldn't extend me any more credit, but I needed sausages, ham and pork to keep the whole show on the road.

'Sorry,' he said.

'What if I gave you my meat-slicer as security?' I asked.

He didn't seem keen but I managed to persuade him to give me another consignment of meat and take the machine, which I didn't even own, as collateral. It bought me some time.

Needless to say I defaulted on my payments to Murray's and they decided to repossess the machine. Denis was under huge pressure to find me. His boss was leaning heavily on him. He chased me all over town for two or three weeks. Three or four times a day he rang the house, rang the office, rang Milltown golf club, rang Fitzwilliam tennis club. I stayed a step ahead of him.

One Sunday afternoon there's a knock on the door and Ingrid tells me there's a detective to see me. He says he's from the fraud squad. I wet myself. With all the schemes I have going to keep the business alive, he could be calling for any number of reasons. I show him into the living room and ask how I can help him.

'A Mr Murray has made a complaint against you,' he says.

'I agree, there is a problem,' I say to him, 'but it's not a problem for the police. It's really for the courts.'

I tell him all about the slicer and he agrees that's a civil rather than a criminal matter and he goes away suggesting I sort it out.

Denis is still pursuing me. My pager is chirping away like some manic songbird. He's resorted now to waiting outside the house for me, so I'm back to driving the streets of the city. One night I come home after eleven o'clock and I see his car parked across my driveway. I pull up and notice that he's fast asleep in the driver's seat. He's exhausted. This thing has beaten him.

I make good my escape. I turn the car round, switch the engine off and freewheel down the hill, so as not to wake him. I decide to stay in a hotel for the night.

Then it hits me, that rare bolt of self-awareness. I think, *You bastard. You absolute shit. That's your friend in that car. This is a guy who soldiered alongside you on the rugby pitch. How could you treat him like this?*

So I pull in, get out of the car and walk back up the hill. Denis is sleeping the sleep of the dead. I tap on the window and wake him up. He slowly gets his bearings. He sees me. 'You bollix!' are the first words that spill from his lips.

'I know, Denis,' I say. 'I know. You hate me and you have every right to. But come in and have a cuppa.'

He follows me into the house and I fix us a pot of tea. 'Denis, I am in trouble,' I tell him. 'I'm in serious shit, I know. I'll sort it out, though.'

'Look, George, it's like this,' he says. 'If I don't have that machine or your money by Monday, I'm out of a job.'

'I'll sort it,' I tell him.

And I did. I cobbled together some money, which I used to pay off Murray's. Months later I landed a big contract and needed the slicer that was still sitting in Donal O'Sullivan's factory. In the midst of my depression, O'Sullivan having heard of my good news, comes wandering up the road and asks me if I need the slicer back. He makes no reference to the debt it is underpinning. Once again someone showed faith in my ability. I wonder why?

Meanwhile, I had VAT and PAYE bills piling up and the Revenue Commissioners wanted to speak with me. I had seven banks and who knows how many hire-purchase companies chasing me. My car was about to be respossessed and I had twenty or thirty other creditors looking for me.

What made it worse was that most of my creditors were like Denis – rugby guys who were friends. Through rugby I had established connections that helped keep my business alive long after it should have expired. But I was going to rugby matches every weekend and having to face guys like the old Lansdowne number 8, Donal Chambers, who was chief executive of Allied Irish Banks Leasing, a company which had repossessed my car from outside my office door and was still on the lookout for the catering truck that, luckily for me, was then travelling around the UK catering for some movie or other. Friends like Mick Pender and Ken Wall at Lombard and Ulster Bank, who had gone out on a limb to save me on so many occasions, were suing me because they had no choice. As time went on my disastrous business career was impinging on every part of my life.

At home, Ingrid was keeping the show on the road, but her love for me was being slowly eroded. She was struggling. She was lecturing at the College of Pharmacy, which made her the main breadwinner, and was raising the children. After Michelle, there were two more, George and Alison.

George was born in Mount Carmel in 1975. I was ecstatic. I really, desperately wanted a son and when the nurse said the words, 'It's a boy,' Ingrid sank back into the pillow and said, 'Thanks be to God.' I think she had visions of us trying for babies until well into our forties.

But young George's arrival did nothing to shake me out of my selfish little world. I let Ingrid take up the entire burden. So she was left trying to figure out how to fit breast-feeding around working full time and running a home. I was an occasional visitor into the children's lives; she did everything.

Ingrid told me she was expecting our third child over dinner one night in Fitzwilliam. It came as a complete surprise to me. With Michelle and George, we had been engaged in the business of what's known as trying for a baby, but Alison was conceived against the odds when there was precious little 'trying' going on. I didn't give Ingrid the reaction she wanted. To me another baby was another mouth to feed. Alison was born in 1980 and when I think of the tremendous pleasure she has brought us, and of how dramatically like me she is in so many different ways, it shames me that I ever thought of her potential existence as a burden.

The problem was that I wasn't making a great fist of fatherhood as it stood. All of the children's birthdays, Christmas and Easter were Ingrid Hook productions. She bought their presents, organized egg hunts at Easter and dressed them up in fancy dress for Hallowe'en. And at the end of the week she didn't know if she was going to get any money from me.

I can say I was there for the big things. I never missed a school play, though it was my style to have to catch a flight back home

94

from somewhere, break the world land-speed record between the airport and the school and come crashing through the doors of the hall just as the curtain was coming up. For me it was always about *getting* there, not *being* there.

I was still gadding about like some errant playboy prince, playing golf and rugby and squash and heading inexorably towards bankruptcy.

It baffles me that Ingrid stayed. I think there were two reasons why. One was that she loved me. The second was that her Austro-German background had taught her that there wasn't a problem in the world that couldn't be fixed by toughing it out.

Ingrid's mother, Louise, was born into a reasonably well-to-do family in Vienna. She married a German who was in the Wehrmacht. In 1941, Hitler tore up his non-aggression pact with Stalin and German Panzer divisions began smashing their way into Russia. Ingrid's father was part of the invading army. Her mother, who had a keen sense of adventure, went along too, serving the army in some kind of clerical capacity. She discovered she was pregnant with Ingrid after the Germans were routed at Stalingrad in 1944 and the German army started retreating from Russia.

It's all there in the history books, the horror of the war on the Russian front. Ingrid's father was among the tens of thousands of soldiers listed as missing in action. The presumption was that he was either dead or captured. There was no body to bury and no one to say they saw him fall. The hope was that he was in a Russian prisoner-of-war camp.

Ingrid's mother managed to make it back to the German-occupied Sudetenland – the modern Czech Republic – where she had an aunt, also called Louise, who lived in Komitau, just south of Prague. Tante Louise lived with her husband, who'd been blinded in the First World War, and it was there that she gave birth to Ingrid.

In October 1944 the Russians swept across the border. The liberated Czechs had a lot of old scores to settle with the Sudeten Germans. All of the German residents of Komitau were rounded up by the Czechoslovakian army and made to stand in a line. The soldiers counted down the line. Every tenth person was plucked out, put up against a wall and shot, while the rest of the town looked on. Ingrid was still a babe in arms and her mother pressed her head into her chest so she wouldn't be scarred by what she saw.

The rest of the town's German population, including Tante Louise, her husband and Ingrid and her mother, were put on a train, their destination unknown. They gathered up whatever they could carry and boarded an old locomotive that chugged east. Then it stopped and they were ordered out somewhere in what was to become East Germany.

Tante Louise – showing the trademark German willpower and resourcefulness that I later saw in her niece – got a handcart and travelled from village to village using her knitting and crocheting skills to put food on the table.

Ingrid's mother eventually made it back to Vienna but the city was devastated. She saw an ad for a post in Manchester with an agency that was run by a German, got the job and packed up what little she had. Just before she left for England, Ingrid was diagnosed with tuberculosis which, in the 1940s, was a killer. There was no real cure other than fresh air and reasonable food and there wasn't much of either in Vienna at the time.

Unable to take a child with TB into Britain, she placed Ingrid with a family in Igls, just outside Innsbruck, promising to come back for her as soon as she'd found her feet. After four years working in Britain she finally managed to obtain a passport for Ingrid.

So little Ingrid arrived in Manchester in 1950, seven years old, without a word of English and with no idea who this woman was who claimed to be her mother. Ingrid's mother enrolled her in a little boarding school in the Lake District, where Ingrid got a fast grounding in English.

Because she was an only child, mother and daughter spent a lot of time together. They talked and played a lot of Scrabble and developed between them an incredible bond which lasts to this day.

Her mother met and fell for a man in Manchester, a typical north-of-England type called Albert Toft, but she wouldn't marry him until she knew for sure that her husband was dead. There were hundreds of thousands of German prisoners of war still in labour camps in Russia, even though the fighting had long since ended. Then, when Konrad Adenauer became Chancellor of the new West Germany, he cut a deal with the Russians, the upshot of which was that the German POWs would be repatriated.

Ingrid's father didn't come back and her mother married Albert. Only in the last couple of years has evidence emerged to pinpoint where Ingrid's father fell on the Russian front.

So that's an insight into the history of the incredible woman I married, the kind of person who sees even the direst situation as something she can and will tough out. She is made of stern stuff and refused to give up, even as I piled indignity upon indignity upon her.

There was no doubt that I loved her. I adored her. That's not just me looking back through rose-tinted glasses now that my life is in some kind of order, and imagining that I cared for my wife. I know I always loved her because I can remember each fleeting moment of happiness in those dark days. The rare peals of laughter; the odd smile that used to send a shiver up my spine. To me she was always the woman I first saw in the green dress at Lytham Squash Club. But I never told her so. I was incapable of communication.

Had I swallowed my pride and told her about the financial trouble we were in, I think she would have saved me from myself. Had she known that this so-called business empire of mine was a million-pound house of cards, she would have persuaded me to do something else. Even unemployment would have been better for us. There wouldn't have been much money coming in but at least I wouldn't have been losing it. I could have eased her burden by doing the housework and collecting the children from school. She would have taken in washing. She would have cleaned houses. Pragmatism is the German way.

My pig-headed pride stopped me telling her how bad things were throughout the 1970s and 1980s. The kernel of the problem was my lack of self-confidence. I never believed I could get another job. Once, in the distant – happy – past, I had been a great salesman. I could have sold insurance. I could have sold *Encyclopaedia Britannica* from door to door. But I was afraid and ashamed to admit my failure. So I kept doing what I was doing.

Sometimes – rarely – I made money. When I made money, I was dangerous. I thought I was a Rockefeller. The memory of one isolated success would become a sump from which I drew encouragement to keep the business going. Boom time was always just beyond the next hill.

When Pope John Paul II visited Ireland in 1979 a congregation of one million people was expected to hear him say Mass in the Phoenix Park. That was one million mouths to feed. John Raftery, who worked for Bord Fáilte, phoned me and every other event caterer in the country to say that they'd need stalls selling mostly sandwiches and hot drinks.

It was one of the few times in all my years in business that I was clever. I said it wasn't for me. John asked if I'd be interested in feeding the 5,000 bishops and priests instead. This was a guaranteed earner: we'd set up a serving area underneath the dais where the altar stood. From there, we'd hand out sandwiches, teas and coffees to the attending clergy. Unlike the original this modern-day feeding of the 5,000 required no miracle with loaves and fishes to succeed. Everyone was given a meal ticket which they could hand to us in exchange for lunch and Bord Fáilte paid us on the basis of how many tickets we collected. Even with my track record, I couldn't lose.

Meanwhile, the caterers who'd seen the Pope's visit as manna from heaven lost their shirts. At Masses up and down the country, priests reminded their parishioners that if they were going to the Phoenix Park to take a packed lunch with them. One caterer I knew arrived with 25,000 sandwiches. He sold 200. In the Bible story, after Jesus divided the five loaves and two fishes between the crowd, the disciples managed to fill eleven baskets with the leftovers. In this case, a JCB arrived the following day to dig a hole in the ground. The leftover ham, cheese and egg sandwiches were dumped in and covered over. There was much wailing and ganshing of teeth, but for once not from me.

The BBC had a large crew on hand to cover the occasion. I'd done quite a bit of location catering for them, so they asked me to look after the team for the duration of the visit. The Pope was staying in the Papal Nuncio's residence on the Cabra Road and being helicoptered to engagements outside of Dublin. The BBC team was also staying at the Nunciature. In the evenings, while I would be feeding them in one room, in the next the Pope would be having supper with Eamon Casey, the Bishop of Galway, and Cardinal O'Fiaich, the Archbishop of Armagh. It's difficult now to picture the late Pontiff as a fit and healthy man, but when I saw him in the house I was surprised at how physically robust he looked for someone close to sixty. Casey and O'Fiaich couldn't keep up with him. I'd open the door of our room and watch this line of nuns running in and out of the main dining room with plates and plates of food. He'd be quaffing wine and ordering more meat. The two boys were bollixed. He kept them up half the night, drinking and talking and eating.

The Man Upstairs might have been sending me a divine message with the Pope's visit: stick to just one thing. If he was, I missed it, of course. Event catering might have been profitable if I had concentrated on just that, but I was chasing rainbows. I wanted a conglomerate when I couldn't even turn a profit.

I had no management skills whatsoever and Matt was struggling under the weight of the burden I left him to carry. Sometimes he would just disappear. Much of his unhappiness, I think, had to do with having to work for someone like me. He believed in quality. Though you'd never credit it from looking at our accounts, I believed in making money. But cutting corners to reduce our overheads was an affront to Matt's professional pride, so we continued delivering a quality product while haemorrhaging money. We were like two guys sitting in the cab of a runaway truck that neither of us was qualified to drive.

★

Every Wednesday at 4.40 p.m. I played golf with Gerry Boyd in Milltown. We must have played more than 500 rounds together during my twenty-five years in catering and not once did he ever mention business, even though I knew he was catching bullets for me. I saw the letters he was getting from head office about this guy George Hook, but he kept defending me.

I was wheeling Ingrid into banks and asking her to sign guarantees that she didn't even read. She trusted me, ducker and diver though I was.

Gerry, Ingrid, Mick Pender – so many people believed me when I said that there'd be better times soon.

During my radio show, on one of the New Year programmes, I talked to a guy who was down on his luck and asked him how Christmas Day had been. He had two ex-wives and two sets of children. He also had two close friends: one was a heroin addict; the other was in Mountjoy prison. On Christmas morning he got up and visited his two families with presents. Then he took his friend the heroin addict a present. Then he visited his other friend in the Joy. On Christmas night he returned to his apartment to eat, on his own, a dinner of spaghetti Bolognese accompanied by a bottle of wine. Then he went to bed early.

To me it sounded hellish – until I recalled my own worst Christmas.

The year 1981 had been a bad one, but in the autumn salvation seemed at hand. I received a call from Alan Jeffers, who was a director of Avenue Investments Ltd, the venture-capital arm of the McGrath family. Paddy McGrath was a member of the Turf Club and chairman of Leopardstown Racecourse. He was also a director of the Bank of Ireland, which at that time happened to be my biggest creditor. His brother Joe was the chairman at the Curragh. So they were familiar with my name and business. Alan indicated that Avenue was interested in taking a stake in my company.

Suddenly it was like my numbers had come up in the lottery. The day that Avenue took a stake in my company would be the day I moved back to Easy Street. Our credibility would go through the roof. No one would ring up wondering when they were going to get paid any more. If Paddy McGrath was involved, they would know they would get their money. Equally elated was my long-suffering friend and bank manager, Gerry Boyd, who immediately arranged for the dogs at Bank of Ireland head office to be called off because the white knight was riding over the horizon.

Avenue was not unaware there were problems; I did not gild the lily in discussions with Alan Jeffers. The problem was that I did not know the extent or the magnitude of the deficiency. I had been living in a dream world for so long that I could not tell the difference between fantasy and reality. But with the contracts I had, it was possible that the company could, with direction, trade its way out of trouble. In a perfect world Avenue would pick up the shares for a song, put in competent people to run it and start making money. First, though, Alan wanted to send in a firm of accountants to assess the extent of the damage.

Peter Fleming, then a partner in the accounting firm Bestow Charlton, carried out the investigation. Whatever Avenue paid him, he earned every penny of it. Following my accounts, such as they were, must have been like decoding hieroglyphics. My business affairs were a maze of twists, turns and dead ends. I'd never bothered with the books. All that interested me through almost twenty years of hand-to-mouth living was whether I could get the money into the bank to meet the cheque I'd written two days earlier. I was buying corned beef by the tonne, thousands of loaves of bread a day, and the paperwork was a mess.

The investigation lasted two months. A few days before Christmas, Peter phoned me and said he was going to see Alan that afternoon. He told me the figures were far worse than he feared. He said that Avenue was prepared to take on a company with major problems; the question was whether it wanted a company with monumental ones. For the first time there was a bottom line. I don't remember what it was. It was a telephone number.

On 23 December Alan asked me to go and see him in his office on Northumberland Road. I sat across the desk from him. He had

Peter's report in front of him. It was as big as the Dublin phone directory. 'We've had a look at this, George,' he said, 'and we're not going to go with it. We've decided not to invest.'

I felt it like a bullet to the brain. I was a dead man. After Christmas, my creditors would start ringing again. The banks would be back on my case. The game was up. That bright dawn that I'd glimpsed had suddenly been scrubbed out.

That night I went to Jury's in Ballsbridge with Peter and Kyran McLaughlin. I've never been able to hold my drink and, after a couple of pints, I was absolutely pissed. I remembered that the next day I was supposed to go and buy the family turkey. I didn't have a bean.

Kyran slipped me some money to pay for Christmas that year.

In the early eighties, England looked like it might offer Dowling and Associates a brighter future than recession-ravaged Ireland. We did the *Ballroom of Romance* for the BBC and now they were throwing regular work our way. Matt and I were spending a lot of our time in England. I rented a mailing address at 150 Regent Street to give the impression that I had a successful business that was based in an upmarket part of London and for an annual fee the mailing address company forwarded any mail received back to me in Dublin.

Producer Kenith Trodd, my contact at the BBC, moved to ITV and wanted to bring us with him. He suggested us as the caterers for his first major production at London Weekend Television. The contract was worth a lot of money but first ITV wanted to see us in action. As a trial they gave us *The Big Match*, with Brian Moore commentating. The match was at Tottenham Hotspur and we set up at White Hart Lane early on the morning of the game. Matt cooked enough breakfasts to line the stomachs of the Russian army but none of the ITV staff came near him. One guy eventually showed up and he noticed Matt stacking eggs in a large crate. 'You use *real* eggs?' he said.

All they'd ever been served by location caterers was powdered eggs.

'Of course we use real eggs,' Matt said.

The guy let this shout out of him, 'These guys use real eggs,' and soon there's a queue of people for breakfast. We got the contract. The eggs clinched the deal.

Then ITV gave us *Live From Her Majesty's*, a Sunday night variety show in the old music-hall tradition, with comedians, singers, dancers and other acts, compèred by Jimmy Tarbuck. There was a tense and often frantic air about the show. Acts would spend all day Sunday rehearsing and then go out to a live television audience of 20 million that night. The tension was always palpable.

When the curtain went up, I was usually upstairs with my feet up after serving dinner, exhausted and relieved that it was over for another week. Occasionally I went downstairs to watch if an old favourite like Max Bygraves was on the stage. One night – it was the third Sunday in February 1984 – Tommy Cooper was on and the crew went down and stood in the wings to see him in action.

I have a lifelong love of biographies, especially about complex or troubled characters, and it always interested me that the great comedians such as Tony Hancock, Spike Milligan and John Cleese were tortured souls. Comedy, they say, is the language of despair. Cooper was like that. He was a genius. He was also a drinker and a depressive.

Everybody stood there in the wings, watching him perform this brilliant, bungled magic routine. Suddenly he hit the deck. Everybody laughed, assuming it to be part of the act. One of the production crew shouted, 'Holy Jesus! Curtain!' and the laughter stopped. Tarbuck rushed over to him with one of the camera crew, who started giving him the kiss of life. It was awful. In a moment it was clear he was dead.

The drip feed of work from ITV was my lifeline but, typically, I messed it up. I brought the lunacy of the way I did my business in Ireland across the water to England. I didn't pay my VAT. Not paying your taxes to Queen Elizabeth was different from not paying your taxes to Charlie Haughey or Garrett Fitzgerald.

One day there is a message at the London office that a Mr

Sampson is looking for me and to return his call urgently. I dial the number and a voice answers, 'Her Majesty's Customs and Excise,' and instantly my blood goes cold. I ask for Mr Sampson and I'm put through.

'It's George Hook here,' I say. 'You were looking for me?'

'Yes,' he says. 'I wonder could you pop in and see me.'

'A bit difficult. I'm in Ireland at the moment.'

'When will you be here again?'

'I'll be over in two weeks.'

'Fine,' he says. 'Let's say a fortnight on Tuesday then. Come at ten o'clock in the morning, if that suits.'

The address he gives me is a big old building up by Cambridge Circus. I ask for Mr Sampson at reception and out comes this old, avuncular type in a cardigan smoking a pipe. 'What's the problem?' I say to him.

'Come and sit down,' he says. He shows me into his office, where there's a young man, only in his early twenties, with a notepad and a pen. 'You don't object to this fellow here taking notes, do you?' he asks.

'Not at all,' I say, 'but why am I here?'

He pushes a piece of paper across the desk to me. It's the invoice I sent to ITV. I'm staring hard at it, knowing what's coming next. 'You charged VAT for it and didn't pay it,' he says.

'I did intend to.'

'That's not the way we work over here, I'm afraid. Now, you've an address in Regent Street but it's not your place of business. You live in Ireland. Your other director, Mr Dowling, also lives in Ireland.'

They've got the goods on me. I'm caught in the act.

'The position is this,' he says. 'We're not going to put you in jail now. You're actually quite free to go if you wish, but I suggest you don't.'

'I'm not going anywhere,' I say.

'Very sensible. We're the Customs and Excise. We can stop you getting on a plane. We can lock you up if we want. Look, as far as we're concerned, this is a cut-and-dried case of VAT fraud.'

'Fraud?'

This is new to me. I'd never considered cheating the Revenue as fraud. In Ireland in the 1970s and 1980s it was what you did to stay in business.

'What do you suggest I do?'

'Well, what I suggest is that you go away from here, get some advice and then come back tomorrow.'

I walk out, convinced now that the roof is about to fall in on my life. I phone our London solicitor and explain my predicament to him and he tells me to come to his office at five o'clock.

'Mr Hook, this is a serious matter,' he says. 'I'll go in there to bat for you tomorrow morning, but I'm not doing anything without a cheque.'

I write him a cheque and we return to Cambridge Circus at ten o'clock the following morning. My solicitor plays the green card and says I'm a simple idiot Irishman over in the Big Smoke who got a bit confused. I'm made to feel like the thick Paddy of stereotype but he's trying to keep me out of the clink.

'Do you think we could cut a deal here?' he asks.

Mr Sampson nods thoughtfully. 'Providing Mr Hook promises to never, ever work in England again,' he says, 'he is free to go.'

I'm not going to jail but I've been served with an exclusion order as far as business is concerned. It's not even necessary, as it happens. Her Majesty's boys got their money anyway by disallowing ITV's VAT claw-back. So ITV ends up out of pocket. A letter arrives a few days later telling me that our relationship is over.

5. A useless bugger

When I open my wallet today, I have credit cards in there with zero balances on them. You couldn't imagine the relief that brings unless you'd lived like I had in the 1970s and 1980s.

A letter arrived from American Express this morning telling me it has approved me for its hunky-dory card: I'm a man of such means and distinction that American Express would be honoured if I would carry one of its pieces of plastic. This is a company that has sued me in three different countries.

Every day there are little reminders like this that I have lived two lives.

Every bank and financial institution with a licence to trade on this island has sued me at some point or other. What kept Dowling and Associates going for twenty catastrophic years was my ability to keep selling them the idea of lending me money. American Express never learned. There were times when its legal department was threatening me with bankruptcy while its sales department was offering me new cards to replace my worthless old ones. And I was never one to turn down an opportunity.

My debts were being ratcheted higher and higher by the day. Two hundred thousand; two hundred and fifty thousand; it didn't matter any more. I was inured to the figure: it was like looking at a phone number. Years before I started my own business I had attended an Irish Management Institute conference where a successful American entrepreneur was extolling his own courage when starting up and talked of owing more money than he could ever repay. The listening executives considered it a virtue. So did I. In the early debt-ridden years I thought I was merely treading the well-worn path of speculation before accumulation.

There were times, though, when my circumstances embarrassed me. Johnny Kinihan, the treasurer of St Mary's RFC, the dearest man, phoned me to say that the cheque for my annual sub had bounced. I didn't even have thirty pounds. Poor Johnny seemed more uncomfortable than I was. 'We have to find a way of keeping you in the club,' he said. In 2004, my old friend Donal Forbes was made captain of Milltown Golf Club and I was asked to speak at his dinner. I talked about the time he was treasurer and he kept me in the club when I couldn't find the money for my annual membership. Don Horgan, who owned the Lansdowne Hotel, cashed a cheque for me for £500 so I could pay the wages one weekend. I promised him it would be safe to lodge it in two weeks' time. Of course, it wasn't. It bounced.

When I owed the butcher, the baker and the candlestick maker, as far as I was concerned there was an element of *caveat vendor* to it: the guy who sold me potatoes did so to make a profit, but ran the risk of making a loss. That was business for you. The only time it was difficult for me was when I was embarrassing friends who were extraordinarily kind to me.

Having a business in London allowed me to widen the circle of banks used to keep the house of cards afloat. Barclays joined the National Westminster and the Bank of Scotland in what was fast becoming a global borrowing and depositing routine. Long before Kenneth Lay at Enron and Bernie Ebbers at WorldCom I was massaging the figures. The only difference was that they became multi-millionaires and I lost my shirt.

I think the moment I saw what I'd become with full clarity came one day after I flew to London, took a taxi from Heathrow to Marble Arch where I lodged some doubtful cheques to meet the 3 p.m. deadline, then turned round and headed straight back again to Dublin. As I arrived home the utter insanity of it dawned on me. I thought, *Hook, you've lost the plot*.

Knowing nothing about the business I was in made me easy prey for sharks and I was vulnerable to being ripped off left, right and centre. For instance, we were shifting tens of thousands of pounds' worth of drink on an average day in Galway or Punchestown but there were no cash registers in the racecourse bars. The only way of keeping tabs on sales was to make sure the spirit bottles were full at the beginning of the day and to check what was in the till against the number of shots gone from each bottle when the bar closed. Now, I wasn't allowed to vet the staff I hired: Number Four Branch of the ITGWU told me who to take on for every race meeting. It didn't matter if I knew a barman to be a thief, or a soak who'd be plastered by the end of the second race. He was protected. You took him on or they shut you down. The vodka and gin scam was a great routine. To make the cash balance at the end of day, the bottles would be topped up with water to pass the stock check. Then at the next race meeting I would face an angry customer accusing me of watering the spirits.

My mother knew I was an easy mark. She'd come to the office and say, 'They're ripping you off, George. They're all ripping you off.' Of course, I never listened.

My mother's behaviour had grown erratic to the point that I believed she was certifiably insane. Her relationship with Ingrid never recovered from the homily she delivered to her on our wedding day and there was always an edge to their relationship. She was forever ringing me to offer her opinion on the various ways that Ingrid was failing as a wife and mother.

Over time her criticisms became more and more vitriolic. She'd call Ingrid the most awful names and say outrageous things about her and her treatment of the children. I didn't recognize it as insanity at the time. I'd just say, 'That's my wife you're talking about. I can't talk to you when you're like this,' and hang up.

When she'd show up at the factory and launch into one of her rants, the staff tended to throw their eyes heavenwards as if to say, 'It's only George's mad mother.'

As it happens, mad or not, she was right about people ripping me off. I used to order chickens by the box-load. Each box was supposed to contain a dozen chickens. She was always at me to count them. I just placated her. One day she came in and, before I could stop her, tore open one of the boxes. There were eleven chickens in it. There were eleven chickens in all the boxes.

Still, if people hadn't been stealing, I'd have been losing it anyway.

★

A few weeks after we shut up shop in England at the suggestion of Her Majesty's Customs and Excise, a new opportunity presented itself. On the June bank holiday weekend in 1984, Ronald Reagan came to Ireland. Reagan had some tenuous ancestral link to Ballyporeen in County Tipperary, which he was keen to exploit to grab the green vote in what was an election year. A photo opportunity it might have been but it was also an opportunity for some of us to turn a quick buck.

There was fairly robust opposition to Reagan's visit, mostly from CND and various groups protesting about American meddling in El Salvador and Nicaragua. A huge security operation was put into force. All police leave was cancelled. More than 7,000 Garda – 70 per cent of the entire force – was involved in securing the President's safety. And Matt and I got the job of feeding them.

Reagan stayed at Ashford Castle in Cong, from where he was flown by helicopter to various venues in Ireland. For the duration, 4,000 Garda worked twelve-hour shifts to form a ring of steel around the castle while he slept. We would feed half the guards at the end of their shift and the other half as they began. It rained almost continually for the visit and the discipline of the Gardaí made a difficult job easy. Looking out of the van all you could see was a seemingly unending line of men in blue patiently waiting to be fed. Thanks largely to Matt's brilliance; not one of them went hungry. We served 4,000 breakfasts and 4,000 dinners for a week and, as usual, we didn't make a penny.

Jim Aiken was the big concert promoter in Ireland in the 1980s and he put a lot of work our way. The big rock acts were even pricklier than movie stars and far more eccentric in their requirements. Agents would hand Jim documents 75 to 100 pages long containing lists of demands. Part of the reason for Jim's extraordinary success was that he spared no expense in making sure those demands was met. And he trusted us because all he ever got back were good reports from the stars we catered for. That was down to Matt's refusal to skimp on quality.

The Rolling Stones always got sparkling mineral water.

Ballygowan wasn't good enough, though. It had to be Vermont White Mountain Water, which wasn't available in Ireland. I had to import it from America before they arrived. They also asked Jim for a table-tennis table – which wasn't used once while they were here – and a slot machine. Every now and then Keith Richards would feed a coin to it, pull the handle and walk away.

The big stadium concerts were hard work. We'd be there for a week or ten days, feeding the enormous cast and crew involved in assembling the stage and putting the show together. We'd cook for the band before rehearsals. Then, on the day of the concert, there might be 2,000 to 3,000 security personnel to be fed.

There were times when it was nearly worth all the trouble. A few weeks after the Reagan visit, Neil Diamond played at Croke Park. Before he left the stadium that night, he stuck his head into the kitchen and told us we were the best caterers he'd ever had in all his years of touring. That meant a lot to me: Neil Diamond thought we were the business. It didn't matter that we'd lost money again. It never occurred to me that compliments from superstars weren't going to put food on my family's table.

At that time I lived every day of my life on the brink of disaster. There was never a day when I rolled out of bed and said, 'Today is going to be a great day.' There were no great days, just different hues of awfulness. I lay awake for hours every night, thinking about it, trying to get some perspective on it all.

Ingrid usually lay awake beside me, though I didn't know that until recently. She knew I was in trouble but had no idea of the scale. I didn't either. I didn't want to. The accounts were such a tangle that it was always difficult to put a figure on it, but by the early eighties I guess that I owed the best part of £1 million. It was certainly more money than I could ever repay by staying honest.

There was no escape from it. Holiday times compounded the misery. We'd arrive in Kerry on a Monday for a week's holiday. By Wednesday I'd announce that I had to drive back to Dublin to sort out some problem or other at work and I'd abandon Ingrid and the children. I would return at some point to try and pick up where I left off.

This summer I took Ingrid to New Zealand for the 2005 Lions Tour and also visited Singapore, Australia and Thailand in a five-week extravaganza. During the planning stage she did not seem to be showing the appropriate level of gratitude for the effort I was making. I chided her gently.

'Have you any idea how much this is costing?' I said.

'Listen' she replied, 'we have never had a decent holiday together, so if you divide it by thirty-five it will look cheap.'

Though my father was long retired from CIÉ his mind was still as sharp as a tack. Two or three mornings a week he came into the office and helped out with paperwork and the payroll, the kind of work he'd been doing all his life. He didn't know the half of what was going on in Dowling and Associates, though. I used to see him filling out tax forms under the misapprehension that I had money to give to the Revenue Commissioners. He saw all the turnover and presumed I was running a successful company.

I started to notice that he'd come in to work with small injuries – a bruise around his eye, or sometimes a scratch on his face, or a mark on his hand. He always had a story to explain the marks away.

One afternoon I was standing on the twelfth tee at Milltown Golf Club when another member, Eamon Beale, came haring across the course to tell me that my father had been rushed to hospital. I presumed it was a heart attack.

I phoned my mother from the clubhouse. 'There you are,' she said. 'He's finally done it. He's tried to kill himself.'

'What are you talking about?' I said, presuming she was having one of her turns.

'Go and see for yourself,' she said. 'He's in the Meath.'

I drove to the hospital like Jackie Stewart to find the old man having his stomach pumped. What my mother said was true. He had taken an overdose.

It was a classic cry for help: he had no intention of dying. He came downstairs to my mother and said, 'I've just taken fifty of your sleeping pills,' and asked her to call an ambulance. He left it tight. They managed to empty his stomach just before the tablets dissolved into his bloodstream.

I was in shock. I associated suicide with young men, not ones in their seventies, and definitely not my father. But then how much did I really know about his life?

When he was conscious again and sitting up in bed he filled in the blanks. It turned out that my mother really was mad. That explained the injuries. She'd been beating him. She had punched him and thrown plates at him. He once woke up in the middle of the night to find her sitting on his chest with a carving knife at his throat.

She was absolutely convinced that he was screwing women behind her back. She thought he was having it off with the twenty-somethings who worked for me. When he would take the dog for a walk, she was convinced it was a ruse to get out of the house and meet other women. She'd go to his coat before he went out and count the coins in his pocket. Then she'd count tham again when he came home. If the amounts didn't match, then it was obvious he was phoning other birds from the call box at the end of the street.

'This can't go on, Dad,' I said.

'I just have to put up with it,' he said. 'That's the vow I made – in sickness and in health.'

I took my mother to see a friend of mine who was a psychiatrist in St John of God's in Stillorgan. He listened to her story, letting her think that it was my father who was under scrutiny.

I rang him the following day.

'George, I am sorry to say she is in a bad way mentally,' he said.

'Well, what do I do?'

'There's nothing you can do. As painful as it is, George, you're going to have to commit her.'

My father wouldn't hear of it. 'In sickness and in health,' he said again.

Then Ingrid played a blinder. She asked to see what medication my mother had been taking and I handed over a veritable chemist's stockroom. Ingrid cast her pharmacist's eye over the labels and spotted it right away. 'You know this is a nuclear cocktail she's been taking?' she said. 'The blue ones are interacting with the pink ones. Your mother's not mad, George, it's a chemical reaction.'

Ingrid persuaded a pharmacist friend to give my mother a placebo. It was an overnight cure. The madness was gone.

There was a disquieting postscript to the story. A few weeks later a man called to the house at Elm Mount Avenue and presented my mother with an unpaid bill from the Burlington Hotel. After that, I think she was convinced once and for all that my father liked to stray.

I don't want to be unkind to his memory, but that unpaid bill is a shadow over my relationship with my father. I think about it from time to time and wonder.

He could have done, I'm sure of that: he looked like Clark Gable and he was a drummer with the third biggest dance band in the country.

And then sometimes a memory comes unbidden from childhood. I'm eight or nine. My mother and I go to the train station to meet my old man after work. We're walking down the hill back towards the city centre. On the opposite side of the road there's a girl, very attractive, probably in her early twenties, whom I recognize from our holidays in Crosshaven. She gives the old man a coquettish little smile. He waves at her.

We walk the rest of the journey in an unbearably tense silence. When we get to the house, my mother goes berserk. There's an unmerciful row in the kitchen. I'm in the living room crying my heart out because I've never heard these two people exchange a cross word before.

I'm not going to sully my father's name by saying that he strayed, but it's easy to see why my mother thought he might have. I think about it from time to time. My mother's suspicions. The day on the road. It's one of those puzzles that I can never resolve. Not every story finishes with the loose ends tied up.

★

One of the qualities I inherited from my father was a head for figures. I wasn't good with money but I was good with dates, phone numbers, totting up sums in my head. I know that I did my Leaving Cert in 1959, that I joined Burroughs in 1963 and that I met Ingrid in 1967. When Bryan O'Neill, a friend from college, came back to Ireland after twenty years in South Africa, I could still call him at his mother's house without having to check the number.

But here's the odd thing. During the course of writing this book, I had to check through old papers to find out that my father died on 19 November 1985 and ask my children to find out that my mother died on 24 October 1994. When you're living a nightmare as I was, these neat, temporal boundaries cease to be important. I didn't live from year to year. I lived for three o'clock, when the banks closed. Twenty-five years of my life passed in a daze.

I can never really excuse the way I neglected my parents in their final years. I was so wrapped up in my own troubles that I allowed them to slip off the radar. In the summer of 1985 my father started getting terrible abdominal pains but my mother never gave him much sympathy. She'd say, 'Ah, you're fine.' That was her way. Eventually they got so bad that he went to see his GP, who listened to his lungs and then made an appointment for him at the Richmond Hospital later in the week. Because of his condition, he also arranged an ambulance to collect him from home at 8 a.m. for his nine o'clock appointment.

My mother phoned me at seven o'clock that night to say she was worried. He still wasn't home. He'd been at the hospital since the morning. I jumped into the car, drove to the hospital and found him sitting on a plastic chair in A&E, doubled up in pain. It was hours since anyone had spoken to him. They'd brought him into A&E and taken some X-rays and left him sitting there for the entire day without a cup of tea or a sandwich or anyone paying him the slightest heed.

I went to the nurses' station and explained the position. One of the nurses said, 'We're overworked, understaffed and we've no beds. Welcome to the health service.'

I stormed off down the corridor, found a payphone and phoned Barry Desmond, who was the Minister for Health and my constituency TD in Dun Laoghaire-Rathdown. He wasn't home but I vented my spleen to his wife. 'My father was a committed trade unionist all his life,' I said, 'and now, at the end of his days, this is how the Labour movement treats him,' and I slammed down the phone. It was very unfair to Mrs Desmond.

I went back to where my father was sitting. After a short time I spotted Sean Murphy, who was a consultant neurologist and a friend of Jack Ormond, my GP. He asked what I was doing there and I told him the story. He immediately talked to the people in A&E, even offering one of his own beds in the neurology ward for my father. Through his help my father finally got a bed in a geriatric ward. Over the coming days he was assessed and his GP's hunch was right: my father had lung cancer, with secondary tumours in the spine.

Instead of making up for lost time, I went back to my normal routine – though you could hardly call it normal, driving around the city at night, safe in the cocoon of my car, unaware that my father was living out the last few weeks of his life and that every day I didn't see him was a wasted opportunity to spend the kind of time with him that he had once spent with me.

Over the years Matt Dowling got to know all of my hiding places, so when I walked into Jury's Coffee Dock just after six o'clock one evening, he was already waiting for me. 'The hospital were looking for you,' he said.

When I got there my father was barely conscious. It was clear he was on the way out. I sat with him for hours, holding his hand, talking into his ear. I said, 'Dad, do you remember when you used to teach me how to play cricket?' and he squeezed my hand. I said, 'Do you remember when you used to take me to the library?' and he squeezed it again. And we communicated like that until he drifted off to sleep.

Jack Ormond, tower of strength that he always was for me, came to the hospital and stayed with me for a long time that night. By now my father was in the last hours and Jack walked me round the block and told me that there was little more I could do. My father would not regain consciousness and I should go home and get some sleep. I would need it in the coming days, he suggested. I stayed until 2 a.m. and then went home. At 5 a.m. a nurse telephoned.

'Your father slipped away during the night.'

I went to the hospital ward where he was laid out on the bed surrounded by a screen. A couple of hours later Arthur collected my mother and brought her to the hospital. Despite everything, he was more of a son to her than I was in her final years.

My father had deeded his body to the medical department in UCD to save us the expense of a funeral. We stood at his bedside crying for an hour and then they came to take him away. We had a funeral Mass in Foxrock church. It all ended as quickly as that.

Rugby was the oasis of happiness in my life. Early one morning in 1986 I was eating breakfast in the Tara Towers Hotel and the lounge was full of American jock types. I asked one of them what they were doing in Ireland.

'We're an American rugby team,' he said. 'From California.'

They were alumni of the University of California at Berkeley near San Francisco – the Old Blues, as they were nicknamed – and they were on a tour of Ireland, playing Blackrock College, Belfast Collegians and Trinity College. I told the guy that I did a bit of rugby coaching myself and he introduced me to their coach, Jeff Hollings, who was a New Zealander. Jeff and I hit it off straight away. He was a computer specialist who had migrated to the United States and played hooker for the budding American national team.

It turned out that Jeff was keen to get his hands on some coaching videos. I was one of the first coaches to use the then-emerging video technology as a coaching aid. It was an expensive exercise at that time: in 1981 the camera and recorder cost £2,000 and a single tape sold for £15. Pretty soon my video library was an expensive but diminishing asset as I kept a record of every game on TV.

Making a coaching tape was an extremely time-consuming

exercise using two videos and two remote controls. There was no editing suite in my sitting room, so each segment had to be painstakingly copied from the original tape to a blank tape in a second recorder. Jeff asked me for some training videos to watch on the bus journeys between games. He and his team were knocked out by them. It felt great to feel appreciated.

About six months later, early in 1987, I got a call from Jeff. There was a rugby coaching conference in the University of Kansas and they wanted me to speak at it. He asked if it would be possible for me to take time away from my business. I put on hold the various billion-dollar takeover bids I was involved in and flew to Lawrence, Kansas, where I made a number of presentations using my videos.

Jeff introduced me to his friend Ron Mayes, a fellow Kiwi who was the coach of the US national team. Ron was a fascinating character, but then you'd expect nothing less of a man whose occupation was an earthquake architect. He designed buildings that were built on ball bearings. When the earth shook, Ron's buildings moved to ride the force of the tremor. He lived, not surprisingly, in San Francisco.

Ron and I had an instant rapport. When the conference ended, I flew to San Francisco and stayed in his house for a few days. One night we went out for dinner. At some point in the evening we found ourselves in the men's room, standing next to each other at the urinals. He turned to me and said, 'You know we're going to the World Cup, George. Well, there's nobody I'd trust more than you to be involved with the American team.'

'Are you offering me a job?' I said.

'Yeah, I'd like you to be part of the team.'

The inaugural Rugby World Cup was taking place in Australia that autumn. Ron already had an assistant in George Betzler, who was the forwards' coach. He wanted me on board as technical advisor to the US Eagles.

The only drawback – apart from being drawn in the same group as Australia and England – was that they couldn't afford to pay me and I'd have to pay my own air fare.

But I said yes. What else was going on in my life?

I said yes to the American offer without mentioning it to Ingrid first. It never occurred to me that she had a right to know that her husband was disappearing to Australia for a month.

As it happened, the job required me to be away longer than that. I went to America three or four times that summer for coaching weekends, each time telling Ingrid that I was going to a meeting for work somewhere in Ireland. I don't know why I told her that. It was madness. I was living in a fantasy world, telling lies even when there was no need to. Another time, in the middle of some crisis or other, I took the Belvedere under-19s to the south of France. I told her I was in Killarney. Lying had become my first instinct. My transformation into Walter Mitty was complete.

In California, I'd order an alarm call for the early hours of the morning. I'd sit up in the bed and, putting on my best wide-awake voice, call Ingrid. It was lunchtime in Ireland. 'It's absolutely bucketing it down here in Tralee,' I'd tell her.

The World Cup was a cosy little daydream that helped get me through a difficult spring and summer. By this time I was ducking and diving to the point where my life was in danger. One day I answered a knock at the door. There were two men standing there. One of them pointed out that I owed the vegetable man £702.50. The other one said, 'Have a cheque for us tomorrow or we'll break your legs,' and then they left.

I had no doubt they meant it. I phoned Kyran in a panic and said, 'I need £702.50.'

'Calm down,' he said. 'What's wrong?'

'Kyran, if I don't find £702.50, they're going to break my legs.'

He didn't even ask who had threatened me. He just wrote me a cheque, gave it to me and I paid the nice men when they returned the following night.

When the Irish Hospital Sweepstakes closed down the Ballsbridge offices, I was served with a notice to quit the ante-building that served as my sandwich factory. The timing couldn't have been worse. I was due to deliver my tender for the school meals contract and in the documents I had to indicate where the sandwich production would take place. There was no time to find alternative premises before the tender date.

I delivered the tender on the due date using the old Sweepstakes address. In July the Corporation wrote to tell me they wanted to inspect the premises. This was a crucial call. The Corporation officials would only want to inspect the premises of the successful, so I knew I had won, but without an approved place of production I would be dead in the water.

I had leased a factory off Baggot Street but it did not have Health Authority certification. I knew I would have it by the time the schools opened in September but I also knew that the Corporation officials, conscious of their responsibility to the city's children, would not accept my undertaking to have it ready.

So I agree a date and a time to show the inspectors around the now-defunct Ballsbridge premises and I get there half an hour before they arrive. I go to one of the security guards, who knows me, and ask if I can borrow a set of keys.

'I've left some of my stuff in the building,' I tell him.

He hands me the keys and I open up. The three inspectors arrive and I take them on a tour of this big, empty husk of a building, where I'm now trespassing.

'Where are all your machines?' one of the inspectors asks.

'I've sent them off to be cleaned,' I tell him. 'That's how important hygiene is to me.'

They tick off the various boxes on their clipboards and a week later I'm told that I have the contract for another year. My relief lasts only as long as it takes me to realize that I have only six weeks to fit out my new factory before the schools reopen in September.

The place I have leased is on Eastmoreland Lane, behind Baggot Street hospital, and the leasehold costs me £5,000. It's a dump. There's no other word for it. There's no way I'll get a health certificate for the place when I inform the Corporation of my change of address. The building needs to be gutted and rebuilt. It needs to be retiled and painted. It needs a false ceiling.

I go to see Ernie Tucker, the Belvedere hooker, who does

ceilings. He's thrilled that I'm putting the work his way. Then I tell him I have no money and he's not so thrilled. I tell him I'll pay him within a matter of weeks. He trusts me because I give him my word. Needless to say, I let him down.

I get Charlie Verso, the old Palmerston referee, to do the tiles. Same deal. He does the work and I spend months hiding from him when he comes looking for the money.

Then I have to get the place painted. Time is tight. It has to be done over the course of one weekend to have it ready when the inspectors arrive to give it the once over. I meet these two young guys who are painters and I ask them to do the job. They want £500 up front. I don't have £500.

It's a Friday afternoon and I head for Gerry Boyd at the bank. He's genuinely happy to see me even though he knows what I'm here for. 'I need five hundred quid,' I tell him.

'Look, I can't give it you, George,' he says. 'You're already up to your neck in debt.'

'I'm going to lose the sandwich contract, Gerry, unless I get this money. I'm going to lose everything.'

'I'm sorry, George. You know I would if I could.'

But I'm one step ahead of him. 'I've an idea,' I say. 'I can write a cheque and take it out to the Bank of Ireland in the airport tonight. They'll give me the £500 if you call them and clear it in advance. They'll phone you to see if there's money to cover the cheque. You tell them it's good. And by the time the cheque arrives back in this branch on Wednesday morning, I promise I'll have the £500 to you to cover it.'

So Gerry agrees to this. He puts his job on the line to help out a proven loser who's caused him nothing but grief in his career. I drive out to the airport that night, cash a cheque for £500 and pay the painters.

Now I have three days to find £500 to save Gerry's job.

On Monday I go to Molloy's electrical shop in Donnybrook and I buy two video recorders. They're expensive – I think they cost about £400 each – but they give them to me on credit. I find a buyer for the machines. A woman who works in the factory knows someone who'll pay £500 for the two. I get the £500 and I give it to Gerry when the bank opens on Wednesday morning.

The problem now is how to pay for the video recorders. Tomorrow will look after itself, I always figured. On 1 September, we reopen for business. We're back making 44,000 sandwiches a day.

The World Cup couldn't come quickly enough. The prospect of pitting my wits against the coaches of two of rugby's superpowers excited me more than anything had in years. I'd never coached above club level before but I knew I had what it takes and that was a feeling that was all too rare for me. I sat down and wrote a thirty-page manual – a World Cup survival guide – in which I said that, to avoid annihilation against England and Australia, the American players had to learn how to scrum properly.

We played a warm-up match against Tunisia in California, where I met most of the American players for the first time. They were all a lot older than I'd expected. Most of them had only taken up rugby in college, in their late teens or early twenties. Most of them were the retirement side of thirty. We were by far the oldest team in the tournament.

But they were a great bunch of guys. Most of them had given up worthwhile careers and worked as barmen or such in order to play rugby. Some of the team had even quit their jobs to go to Australia. Like everyone else in 1987, they were amateurs but they had none of the perks associated with playing international rugby. The parent body, the USARFU, had no money either. However, for the duration of the World Cup they were on a daily allowance of $30 from the organizers, giving birth to the chant of, 'Per diem, per diem, per diem,' which became our unofficial World Cup theme song.

Our first game was against Japan in Brisbane and the result would determine the success or failure of our participation in the tournament. The best we could hope for against England and Australia was to keep the score down to a respectable level. But ultimately, we would be judged by what we did against Japan. Whoever lost was going to finish bottom of the group.

The American players had never really learned defence before. I got to work with them for a couple of weeks before the tournament began and put in place a defensive system. It was rudimentary enough but to the Americans it was like splitting the atom.

They picked it up quickly, though. Our two wings certainly had the right credentials. Gary Hein was only 19 but he'd been the defensive captain for the Cal Berkeley American football team. Mike Purcell was the American collegiate wrestling champion. It came easily to them.

We travelled to Brisbane. The American budget didn't stretch to a hotel room for me. However, the organizers provided each country with a team room. The hotel put a bed in it and that's where I slept, making myself scarce when players wanted to come in for physiotherapy.

Two nights before the match I was shocked to discover that none of the players knew the words to the American national anthem. I couldn't believe it. 'What are you going to be doing,' I asked them, 'when they play "The Star Spangled Banner" and the eyes of the world are looking at you?'

Ed Burlingham, our lock and captain, took the rest of the boys into the corner and they ransacked their memories for bits of the song they had learned as kids. Everyone could chip in with a line or two, and, between them, they came up with the words. We all learned it off and practised it together.

'We're going to go out there,' I told them in the dressing room, 'and we're going to sing this song like it never existed before.'

I gave them a speech before they ran out onto the pitch. I hadn't a note in front of me but, in tenor, I was aiming for something along the lines of the Gettysburg Address. I scoured my memory bank for historical references I thought might strike a chord. General John J. Pershing. General George Custer. General Douglas MacArthur.

They went out onto the field and they sang the national anthem with me joining in the grandstand. RTÉ was taking the live feed from Australian television. Not many people in Ireland knew I was involved with the American team until they saw me on television, standing ramrod straight, with my hand on my left breast, belting out the words of 'The Star Spangled Banner' in Ballymore, Queensland.

We beat Japan 21–18. What I remember most vividly about the game is the final ten minutes, when we were three points in front and the Japanese were storming our line. We didn't get out of our own 22. It was ten minutes of hard-hat defending, but we managed to keep them out and we won.

It was a rare enough feeling for the Americans. It would be sixteen years before they won their next World Cup match.

The match had been played in a fairly spiky atmosphere. The referee had penalized us repeatedly for being offside and for putting the ball into the scrum crooked and the American players and management got pretty irritated about it. The day after the match the entire tour party went on an all-day excursion. I passed on it and spent the day in my room, analysing the video of the match. Every time the referee put the whistle to his lips, I paused and rewound again and again, and took notes.

Then I got Ron to call a team meeting. I put the tape on and talked the players through every decision the referee had made. He was never wrong. I pointed my finger at individual players, said, 'Brian Vizard, what were you complaining for? You *were* offside, you fucking eejit.'

No one had ever done it for them before.

The following morning we looked at the issue of the put-in. I got our first-and second-choice scrums to pack down and invited an international referee to watch our scrum-half, Dave Saunders, put the ball in. I told him the way I wanted him to put the ball in and he did it. The referee said it was fine. Then I suggested he try it the way he had against Japan. The referee blew the whistle.

What I'd discovered from watching videos was that Australia, England and New Zealand were all putting the ball in dead straight but on their side of the scrum. What we were doing was standing in the centre and putting it in crooked.

We did endless repetitions until Dave learned to do it my way. He wasn't penalized again in the tournament. After that I felt the players were looking at me differently. They knew I wasn't a bluffer. I knew my stuff.

I was quite possibly the only man in Australia outside the confines of a secure institution who believed we could beat England. The men in white were riven by in-fighting. Their backroom team was a salad of conflicting characters and personalities. The manager was Malcolm Weston, the old England and Lions centre, who wanted so badly to be liked by the players that all twenty-seven of them were convinced they were going to be picked, so that generated bitching and backbiting amongst the squad. The coach was Martin Green, who was Cambridge educated and had a Jewish background, while the assistant coach was a hard-nosed, cloth-capped Lancastrian from Orrel called Des Seabrook.

They were coming at it from three different directions. It was an open secret that morale in the England camp was in tatters. If we could just get ahead early, I believed we could really rattle them.

Next up, though, was Australia on a Wednesday night in Ballymore. No one quite shared my optimism about the England match but it was still considered the more winnable of our two remaining games.

We knew the players didn't have the strength to run around after the Australians for eighty minutes, and then do the same against England four days later, so we named a second-string team for the midweek game. The Australian media went berserk. They said it was an insult to them and David Campese was going to punish us by scoring nine tries.

I was sent out to explain it to the press. Anyone who has ever watched Australian television will know that they don't believe in pulling punches. 'How could you possibly do this?' One television reporter asked me.

'Look,' I said, 'we're here to beat England. We don't give a bugger about Australia.'

Not surprisingly, it didn't help matters.

Australia beat us 47–12 but we were magnificent. Campese didn't score one try, never mind nine, while our full-back, Ray

Nelson, scored what was voted the third best try of the tournament. But the most impressive aspect of our performance was how well we defended. It was encapsulated in one memorable moment in the second half, when Steve Tuynman, the Australian back-row, was steaming forward to score in the corner and Gary Hein, with less than a dozen rugby games under his belt, put in a tackle that rivalled a Scud missile. Hein put Tuynman not only over the line but also over the advertising hoardings and into the crowd.

Alan Jones, the Australian coach who was behind me, jumped up and shouted, 'Oh shit!' and rushed down to the side of pitch, where Tuynman was suffering from nothing more serious than dizziness and a badly bruised ego.

After the match we flew to Sydney to prepare for the England game. Australia had Japan next and just happened to be on the same flight. As soon as we were airborne, I went looking for Jones and I sat in beside him. We chatted away. He asked me how I thought we'd done so far. I said I thought we'd done well. Our only problem was that we couldn't win our own scrum ball. You can lift as many weights as you like in training, but if you can't master the art of scrummaging, then it was no good to you.

He agreed with me. Then I did something very cheeky. I asked him could he find a team for our pack to practise against in Sydney.

'I'll do better than that, mate,' he said. 'I'll give you my reserve pack.'

The day before we played England we were practising in Sydney when four taxis pulled up alongside the pitch. The entire Australian reserve forward pack got out, along with their coach, whose first words to me were, 'What do you want us to do?'

It was an extraordinary act of kindness by the Australians. There was nothing they could learn from us. They genuinely wanted to pass on what they knew to help one of the weaker rugby nations.

Looking back, I don't think the players really shared my belief that we could beat England. On the last page of the training programme I drew up for them before we went to Australia I wrote three words: 'Scrum, scrum, scrum.'

Somehow, it never sunk in. They didn't practise it enough. So much for giving England an early jolt. We lost our first four scrums against the head. We couldn't win any possession. England took ownership of the ball and we couldn't get our hands on it. Then we had an out-half who was English but lived in America and I think the unreality of playing against his own country got to him. In the end we lost 34–6.

It could have been worse.

I flew back to Ireland clutching a rugby ball signed by the entire American squad and with a head filled with happy memories. I arrived back to earth with a bump. The World Cup was just a brief intermission in the horror story of my life. While I was living the fantasy that I was one of the world's leading rugby coaches, locking tactical horns with the big boys, back in Foxrock the phone had been cut off again. What made it worse was that Ingrid's mother and stepfather were staying in the house. Albert, the blunt Lancastrian, always saw me for what I was. One night, as they flicked between channels on the television, my face had suddenly filled the screen. 'There he is,' Albert shouted, 'the useless bugger.'

When I got back Ingrid was furious with me and I knew I'd done damage to my marriage. The phone was still cut off.

I just stepped back onto the treadmill. Telling lies; writing cheques I couldn't honour; hiding; driving around the city at eleven o'clock at night, frightened of who I might meet if I went home.

6. Breakdown

I can't say with any degree of certainty when I decided to kill myself. Rock bottom was 1988 and 1989, so it must have been then. It wasn't a single incident that brought me to the precipice but the relentless accrual of setbacks, heartbreaks, mistakes, disappointments and regrets. Rock bottom culminated in an act that was so selfish that I didn't think I deserved to live any more: a mistake too monstrous for forgiveness.

Dowling and Associates was continuing to skitter from one disaster to the next. Matt was struggling to hold the seams of the business together. I hired a chief executive, Des English, who came from a senior position in one of the Smurfit companies. He could have been the best chief executive in the world, but the business was such a shambles that Michael Smurfit himself could not have turned it round. One afternoon Gerry and I were playing golf in Milltown. We were walking down the eighth fairway when Des came running after me. John Roe of Egan Wholesale had told him that he wouldn't be giving us any meat the next day on account of what we already owed him. I told Des I didn't want to know. He said there was no meat to make the sandwiches. I didn't even look at him. I just said it again: 'I don't want to know.'

My way of coping was to disappear. I think that's what I was really doing at the World Cup: I was hiding in plain view. I had reached the point where I no longer cared. Mentally, I had stepped away from it. I had to. It was the only way to stop myself from going over the edge.

On the other hand, looking back, maybe my retreat into my own little world was a sign that I was already having some sort of breakdown.

★

Without Elliot's Cash and Carry, Dowling and Associates would have folded like an accordion. I was using 10,000 loaves of bread a week; I was buying corned beef, cheese and butter by the tonne; I was using thousands of pots of jam; and all of it was on tick.

Elliot's was a family-run business. I knew Peter Elliot, the manager, through rugby. He was hooker and captain of the St Mary's fifth team that I coached to win the Winters Cup. They were a small operation and they depended on my paying them on time. But then, of course, the inevitable happened and I missed a couple of payments. I owed them £50,000. I ducked Peter for as long as I could but he finally caught up with me and told me that unless I paid him the business was going to go down the pan.

I did a terrible thing: I told Peter that I'd give him the deeds to a house as collateral against what I owed him. If the debt wasn't settled within three months, then he could sell it. I wasn't talking about my house, though. It was my mother's house. My parents had decided some years earlier to deed the house in Beaumont into my name.

This was one of those rare moments of clarity when I caught a glimpse of what I'd become: a man prepared to sell the roof over his mother's head to save his own hide. I don't know if she had an inkling of what was happening. About a week after I handed Peter the deeds, a letter arrived for me in Beaumont with the name of our solicitors stamped on the envelope. She handed it to me, unopened, and said, 'I could go into an old ladies' home if you have to sell the house,' and it floored me like an uppercut. In her life she sacrificed all the things that would have made her life more bearable and she was utterly selfless to the end. I couldn't look her in the eye.

'You're not going into an old ladies' home,' I said. But, of course, that was no longer in my hands.

Uncle Tommy, at whom I had looked up in vertiginous wonder as a boy, got cancer. The doctors said there was no hope for him. He was back in Cork, having taken over our old house at 79 Albert Road, to care for Molly until she died. When Molly had been released from the asylum she had lived with my grandmother at number 88 and then she moved in with Tommy after the old lady died. Now my mother went back to Cork to care for him in his final months.

There was no chance of me scraping together enough money to buy back the deeds from Elliot's. A deadline was set and the days passed like sand through an hourglass. Business was bad. I owed everybody. I must have been hiding from a dozen people at that point. One night I was driving around the city. Someone was parked outside the driveway at home. I never found out who it was but I knew I couldn't go home. At about 11.30 p.m. I checked into a little bed and breakfast opposite Larry Murphy's on Lower Baggot Street and spent the night there in despair. I'll always remember that night as a staging post on the road to the bad place I was headed.

The deadline passed. No hard feelings, Peter said, but they had to take possession of the house. I gave him my set of keys and he sent a man out to change all the locks. I knew I'd reached rock bottom. I'd messed around everyone who cared about me – Ingrid, Gerry Boyd, Mick Pender, Ken Wall and all the other people who tried might and main to get me on the straight and narrow. Now this woman, who threw me over her shoulder and carried me to the South Infirmary when I cut my foot, who pulled me, coughing and choking, from the Lough, was about to be put out onto the street because of me. I had no respect left for myself.

I was driving past the Tara Towers in Booterstown one night and this big petrol tanker was coming towards me on the opposite side of the road. I remember thinking that all I had to do was pull the steering wheel to the right, plough into the tanker and it would all be over. It would look like an accident. One flick of an arm could put me out of my misery once and for all. But I kept driving straight. The tanker passed. The feeling didn't.

A few nights later I was driving around again, insulated in my little bubble. Just after eleven o'clock I decided to go home. I turned off the Stillorgan dual carriageway at Foxrock church, but instead of turning left again into Foxrock Park, I kept driving straight down Kill Lane, through the Deansgrange crossroads and past Baker's Corner, towards Dun Laoghaire. I looked at my watch. It was 11.15 p.m. I thought I'd give it another half an hour.

I turned right at the bottom of York Road and followed the seafront until I reached Dun Laoghaire pier. I parked the car at the side of the road and got out. I'd been driving for five hours, breathing in recycled air, listening to my own thoughts. I was stiff. A walk would clear my lungs and my mind. I put on my coat and started walking towards the end of the pier.

I remember thinking, *What if some fellas jump out of the darkness and mug me?* and then thinking what a wasted job they'd have. I was skint. I laughed, alone in the dark.

I reached the end of the pier. It was freezing. All around me was black. I had the same thought as I'd had the night I almost ploughed into the petrol tanker. I thought, *This is it, George. You came here for a reason.*

I took off my coat, then a jacket I had on underneath. I felt the rapier thrust of the cold cut through me. I took off my tie. I sat down on the cold ground and took off my shoes and socks. I stood up, pulled down my trousers and stepped out of them. I walked to the edge, in my underpants, with my shirttails flapping at the back of my legs, and I stared down into the water.

I remember thinking that this was definitely the right thing to do. I thought about Ingrid and the children. I was leaving them without a dime. Every insurance policy I'd ever taken out I'd either hocked or let lapse. But I thought they'd still be better off with me dead. I couldn't drag them down any more.

There was only one step left now and that was the one I was about to take off the end of the pier. Then it would be done. I looked down into the water. A memory surfaced. I'm a child and I'm lying at the bottom of the Lough in Cork and I'm looking at the froth of the water as it starts to fill my lungs. I stood there and thought about drowning, shivering in the bleak cold, for what must have been an hour. I went looking for my clothes. I put them on in a daze.

I walked back to the car with my hands in my pockets. Failing to step off the pier was not so much a decision as another failure.

There was no flash of insight telling me that now was the time to turn my life round. I wasn't Jimmy Stewart being persuaded off the bridge by the thought of what a terrible loss he'd be to the world. I'd simply chickened out. But I knew I'd be back there again.

I turned the key in the ignition and I thought, *A new day starts tomorrow*, but it was a thought that filled me with nothing but despair.

The next morning I phoned my good friend Simon O'Leary and told him some of what I was feeling. We arranged to meet that afternoon in the Cumberland Inn in Dun Laoghaire, which took me on the same route as the night before. We ordered a couple of pints of stout and I told him, 'I nearly topped myself last night.'

Simon just nodded. Being a barrister, he had this way of detaching himself, of looking at a problem analytically, which is why I chose him to talk to ahead of all my other friends. He's not the gregarious, back-slapping, palsy-walsy type. He can be diffident to the point of seeming unsympathetic. Sympathy wasn't what I needed.

We had two or three pints of Guinness. Simon listened while I emptied myself to him. Then he talked sense to me. We drew up a sort of spreadsheet of my life to date. Simon pointed out that I had excelled or at least had been more than competent at everything I had put my mind to before I made one bad move, the move into catering. He suggested that I should try to get back to the things I was good at. This was what I needed to hear.

And that was it. I didn't wake up the next morning and think, *Today is going to be a great day*. It was years and years and years before I ever thought that. But I realized now what I had to do to sort myself out.

Tommy died. My mother was coming back to Dublin in two days to a house that was no longer hers. The Elliots were wondering when I was going to clear her things out of the house.

I went to see Mick Pender at Guinness and Mahon. I told him straight out that I needed forty grand. He'd heard a hell of a lot of urgent cash pleas from me over the years but I clearly hadn't lost my ability to surprise him. 'Forty grand?' he said, shifting uncomfortably in his seat.

'Forty grand.'

'I can't give you forty grand, George. Loans that size have to be approved by the board. Look at your credit history. They're not going to give it to you.'

'Mick, this is my mother's house,' I said, and I told him what I'd done. It says a lot about me that he didn't seem too surprised about that.

'I'll tell you what I'll do for you,' he said. 'You write a cheque for forty grand and give it to the boys. I'll see that it's paid. I'll keep it away from the board for as long as I can. But the day it hits the board, George, you have to follow through.'

'I will,' I told him.

'I believe you, George, because I trust you. I'm approving you for an overdraft of forty grand.'

I went to see Peter Elliot the following day and handed him the cheque. I got back the deeds and the new keys on my way to Heuston station to collect my mother off the Cork train.

'How are you?' I asked her.

'Sad,' she said. 'How are you keeping?'

'Same as usual. Oh, while you were away, I put new locks on all the doors. I was just worried about your security.'

'Thanks, George.'

I got away with it by the skin of my teeth, but in another way I didn't. It scarred me. The lengths to which I was prepared to go to save myself remain a shadow on my being.

Same as ever, the debt hadn't gone away. I'd just passed it around, like I always did. Some months later, Mick phoned me in a panic. 'George,' he said, 'I have to have the forty grand by Wednesday, otherwise I don't have a job.'

There was an audit on. The men with the green pens and the clipboards were arriving from England and this £40,000 overdraft he'd extended me was going to be discovered. To me now, this wasn't a straight bank loan. It wasn't like owing money to the Bank of Ireland or to AIB or the government or big business. It was a debt of honour.

I phoned a solicitor friend who was bailing me out on some other issue and asked his assistance. That day we did the rounds of some financial institutions.

My first port of call was to the Trustee Savings Bank. 'What do you want forty grand for?' the manager said.

'You want the truth?' I asked.

'Yes.'

'To give it to another bank.'

'We don't lend money to people to pay off bank loans, George. Sorry.'

Then I phoned a top banker, someone I knew through Milltown Golf Club. Of course, not a single penny of my money had ever seen the inside of the bank's vault.

'Can I come in to see you?' I asked. 'In about half an hour?'

'Sure. What's it about?'

'I need, er, thirty grand,' I said.

'Come in at two o'clock,' he said.

I went to see him. I said I couldn't tell him what the money was for. He debated the issue in his mind and said, 'OK.' I left the bank with a cheque for £30,000. People decry the old-boy network but it saved my life. That man joined a long queue of people who unselfishly took risks to help me. Every year I live is a testament to their good will.

I was still short £10,000. My solicitor friend's secretary came up with an idea. She suggested she call next door to the Ulster Bank and put a case for me getting an overdraft of £10,000. As the manager made out the bank draft, he said, 'I presume we're going to see this guy again?'

I brought the £40,000 to Mick and that crisis passed. Now I had two more debts, and to my credit I cleared them in almost the suggested repayment timeframe. Some favours were just too big to be ignored.

★

Up to this point in my life, fear of confrontation had been my main motive for hiding from people. Now, I was trying to hide from myself, from my overwhelming feelings of failure and inadequacy. Churchill gave a name to such depression: the Black Dog.

Mine was not the conventional kind of depression, though.

During the Second World War, the Americans decided not to rotate their troops after the Normandy landings, so the veterans never got a break, unless they were wounded or they broke down. Far more broke down than were wounded. The medics of the Second World War, unlike their predecessors in 1914–18, knew that men do not have unlimited courage. Constant exposure to pressure causes the supply to run down.

In the twenty-one years up to 1989, I suffered more stress than most people will know in their entire lives. I brought it all on myself. If procrastination were an Olympic event, I'd be sitting at home wondering whether or not I should go. I have this awful inability to say no to people. Someone invites me to dinner and, even as I'm saying yes, I know that I have something else on that night. So for a week or two weeks I keep up the pretence that I intend going. I don't like telling people what they don't want to hear, so I don't, right up until the last minute, when I cancel, offering some lame excuse. I recognize that part of me wants too much to be liked. It's a personality flaw. I'm a moral coward. I've never been able to make tough calls. That makes me the worst kind of person to be in business.

Decisiveness is a quality I envy in others. Eddie O'Sullivan has it. Garrett Harte, the producer of *The Right Hook* on Newstalk 106, has it. If Eddie has a problem, he confronts it. Usually head-on. He picks up the phone. He does what he has to do. Garrett likewise. I'll think of ten other things to do rather than have that unpleasant conversation.

By 1989 my bank of courage was empty. If I felt pressure, I just shut down, like a computer slipping into standby mode. I'd come home from work in the middle of the day, draw the curtains, lock all the doors and windows, crawl into bed and put a pillow over my head. The phone would ring all day. I'd turn down the volume on the answering machine so as not to have to hear who was looking for me. I never listened to the messages. I rewound the tape and recorded over them.

My personal relationships were all coming apart. I couldn't look my mother in the eye knowing what I'd done behind her back. I spent less time with my wife and children than a father with visitation rights. Ingrid had started keeping an *Irish Times* Year Planner pinned to the back of the kitchen door. She marked each day with a triangle, a circle or a square, to indicate how much time I spent at home. I can't remember the exact code. I think a circle meant that I came home at a reasonable hour and ate dinner with them, a square meant that I missed dinner but came home either late that night or in the early hours, and a triangle meant that I didn't come home at all. There were very few circles. The planner was usually a mass of triangles and squares.

A firm line had been drawn under my relationship with Arthur and Frances. If they haven't appeared anywhere in the account of my adult life it's not that I've airbrushed them out of it. They just didn't figure in my life, nor I in theirs. Once I left home, I rarely saw them. We just dropped out of one another's consciousness.

Arthur left school early to become an apprentice barman in the Royal Hibernian Hotel in Dublin. He won the All Ireland cocktail-making championships with a concoction of his own invention and landed a plum job in the airport bar. Frances married a man from a Republican family from Dundalk, who, strangely, also happened to be the governor of the Maze Prison in Lisburn. One day she walked out of a shop in Portadown to find her car surrounded by RUC and army personnel. A limpet bomb had been attached to its underside. Thankfully it had failed to go off. For their own protection, the family moved abroad and I haven't set eyes on Frances since.

We fell out over Tommy's inheritance, a miserly ten grand. Before he died he gave it to me and asked me to do something with it. I put it into a bank account in Tommy's name. I don't think it was the money that bothered them as much as the sense of being frozen out, being made to feel less than fully part of the family. That was the last time we spoke.

I feel a deep sense of sadness at our estrangement. I can only imagine how awful childhood was for them, the trauma of losing the woman they knew as their mother, being indoctrinated into calling this other person Mammy and then it all coming out in the wash. They were doubly hard done by. Ireland of the forties and fifties did terrible damage to people.

Rugby was my sanctuary. Coaching was the only successful part of my life. It also offered a semblance of normality to my disappearances.

I came to training at Old Belvedere one night in September 1989 to find a man waiting for me. He was a diffident sort of guy. 'Hello, George,' he said, like he expected me to know him. 'John Callanan. Chairman of the Connacht selectors.'

'Hello, John. How are you?'

'Well,' he said, 'I've a bit of a problem, actually. We have a coach, who is primarily a forward coach. We were wondering whether you'd be prepared to coach our backs.'

Connacht had a huge game on the horizon against New Zealand, who'd won the World Cup the previous year. They were touring Britain and Ireland. Between tests, they had arranged to play the provinces. Before the All Blacks arrived, Connacht had to face the Inter-provincial Championships and the traditional ritual slaughter at the hands of Munster, Leinster and Ulster. I would have no formal title but would be the de facto assistant coach to Dec McDermott. My ego could not resist the chance to pit my wits against the mighty All Blacks.

We didn't have much to work with. We had a very good fullback in Jim Staples from London Irish. Eric Elwood was a 19-year-old young fly-half at Galwegians who was competing for the number 10 shirt with Cedric Cruess-Callaghan, who was playing for me at Old Belvedere. I thought Callaghan had more experience but he failed to take his chance during the Inter-provincial Championship and the youngster got his break in the biggest match of that or any other season up to then.

Now that the game is professional, it's difficult for people to comprehend just how difficult it was for Connacht in those days. Less than half of the side actually lived in Connacht, so we were rarely together as a team. The night before a match we'd have our one and only training session in Athlone, which was halfway between Galway and Dublin, where most of the players lived. Five or six would always arrive late, saying they were stuck in traffic. There was no money. There was no organization. If Roy Keane had spent a weekend with us, he would have thought Saipan was paradise.

Ulster came to Galway. Somebody lost the keys to the dressing room. Fifteen minutes before kick-off the players were still standing around in their civvies at the back of the stand. The players were a fatalistic lot, being used to it over the years. I was incandescent with rage. Every organized bone in my body was trembling with anger at such shabby treatment.

Willie Anderson, the Ulster captain, shrewdly used the shambles to psyche up his team. This wasn't incompetence, he said, this was a studied insult to the loyal sons of Ulster. He didn't believe that for a minute, of course. He did it to rouse his players. It was clever. The bad news for us was that somebody found the keys and Ulster trod us into the ground. Then Munster and Leinster did likewise. The traditional Connacht Triple Crown.

We had three weeks to prepare for the All Blacks. Had we thought enough about it, we'd have been frightened to death. This was the team of Wayne Shelford, Grant Fox and Sean Fitzpatrick. The reserve hooker, Warren Gatland, was selected to play against Connacht. The All Blacks had run in eight tries against Wales, who had beaten Ireland in the semi-final of the 1987 World Cup.

We had a second row called Aidan Higgins, known as 'Tank'. A week before the match we trained in Athlone and 'Tank' couldn't complete a lap of the pitch. He weighed more than twenty stone. Not twenty stone of brawn. Just twenty stone. He had a vertical jump of about three inches. There was no lifting him, even if lifting had been allowed.

Though I was hired to work with the backs there was often a crossover between Dec McDermott and me. There's very little innovation in rugby and I had plagiarized a lineout variation from the Japanese, who'd used it to offset their opponents' height advantage at the World Cup. We stood Higgins at the front of the lineout. The hooker made out that he was going to throw the ball long but dropped it in front of 'Tank' instead. He would fall on top of the ball and then we'd ruck over it.

When the All Blacks were defending their opponents' put-in at the scrum, they stood their number 8 off, giving them the advantage of an extra defender. I told our number 8, Noel Mannion, to try it.

'You can't do that,' he said. 'You can't have seven against eight.'

'Just try it,' I said.

I also borrowed from Australia, who had used a defensive system that I thought was genius. When the ball came out of the scrum, their scrum-half – instead of following his opposite number – ran at the opposition out-half. The Australian out-half ran at the opposition centre. So they always had a man over.

I taught it to the backs. We performed a cut-and-shut of the Australian and New Zealand systems. With an extra man either side of the scrum, we would make it very difficult for teams to score against us. That was the theory.

The All Blacks arrived. Their new weapon was the rolling maul. Nobody in the northern hemisphere had seen it before. A week before they came to Galway, they gave a devastating demonstration of how it worked at Lansdowne Road, when they slow-walked the Leinster pack from their own 22 all the way over the Leinster line. It was like Blitzkrieg. It was unstoppable.

We were playing them on a Tuesday night. We assembled in Galway the Saturday before the game. The players would be together for four days, the longest preparation for a match that any of them had known.

I brought young George to Galway with me. We stayed in the

Great Southern Corrib Hotel. Over a few frames of snooker one afternoon, we struck up a great rapport with two Welsh guys, who, it turned out, were the referee and the assistant referee for the match. We became great pals as we killed the interminable, nerve-jangling days before the game.

The usual attendance at Connacht matches was the traditional two men and a dog. The visit of the All Blacks guaranteed a full house. We felt like we were hitting Broadway. I saw Noel Mannion and Noel McCarthy, the captain, in Eyre Square on the morning of the game, surrounded by people. The air crackled with excitement.

Dec had his moment alone with the players before kick-off. I stood leaning against a wall in the corridor while he gave them their team talk in the dressing room. I was in the middle of a daydream when I heard my name.

'Can I have a word?'

It was the referee.

'What's wrong?' I said.

'Your out-half can't play.'

'Eric? What's wrong with him.'

'Nothing wrong with *him*,' he said. 'It's his boots.'

He held them up, at arm's length, regarding them as if they were nuclear waste. I've never seen boots like them. The studs had jagged edges. The nails were showing through the soles. They were caked with mud.

I couldn't believe it. He was 19 years old and making his debut for his province against the best team in the world. Jimmy Davidson, the Ireland coach, was in the stand. Had it been me, I'd have had brand-new studs. I'd have had brand-new laces. I'd have polished my boots to the point where the dazzle from them interfered with the navigational equipment of passing aircraft. What I see now, but was in no humour to see at the time, was that this demonstrated the guy's supreme self-confidence. The All Blacks. Big deal. He didn't give a hoot. That was great. But now we had a problem.

There were forty minutes left before kick-off. Someone

suggested I get a taxi into town and pick up the first pair of size tens I laid eyes on.

'I can't,' I said. 'There are thousands of people on their way to the ground. Can you imagine what the traffic's like?'

I went for humility. I went to the referee's room and pleaded with his better nature. 'It's the All Blacks,' I said. 'Give us a break.'

He sighed. 'Do what you can with them,' he said.

I thanked him, then begged as many matchboxes as I could and used the sandpaper edges to smooth down the jagged studs. I banged the nails out of view. I rubbed them with a cloth. Then I brought them back to the referee.

'They'll do,' he said.

The All Blacks proceeded to knock the stuffing out of us. It was what we expected. We lost the war but we won the odd battle and there was a kind of valour in that. They didn't score a try from a rolling maul because the first-up tackling never allowed them to stay on their feet with the ball.

In that regard, Noel McCarthy and Mick Fitzgibbon deserved Purple Hearts for their performances in the pack. They played rugby with no regard for personal safety. Fitzgibbon was the bravest player I have ever met. Wet through, Mick cannot have weighed much over thirteen stone. When he took off his shirt, he looked like he'd just walked out of Auschwitz. He was thin and knotty with ribs like accordion keys. His shoulders had seen so many dislocations that the bones stuck out at freakish angles. Yet when he hit you, you felt like you'd been hit by a rhinoceros.

At the dinner, Grant Fox told me that they knew they'd been in a match. That was victory enough for us. We lost by 40 points to 6, which compared favourably with Leinster and Munster who had lost by 36–9 and 31–9, respectively. Even Ireland could only score six points against the black juggernaut.

After the post-match banquet, we went on a pub-crawl. I was wasted on the second or third leg. I decided to go back to the hotel. I had young George with me. He wasn't ready for bed. 'Can I stay?' he said. 'Please!'

Aidan Higgins said, 'I'll look after him.'

So, at ten o'clock, I went back to the hotel, leaving my 13-year-old son in a pub called The Hole in the Wall, in the company of a twenty-stone second-row who drank pints of Guinness in three mouthfuls. As I headed off, I heard 'Tank' say, 'Your job tonight, young George, is to count how many pints I drink.'

At four o'clock in the morning, I heard the door open. I opened my eyes and George was sitting on the end of my bed.

He said, 'Twenty, Dad!'

Dec was quitting after the New Zealand match and, as his de facto assistant, I was best placed to get the job. Typical of me, I sat down and wrote a thirty-page submission to the Connacht branch on why I was the right man for the job. I laid down on paper the changes I would make. I devised a brand-new training regimen. John Callanan said that as far as he was concerned there was no better man for the job. I thought I was a shoo-in.

Two weeks later he phoned me. 'You didn't get it,' he said.

'Who did?' I said.

'Ciaran Fitzgerald.'

I couldn't believe it. Ciaran Fitzgerald had only retired from playing a year or two earlier. I wanted to ring someone to vent my spleen but then I remembered a piece of advice my father gave once gave me. Doors open, he said, and doors close, but never slam one shut yourself. Six weeks later, Jimmy Davidson resigned as Ireland coach and Ciaran Fitzgerald quit to go and manage Ireland. I got a call to say the Connacht job was mine if I was still interested.

In that moment, I felt almost Churchillian. There comes a time in everyone's life — as there did, briefly, in Winston Churchill's — when you know that your moment has arrived. You feel that you were made for the opportunity that has presented itself. That's how I felt. It was as if all the years I'd spent coaching teams had been building towards this day. I was excited by the challenge.

The season was only a month away. I still hadn't found myself an assistant. I knew I wanted someone who was local. Bringing in another Dublin or Cork face would make it seem less of a

Connacht team. 'I've an idea,' John said to me. 'What about Eddie O'Sullivan?'

I looked at him. 'Who is Eddie O'Sullivan?' I said.

'He's a fella who lives in Moylough village,' he said, 'about twenty miles outside Galway. He's a teacher in the local convent but he's on sabbatical to the IRFU at the minute as a development officer.'

'So what good is he to me then?'

'You could ask to have him released to assist you, as part of his own technical development.'

A few days later I was back in Dublin and I called into the IRFU headquarters on Lansdowne Road to have a word with the director of rugby, George Spotswood, who'd got the job that I applied for some years before. He was in his office. We chatted for a few minutes. 'Is Eddie O'Sullivan here?' I said.

'Next door,' George said, and in that moment a sliding door opened off to my left and through it came Willie Anderson, all 6′6″ of him, blocking out the daylight in the room. He shook my hand and fractured a few metacarpals in the process. He said, 'This is Eddie O'Sullivan,' and he spun round and introduced me to my new assistant.

Short was my first impression. Everyone was short next to Willie, but Eddie really was short. Then it was his crew cut. Then his muscles. He clearly worked out a lot. I knew nothing else about him, except that he had been at the University of Limerick with Tony Ward. He had played on the wing for Munster and scored a try against Australia. It being foggy, though, nobody saw it.

'Has somebody told you?' I said.

'Yeah,' he said.

'Will you think about it?'

'Yeah.'

'Obviously this isn't the place to discuss it but I'll be back in Galway next week. We can talk then.'

We arranged to meet in the Great Southern in Eyre Square. I ordered a pot of coffee and Eddie put me on the back foot straight away. 'What's your plan for this team, George?'

Was he interviewing me or was I interviewing him?

'I haven't quite worked it out yet. I've a vague idea where I'm going. I know where our weaknesses were last season and I know how to fix one or two of them.'

As I talked, he produced a manila folder and started pulling pieces of paper out of it. 'This is my plan for the lineouts,' he said, 'and this is what I want to do with the scrum. And when we attack the opposition, I want to attack them at these pressure points – here, here and here. And here's my idea for the defence . . .' and as I watched this mountain of papers build up on the table in front of me, I said to myself, '*This* is the man!'

There was an immediate fellow feeling between us. A couple of weeks later I took him to dinner at Milltown Golf Club. Eddie loves his wine and he started by discussing the relative values of Chianti and Sauvignon blanc. All I knew was that they were two different colours. 'Why don't we order a bottle of white for the fish and a bottle of red for the meat?' I said, and Eddie said, 'OK,' looking at me like I was some kind of philistine.

Eddie could hold his drink. I couldn't. Dinner stretched out over hours. Between courses we improvised little tactical situations. The salt and pepper shakers were Connacht. The sugar cubes were Munster. We discovered that we thought similarly about so many different things. There was an intellectual symbiosis between us. 'To hell with the expense,' I said, 'let's have a dessert wine.'

An hour later, Eddie helped carry me like a drunken sailor out of the most important rugby meeting of my life.

I made plans for a get-to-know-you weekend with the players in August. I cast my net wide, inviting anyone and everyone with a chance of making the team. Forty showed their faces. Most of them knew me from the previous year but I got the impression that they were sizing me up as much as I was sizing them up. In their eyes, I was a coach who had never played at a high level, and though I had coached a lot of teams, I had never won anything more than a couple of cups at under-19 level.

I knew that if I didn't crack it from day one, I was a schoolteacher without the respect of his class. There were some new boys in the squad, among them Mark Egan from Trinity and John Duffy from Wanderers. Eddie and I spent the week before planning a schedule for training that would, I hoped, knock the players' socks off.

Ciaran Fitzgerald decided to call an Ireland squad session for that weekend. It didn't affect us very much; Noel Mannion was our only squad member. However, Ciaran had appointed Eddie as his fitness expert and he wanted him in Dublin on the Saturday. John made a call and explained that he was needed in Connacht but Ciaran wouldn't release him. I understood where he was coming from; he had his own problems.

I was in a flap when I met Eddie. 'What do I do now?' I said.

And for the first of what would amount to hundreds of times over the next five years, he said, 'You can *do* this, George. You *know* this stuff. You know it as well as I do. Better in some places.'

It was unbelievable. I can only imagine what it's like in the Ireland dressing room now. He has this way of filling you with confidence just by his belief in you.

I said I'd take the Saturday session. Eddie was sure he could get away and be in Galway for the Sunday session. Putting forty players – backs and forwards – through a session is difficult to do but I was in my element. There was the sound of authority in my voice. The session was interesting, innovative and on time. The players were looking at each other, thinking, *This isn't how Connacht sessions are meant to be.*

The players trained well that day and I ended the session before time. Eddie was a firm believer in finishing training early rather than late.

Coaching in the amateur era wasn't terribly sophisticated. Players would be ordered to do ten laps of the pitch and then on the ninth lap the coach would shout, 'Three more!' I always remember Danny Blanchflower saying that when he was at Barnsley, the manager would not give the players a ball at training. The idea was that by the time the game came round on Saturday they would be hungry for the ball.

I went back to the hotel. The phone rang late that night. It was Eddie. 'Sorry, George, Ciaran won't let me go.'

I had put off a lot of the technical work involving the backs and forwards until the following day. Now I had to do it myself. Standing on my own two feet did me no harm.

The fact that the club had no money increased the sense of adventure. When we went to Belfast, Limerick or Dublin to play in the Inter-provincial Championship, the Connacht branch very thoughtfully asked hotel reception to cut off the phones to the rooms. The players had to use the payphone in the lobby to talk to their girlfriends, wives and children. The Europe Hotel in Belfast had dirty movies on pay per view. Not for us, though. The branch had the hotel staff cut the feed, not out of fear for our mortal souls, but because they couldn't afford the charge.

Eddie and I were first in charge for a game against Spain in Galway. We all got terribly excited about it. The European Cup hadn't been dreamt about in those days. There was no Celtic League. Connacht invariably played three matches a year – against Munster, Leinster and Ulster – and success was losing the three matches by the lowest possible aggregate. Playing Spain, an international side even of the second rank, was something to get excited about.

I'd never met anyone who was as focused as Eddie. He was the finest professional with a small 'p' I ever met in the amateur game. It was his idea to bring in Liam Hennessy, to improve the team's fitness. At that time, Liam was a PE teacher in St Columba's in Dublin. Like Eddie, he had a head brimming with innovative ideas. You could have run a small town on the energy coming off these two guys. Liam started testing the players for body-fat content, developing advanced training routines and establishing off-season programmes. It was a quantum leap forward in Connacht. He also reduced the speed at which players dehydrated. Normally when players finished a game, they had a beer. Now, under Hennessy, they had water, brown bread and bananas, which Liam had worked out contained all the right nutrients to put back whatever the game had taken out of them. We were aeons ahead of many teams and recovery rates quickened and injuries decreased.

We gave a young blond kid called Simon Geoghegan his first start in that Spanish game. Jim Staples tipped me off about him, said he was a bit special. I already had an idea, having coached him for the Ireland Students' team.

We beat Spain, scoring three or four tries in the process and playing the kind of rugby that must have looked like a foreign game to the people in the ground. Rugby in Connacht was always about grunt and grind. Now they were watching back play. Geoghegan was outstanding.

I had a couple of pints with the players back at the hotel, then told them there was a team meeting at 10 a.m. the following day. Every set of eyes in the room did an eight-ball roll. Then I went up to my room to analyse the tape of the game. I spent four and a half hours in front of the television, pausing, rewinding and scribbling notes. At 3 a.m. I crawled into bed, exhausted.

My eyes had only just closed when the phone beside the bed rang. It was the desk sergeant in the local Garda station. 'I've one of your fellas here,' he said.

'One of my . . . players?'

'Disturbing the peace. Look, it's not a big deal. I'll release him, but it has to be into your custody.'

I drove to the station and there he was – the name shall remain secret – in the clink. It turned out he'd thrown a rock at a door or something. We drove back to the hotel. I had a couple of fitful hours of sleep, then got up, got dressed and was standing in Eyre Square at 7 a.m. when the truck arrived from Dublin with the morning papers.

The CAO results for university places were published that morning. Michelle was waiting for hers but was in Florida on holiday with her friend and her family. I pulled an *Irish Times* out of a stack that had been left outside a shop. I checked her exam number against the results in the paper, then phoned her from the lobby of the hotel to tell her she'd got the points she needed to do European studies in Trinity College.

It was years since I'd felt as good about life as I did before the team meeting that morning. It was like a pall was lifting from over me.

The players didn't have to be roused from their beds to make the 10 a.m. meeting. They all showed up, still half-cut admittedly, but they were there. I went through the video of the game with them, using the counter to mark incidents in the game that I wanted to talk about.

The video meant there was no place to hide for the players. They knew how much effort it took to prepare for that meeting. I could sense that players were looking at each other and thinking, *We have just beaten Spain. Where did we get this guy from?*

It was a great start but then we went into virtual hibernation waiting for the Inter-pros to come around. Our first match was against Munster in Thomond Park in Limerick. There was little or no opportunity to get the players together before the match. I arranged a training session for Wanderers ground on Merrion Road in Dublin on a Sunday afternoon, a week prior to the game. There was a full All Ireland League programme on the previous day. Every player was under instructions to ring me once his match was over and tell me how he'd come through it. I sat by the phone all afternoon. By the end of it, I had my head in my hands. I wasn't looking at an injury list as much as a body count. Ray Hernan, one of our centres, got crocked playing for Mary's. Davy Henshaw, our tight head, hurt himself playing for Athlone. The news wasn't good on a couple of others.

It was 6.30 p.m. on the night before what would be our only proper squad session for the match against Munster.

I had an idea. I picked up the phone and rang London Irish. There must have been six teams playing at Sunbury that day and I could barely make my voice heard over the background noise. I asked to speak to Jim Staples. Eventually he came to the phone.

'How are you, George?' he said. 'I'm just getting ready to hit the airport.'

He and Geoghegan were flying to Dublin that night.

'Don't go yet,' I said. 'Is David Curtis there with you?'

'He's here, yeah. Why?'

'Would he come over with you?'

'What do you mean, come over? To Dublin?'

'Trust me, Jim. Is he there?'

'I'm looking at him. I'll put him on to you.'

I'd only laid eyes on David Curtis once before, at the Varsity match in Twickenham, where he played in the centre for Oxford. He was brilliant that day. He was born in Harare, Zimbabwe, but it said in the programme notes that his father had played for Ireland. I had a ticket for the tea and buns in the stand after the match and I went down and got chatting to him. The family roots were in Sligo. It turned out that not only had his father, Brian, played for Ireland, but his grandfather was a Protestant clergyman who led the forward line for the Irish Free State. I don't know how good Canon Curtis was, but his grandson was outstanding. When he graduated, he signed for London Irish, which was now top of the English second division and heading for the first.

'Hello, this is David Curtis.'

I recognized the Zimbabwean accent right away. 'David, you probably don't remember me but I met you once very briefly. I just wondered if you'd be interested in playing for Connacht?'

'Connacht? Of course.'

He'd heard of us. That was a relief. 'OK, here's the deal. There'll be a ticket waiting for you at Heathrow. Get a cab with Jim and Simon. We're staying in the Mount Herbert Hotel on Lansdowne Road. You're staying in Jim's room. Tell him.'

'OK.'

'Now, I have a slight problem. I've no approval from the selection committee to pick you. If anyone asks you who you are, you're a friend of Jim's and you're just over for the weekend. Are you an early riser?'

'Er, I can be, yeah.'

'Good, I'll meet you for breakfast in the Mount Herbert at eight o'clock in the morning.'

I booked a return ticket in his name using my credit card. The lack of organization in Connacht was a blessing in some ways. There were no officials hanging around the team hotel, so no one knew about my solo run.

Training was on Merrion Road in the afternoon. Eddie

O'Sullivan arrived. 'Have a look at your man,' I said, nodding at Dave, who was going through a few drills with the other backs.

'Who is he?'

I gave him his résumé. 'Take a look at him, will you? I think he may be OK.'

Eddie took the backs to one end of the ground and I took the forwards to the other. Twenty minutes into the session, Eddie came down to me. 'Your man's the business,' he said.

'You mean, if I were to pick him, you'd be happy?'

'Absolutely.'

'Good,' I said, 'because I haven't got permission for him yet.'

Right on cue, I looked up and saw John Callanan, the chairman of the selectors, ambling up the driveway of Wanderers. I think John is the most genuine, trustworthy person I've met in a lifetime in rugby. I could tell from his puzzled look that he'd noticed David. 'Hi, John,' I said.

'Who's your man?'

'There's something I want to talk to you about, John. I want the new guy on the team.'

'George, you should know enough to know it doesn't work like that.'

'Ray Hernan cried off at six o'clock last night, John. I want him.'

'Well, I'd better go home and make some phone calls then.'

There were five members on the selection committee. John and I were two. This would need to be unanimous. Ciaran Smith, the ex-Corinthians and Mary's fly-half, was one of the committee that agreed to select Curtis as the replacement. That night, I was sitting at home when the phone rang. 'George,' Ciaran said, 'I think you'd better tell me who this guy is who I've just voted for, in case anyone asks me.'

A few days later, the *Connacht Tribune* published an article that was scathing of me for bringing in outsiders. To be honest, I wouldn't have cared less if David had been Martian, as long as he could do a job for me, but the newspaper hadn't even bothered to check David's history. At least Sean Diffley in the *Irish Independent* remembered David's father playing wing-forward for Ireland just after the war.

We went to Limerick the following weekend to play Munster. We arrived at the hotel and went to check in. The girl at reception checked the computer and said, 'We've a reservation for you, Mr Hook, but none for any Eddie O'Sullivan.'

Eddie blew a gasket. 'I'm fucking out of here,' he said. Then he turned and stormed out. I was rooted to the floor with shock. My assistant coach of only one match is spouting resignation. It was the first time I ever saw the hypersensitive side to his personality. Eddie feels every slight. He feels imagined slights. When Eddie reads an article about himself in a newspaper, he doesn't just read the words, he studies the punctuation, agonizing over every comma and semicolon, wondering if it makes the thrust of the sentence positive or negative.

I chased after him and caught up with him in the car park. He had his keys in his hand. 'Ah, for heaven's sake, Eddie,' I said. 'Come back in. You know the branch have no money. They've just doubled us up in one room.'

Eddie calmed down and we roomed together for what was the first of many times over the next six years.

We seemingly didn't have a prayer against Munster. They had Ralph Keyes and Michael Bradley. We had a centre and a tight head that were meeting their team-mates for only the second time. This was Thomond Park, with Noel Murphy, Tommy Kiernan and all the greats looking down at us from the stand.

We went out and beat the hell out of them. We lost. The result was a travesty. The referee had a nightmare. Ralph was given three points for a drop goal attempt that sailed wide. Eric Elwood had a perfectly good drop goal denied. For long tracts of the game, we had them on the rack.

Simon Geoghegan scored a wonderful try that came straight off the shop floor at London Irish. We had a scrum somewhere around the halfway line. Jim Staples went to out-half, in effect down the blind side. When the ball alighted from the scrum, they skipped him and went to David Curtis, who flipped the ball to Simon to run fifty metres and put the ball down under the posts. It was easier to score the conversion than to miss it but Derek Holland somehow put it wide.

I don't know what happened. It was like we couldn't believe what we were doing to the mighty Munster in their own backyard. It was a guilty pleasure that no one felt quite right enjoying.

My relationship with Eric never recovered from the time I argued against him for the Inter-provincials. He was right and I was wrong. He was a far better player than I thought he was. On the debit side, his occasional rushes of blood cost us matches we could have won. In the second half of the Munster match, we were stubbornly defending our own line when Eric decided to try to chip Ralph to put Simon in for an eighty-yard try. It was stupid and reckless. Ralph charged the ball down and Munster scored and kicked the conversion.

I was like an antichrist on the sideline. After all our hard work, we were six points behind going into the final minute. We went back down their end. David Curtis looped around three of their guys to score a beautiful try in the corner, presenting Eric with the kick to beat Munster.

I didn't blame him for missing it. It was from the touchline and the breeze made the angle impossible. But I did blame his careless-ness for costing us a famous victory. Afterwards, Eddie and I went for a cup of tea under the stand. A whole procession of people stopped by to tell us what a great job we did. We were inconsolable. A moral victory was no kind of victory at all.

I cheered up. Tommy Kiernan, who I knew from school, wanted to congratulate me on discovering David Curtis. He did it in a way that was typically Tommy. 'And the fucking British Empire is playing for Connacht now, is it?'

I could do nothing but laugh.

We regrouped. A week later, we played Leinster in Galway. We beat them up and down the pitch but we made a mess of it. Ray Hernan's kid brother – who was as Connacht as Connacht could be – lined out for Leinster and scored two tries. We lost by two points.

Our last game was against Ulster at Ravenhill. Before the match, we lost David. Fifteen minutes in, we lost Jim. It was like taking the guns off the destroyer. Ulster were better than us but we ran them all the way. We were only a handful of points behind in the closing minutes but the players didn't know how far behind we were or how much time was left. I was screaming at Noel McCarthy, our captain, to try to make myself heard. We spent the last five minutes taking short penalties and running them to try to breach the Ulster line. A couple of them were right in front of the posts. If we'd kicked them, we'd have won. We lost by two points again.

It was extraordinary. We finished bottom of the championship, having played three and lost three by a combined aggregate of just five points. We could conceivably have won all three matches. Max Boyce would have been writing arias about us. Instead, we were nobodies.

The following autumn, Ciaran Fitzgerald resigned as Ireland coach. Those five points, I believe, cost Eddie and me the job of replacing him.

I wouldn't have made a good Ireland coach. At that point in his life maybe Eddie wouldn't have either. But as a double act we were better than all the alternatives. We had achieved more with fewer resources than anyone else around.

How many Connacht players are in the Ireland team today? How many were in it before Eddie and I took over? The Ciaran Fitzgeralds, Mick Molloys and Ray McLoughlins came around once a generation. Three months after we finished bottom in the Inter-provincial Championship, Jim Staples, Simon Geoghegan and David Curtis were all in the Ireland back line. It was 1991 – the start of a World Cup year – and Connacht had three players on the team.

Other players got their first caps on the strength of their performances for us. There was Mick Fitzgibbon and Neville Furlong, who scored two tries against the All Blacks on a tour of New Zealand. I felt an immense sense of pride that day. Neville was our creation. He was an average enough rugby player who took the

Liam Hennessy fitness book and devoured it whole. He turned himself into a machine. I remember once at a summer training camp he took his shirt off for some fitness test or other and my jaw hit the floor. He belonged on the stage at a Mister Universe contest.

We toured England in the summer of 1991 and played three matches in the space of a week. The English players couldn't believe our itinerary. And yet the games took little or nothing out of the players because of our approach to fitness.

We were miles ahead of the posse. We were the best men for the Ireland job.

7. Running away to America

The business was in its final death throes in 1991. I'd been served with enough writs to wallpaper my living room and I'd held off the banks for a long time, but the time of reckoning had come. The house in Foxrock was safe – family homes were protected in law – but, being in my name, my mother's house in Beaumont was at risk. All my chickens had come home to roost.

People rallied round me. An emergency meeting of the Friends of George Hook convened in my accountant, Andy Butler's, office. Andy, Kyran McLaughlin and a solicitor, Brian McLoughlin were there, together with Bryan O'Neill who was not only financial controller at Dowling and Associates but also a good friend. Naturally, I was there, but I might as well not have been. I sat at one of the tables, mute, while they talked about what they were going to do to extricate me from the mess I'd made of my life. It was as if they were talking about a retarded child: I was the object of the discussion but seemingly incapable of making any contribution. Everything was being done for my benefit, and without charge, but it remains the low point of my life.

I was the beneficial owner of my mother's house and therefore, with my debts, it could be seized by a creditor and result in her eviction. To protect my mother, Kyran agreed to buy her house for £60,000. (That amount was arrived at after independent valuation.) My mother could continue living there but when she died, the property would revert to Kyran. The house wasn't a prize addition to Kyran's property portfolio. He bought it simply because he was my friend and, for the umpteenth time in our lives, he wanted to bail me out. He wrote out a cheque for £60,000, which I never saw. Andy Butler and Bryan O'Neill then leveraged that money to settle debts many times a multiple of that number.

Although most of my financial troubles had gone away, I still carried a substantial debt for a man with no income. Then in the space of a month during that summer, London Irish asked me to coach the first team, Portobello College wanted me to lecture in marketing and the Irish Museum of Modern Art in Kilmainham offered me the job of marketing manager. All the jobs had flexible time schedules and, bedazzled by the prospect of a substantial income, I accepted them all. My master plan was to do the morning lectures at the college, then zip across to Kilmainham to set up the marketing plans before flying out to London on Thursday to run the session at London Irish that evening and stay until Sunday to take in the game. Naturally it did not work and my careers as a lecturer and manager were short-lived.

The London Irish job came about because Jim Staples had been appointed the new captain at the club. The 'Exiles' had just secured promotion to the first division of English club rugby. Simon Geoghegan and David Curtis and Jim had all been part of the Connacht team during my first season in charge and were keen to bring me to the club even though I would be commuting from Ireland to do the job. I agreed to take it on, but on condition that I could have Eddie O'Sullivan as my assistant. 'We are a team,' I said, and Jim agreed. Eddie and I flew to London and met the team manager, Kieran McCarthy to complete the deal.

London Irish has had more committees than Italy has had post-war governments. When I played for them in the early 1960s, I went to the AGM one year and saw the secretary shafted. It was like watching badger-baiting. That was the nature of the place. The membership was drawn from such disparate backgrounds – the Irish Catholics, the Irish Protestants and the English – all with their own beliefs and values and petty prejudices that keeping the peace at Sunbury was like trying to hold Yugoslavia together after Tito. Impossible.

The internecine warfare that was never far below the surface was demonstrated when I was invited to the club dinner at the Kensington Tara Hotel. At the drinks reception, I suddenly realized that not only the club committee but also the current coach of the team did not know of my impending arrival. Little did I think that

I would be the victim of a similar situation within twelve months and even the great Clive Woodward would be unable to break the cycle of coups that was the lifeblood of the amateur era at the 'Exiles' club. He had to walk away after his sojourn in charge.

Later that summer, I flew once more to London to meet two heavyweights from the committee. Despite being taken to an expensive dinner in the West End, it was perfectly obvious that Roger McKibbin and Mariott Irons were less than enchanted with the fait accompli of my arrival as coach. By the time the brandy and cigars arrived, the argument boiled down to one key issue – could I keep London Irish in the top flight? The history of league rugby in England was littered with examples of promoted clubs going straight back down the following year.

Eddie agreed to join me. At that point, he was not only Ireland's fitness co-ordinator for the upcoming World Cup but he was also coaching Blackrock and holding down a full-time teaching job in the Convent of the Holy Rosary in Mountbellew in Co. Galway. I often wonder if his famous insomnia goes back to those years. On Tuesdays and Thursdays, he finished school at 3.45 p.m. and drove to Dublin to coach Blackrock. When the sessions were over, he drove home again. When he joined me in London Irish he'd leave school and drive to Dublin to catch an early evening flight to London. I'd pick him up at Heathrow and we'd take the back roads to Sunbury, where he'd train the backs for a couple of hours. I'd take him back to Heathrow, where he'd catch the 11 p.m. flight back to Dublin and then drive home to get a couple of hours' sleep before school the next day. He was indefatigable.

Like most team sports, players that are good enough to compete in the lower divisions rarely make it in the more rarefied atmosphere of the top level. The plan was for a summer of recruitment. I persuaded international Tom Clancy to leave Lansdowne while McCarthy delivered Matt Keenan, a second row from Auckland who had played for Western Samoa in the 1987 World Cup and a host of others including Oxford University number 8 Mark Egan and prop Gary Halpin from Wanderers.

McCarthy identified David Peglar at Wasps as a key target. He was a superb captain and a natural leader but had missed a season because of a bad ankle injury and did not seem to be in Wasps' future plans. He had a superb track record as an open-side flanker and captain. I met him at his office and when he agreed to come to Sunbury I was elated not just to sign a quality player but that an Englishman who did not know my background would commit because he liked what he saw and was motivated by my ideas.

On paper we had a team but the Rugby World Cup was scheduled for October and Curtis, Geoghegan, Staples and Saunders were all in the Irish squad together with Eddie in the management team. They would not be available until after the competition. There was more bad news as the season opened, for one reason or another most of the new signings were not yet on board and crucially David Peglar's ankle still required treatment. His absence was very damaging because he might have provided leadership while Staples was away.

So we went into friendly games with the bulk of the side from the previous year's squad. They knew they were only keeping the places warm for the big signings so morale was poor. We lost most of the games and we were humiliated on the morning of the World Cup Final when we lost to London Scottish by over fifty points. What made it worse was that many people from Ireland decided to come to the game before travelling on to Twickenham for the final.

The following week brought good and bad news. The good news was we had all our top players back and in training. The bad news was we had two weeks and one warm-up game before the opening league game against champions Bath at Sunbury. We succeeded in beating the British Universities, who were no test, and then faced the music in front of the BBC cameras and a packed attendance a week later.

It may have been my finest hour. It was an extraordinary achievement to lose to Bath by just a couple of points with a group of players who had been together little over a week. Coaching careers hang by a thread and my year could have been totally different had Rob Saunders been able to play at scrum-half. In the final minute we had the game for the taking with Geoghegan free on the right. The second-team scrum-half went left; the opportunity was lost and with it my chance of an historic victory.

Amateur bodies work in mysterious ways. While I was at Sunbury I was also coaching Connacht in the Inter-provincial Championship and the Irish Students who were preparing for the first-ever Student World Cup in South Africa. Connacht were incredibly good to me and accepted the situation but the IRFU dumped me as coach to the Students team without a word. My first intimation that I was persona non grata was when I read the announcement of the travelling party in a newspaper.

With a couple of games to go in the Premiership we looked certain to avoid the drop. Then in the build-up to the Saracens game, I was consumed by my old demons. I had, as was my wont, subsidized my new career by increasing my borrowings. I was facing an interest bill at the bank. Some years earlier I had taken an Old Belvedere team to the Dubai seven-a-side tournament. We had been hosted by the Irish community in the emirate and they now invited me to speak at their St Patrick's Day dinner. To avoid clashing with Ramadan, that year it was to be in late March rather than on the 17th. There was a fee involved so I went.

Less than a week before we were due to play Saracens I got on a plane for the United Arab Emirates without telling anybody, preferring to phone Kieran McCarthy when I arrived. It was stupid but I was once more under self-inflicted pressure because I had concentrated on coaching instead of getting paid.

I came home from my three-day break and watched helplessly as Saracens took us apart on the Saturday. However, it was not a fatal blow as we were almost safe from relegation. Almost, but not quite. When the rugby results came off the teleprinter, bottom had beaten top in almost every other match that day. If the same thing happened on Easter weekend, we could still go down. Our final game of the season was away to Bristol, the aristocrats of West Country rugby.

★

All season the out-half position had been our Achilles heel. We tried various options – even David Curtis, who was the Irish centre, filled in for some games – but we needed him in midfield against Bristol. A week before the most important game in my and the club's life, we had nobody at number 10. Bristol and London Irish had been playing each other for over a hundred years. In that time 'the Irish' had won on just five occasions and only twice away from home. The odds against staying up were getting longer.

That season, the London Irish under-19s had two schoolboy international fly halves. One was Paul Burke (now with Munster), the other was Owen Cobbe. Paul was the better of the two. He'd played for England at schools level, even though he was as Irish as Paddy's pig. His parents were ex-pats who owned a pub in London. I met him at the club and told him I wanted to name him in the team for the final game of the season. He shifted uncomfortably in his seat. He was still only 19 years of age.

'I don't know if I'm ready for this,' he said.

'I don't know if you are either, Paul,' I said. 'However, I have seen enough of you to believe that you can do it.'

'No,' he said. 'I'm not ready. I don't want to play.'

Owen Cobbe had gone to Pres Bray and was Paul Burke's opposite number at fly-half when Ireland had played England the previous year. At London Irish, though, Paul was adjudged the better kicker and Cobbe was accommodated in the centre. He was my second and last hope. I called him in. 'Cobbie,' I said, 'I want you to play against Bristol.'

He didn't blink. 'Fine,' he said. It was an astonishing display of confidence by a youngster who had never played above age-grade rugby. Perhaps he'd misunderstood.

'I want you to play against Bristol,' I repeated. '*In* Bristol. And we have to win to stay in the top division. You're OK with that?'

'Fine, yeah,' he said again.

Eddie arrived over on the Monday. It was Easter week. I pointed Cobbie out to him. 'That's the guy I've got for fly-half there,' I said. 'Have a look at him, will you?'

'OK,' Eddie said. 'I'll tell you in ten minutes,' and he went down to the far end of the pitch to work with the backs while I worked with the forwards on their lineouts. A few minutes later Eddie arrived down and gave me a barely perceptible nod.

'He's OK?' I said.

'He's OK.'

We had one more problem. The season should have been done and dusted at that point. Snow had wiped out a weekend of fixtures earlier in the winter, and all those postponed games were being played one week after the season should have ended. David Peglar, on the assumption that the game would be unimportant, had agreed to play for his local junior team on a tour to Cork over the holiday weekend. He'd given his word that he'd play. A council of war took place in Kieran McCarthy's office in Sunbury. We called Peglar in Ireland.

'David,' I said to him, 'all our lives are on the line here.'

'George,' he said, 'if you can get me back, I'll play.'

We had to have David in the team. We discussed chartering a plane to have him flown from Cork to Bristol immediately after the tournament but eventually he decided to come by a scheduled flight after his club agreed that he could miss the last match of the tour. The timings were tight but we offered up novenas that fog or mechanical breakdown would not screw up the whole plan. We needed him.

The match against Bristol was an epic encounter: the unstoppable force meeting the immovable object. Cobbie played like a fifty-cap veteran. There's one image of him that I carry with me to this day. Bristol were encamped ten metres from our line and the ball squirted out of a ruck a few yards in front of him. There were three Bristol players stampeding towards him but he threw himself on it and took a terrible shellacking. I've never seen such unswerving bravery in an 18-year-old.

Apart from Cobbie, David Curtis was outstanding. Knowing how raw Cobbie was, he kept calling for the ball in difficult situations and taking the tackles for him. It was one of those days that reminded me why I fell in love with rugby. For only the third time in a century, we beat Bristol on their own patch. As it happened, the other results went our way, so we not only stayed up, we stayed up comfortably. But even had all our rivals won, we had saved ourselves by our own efforts. I couldn't have been more proud.

Soon after the season ended, Kieran McCarthy and I were called to a meeting with Roger McKibbin, Mariott Irons and the club president to review the season. They were clearly dissatisfied with the way it had gone. I felt they were out of touch and had no idea just how competitive the top flight was and what had been required to survive.

I pointed out that, apart from the momentous victory at Bristol, we had beaten Wasps, who were champions two years ago, Rosslyn Park and Nottingham. We had drawn with Northampton away and also with Rugby. 'What more did you want?' I asked. Eight months previously, in a restaurant in the West End, all they had wanted was to avoid relegation. Now, of course, they demanded instant success. I knew that my time was up with this particular group.

Then salvation appeared on the horizon in the form of the traditional end-of-the season coup. London Irish was in serious financial trouble and Ray O'Rourke, an Irish construction magnate, had put money on the table to bail us out. He'd always been good to the club, directly and indirectly, offering sponsorship and giving players jobs. David Curtis worked for him as an engineer, as did Tom Clancy. Now that he effectively owned the club he wanted new faces on the committee. McKibbin and Irons were ousted. I felt a little bit more secure about my own future once Irons and McKibbin had been shown the door.

Paul Collins, the former Ireland back row, was the new captain and he worked for O'Rourke as his financial controller. I met him for lunch in a pub near O'Rourke's offices in east London. Paul said they wanted me to coach the team the following season. However, within weeks O'Rourke and Collins unveiled Hika Reid, the ex-All Black hooker, as coach and I received the news of my departure in the usual manner: third hand. It turned out that my last action as coach had been to hold a team meeting in Sunbury and hand out training programmes for the summer.

Then I made a stupid error, a mirror image of the mistake I made when Pat Campbell sacked me, and decided to strike out on my own. I saw an ad for a coaching position at Fylde, the club in Lancashire where I'd met Ingrid twenty-five years earlier and where my old friend from the Preston branch of Burroughs was a former president. Fylde had just been promoted from the third division to the second. It was a comedown for me but not quite as humiliating as going home would have been. Pride was too important to me.

I got an interview and got the job. Bill Beaumont, the former England and Lions star, was the director of rugby at Fylde and he put together a package for me. I was quite underwhelmed by it but these were the first, tentative days of the professional era. Professionalism in rugby was in a very grey area. Like tennis and athletics in the sixties it was the era of 'shamateurism'. The legislators were frantically putting their fingers in the dyke against a tidal wave of under-the-counter payments. Coaching directors who did not, apparently, have a 'hands-on' involvement with the team could be paid, but putting on a tracksuit and getting your hands dirty for money was verboten. Clubs all over Ireland imported Kiwis and Springboks to coach their teams but filled out a meaningless form for the IRFU to say these guys merely 'directed' things. Similarly, foreign players reputedly came to Ireland for the love of the game and not the cash.

There were rumours about who was getting paid what and where but nobody knew for sure. I still had the naïve idea that I could accept money and remain a Corinthian if I persuaded myself that it was expenses. This naïveté was the reason I worked for a season at London Irish without making an issue of money. But now I had to make an issue of it. I'd had no wages for almost a year and I'd racked up even more debts. I had hoped to get some compensation for my efforts and my commitment. I phoned the London Irish.

A month later a senior club representative called me to arrange a meeting. I pointed out that I had kept the club in the first division and deserved some credit for that, since I would no doubt have been blamed had the club been relegated.

We arranged to meet one lunchtime at a hotel close to Heathrow. We ate lunch. We ordered coffee. The man pulled out a cheque and placed it face down on the table. I presumed that a figure close to a year's salary would be realistic, and that was what I expected to see on the cheque, but the amount – £15,000 – would barely have covered my expenses for the year.

I drove the three and a half hours back to Lancashire, stopping only once, at a branch of the National Westminster Bank to deposit the cheque by credit transfer against my overdraft. There was, sadly, still a debit balance remaining which would be a problem for another day. Nevertheless, I was £15,000 better off than I might have been had I not raised the issue. Still, when I'd met the London Irish representative, I had been putty in his hands. Confrontation was never my strong suit.

The upside of coaching Fylde was that I was staying with Tom Windridge, one of the dearest men I've ever met, wonderfully warm and hospitable. He gave me a bed and three meals a day for twenty pounds a week, which I had to force him to take on pain of terminating our friendship.

The downside was that I was working with a team that couldn't knock their way out of a wet paper bag. We won only one match that season and finished it back in the third division again, a fall from which the club has never recovered.

I'll admit only limited liability for that. There were demographic problems that I could not control. The club is based in Lytham St Anne's, a sleepy retirement town where the average age of the population is in three figures and the number one sport is dominoes. Well, maybe not, but it wasn't exactly awash with young, fit rugby players.

The club wasn't built to survive the professional era. I found out in time that neither was the coach. Just like Fylde, I belonged to a different age. What I didn't grasp was that in the professional era – I was paid now by monthly direct transfer – the club owned you. I had always enjoyed the sense of being a servant to the clubs I coached. I didn't know how to act as an employee, especially when the club secretary, who was my nominal boss, was a chartered accountant with the personality and charm of a revenue inspector.

At London Irish, at least I had a support team to take some of the flak. But I didn't have a Kieran McCarthy or a Jim Staples at Fylde. As a full-time, fully paid coach, results were down to me.

Bill Beaumont and I remain friends to this day but we had completely different ideas on rugby. I had just come from the first division, which then as now was fiercely competitive. The gulf between it and the lower reaches of the second division was massive. I was used to working with players of high skill levels, at Fylde they were below average. The job of a coach is to improve his players, but sometimes the task can be too great. As Winston Churchill put it: 'Give us the tools and we can finish the job.' Fylde had neither the resources nor the players to survive. Bill was simply too nice a guy to recognize that Fylde's time was over.

Meanwhile, in an effort to help the club escape relegation for the second time, I was trampling all over people's sensibilities, changing the defence, reorganizing training sessions, bringing in new faces. No one ever really understood what I was trying to do. It was like going from managing Arsenal to managing Rushden and Diamonds. The credibility gap was too wide.

Then there was the fact that I was miserable after Sunbury, like a lover scorned. Fylde got me on the rebound. We were never going to make each other happy.

In November 1992, the Black Dog of depression came wagging its way back into my life. I disappeared. I drove to Manchester airport, looked up at the departures board and got on the next plane out of town. It was to London. I checked into the Ryan Hotel in the East End, locked the door of my room and got into bed with the pillow wrapped tight over my head. I didn't even phone Tom to tell him where I was. After twenty-four hours Tom reported me missing. The police found my car at the airport and said there was nothing to worry about. I'd probably gone back to Ireland.

Nothing to worry about? Who was going to give the team talk on Saturday?

I stayed in the hotel for five days, removing my head from under the pillow only to eat room-service dinners. After a few days of this, I got up the courage to pick up the phone to tell Bill that I was coming back.

At the end of the season, I returned home. It wasn't like I had much choice. The atmosphere in the house was icy. For two years Ingrid had been on her own. I'd fly home on a Wednesday morning, when she was at work and the children were at school. We'd spend Wednesday night together as a family and on Thursday afternoon I'd go back to England. Ingrid might as well have been a widow; at least she'd have had a pension. After two years living like that, there was little or no communication between us.

I'd been a bit-part player in my mother's life, too. I still feel a deep sense of shame at the way I just picked up the tempo of my life again after my father died without it ever occurring to me that I should spend a lot more time with her. The number of times I saw her in the eight years she was a widow shames me. I fluttered in and out of her life as ephemerally as a butterfly. Sometimes I'd appear on the scene and take her out to lunch, which she loved, or the chiropodist, but I didn't absorb the lesson of my father's death, that these moments are precious. There was always something more important to do. Meanwhile, she was lonely and alone.

One morning she phoned and said that she needed to talk to me. I drove to Beaumont to see her. We sat in the living room and in calm, measured tones she told me that she had a plan to end her life – she had been saving her sleeping pills so she could decide when and how to die – and she explained the rationale behind it.

'George,' she said, 'I'm well into my eighties now and I'm not enjoying life any more. My husband is dead. I haven't many friends. I'm on my own. What we're going to do is this. We're going to go for a nice lunch somewhere and talk about old times. Then we're going to come back here, make a pot of tea and I'm going to take the pills. And you can hold my hand while I go to sleep.'

There wasn't a shred of self-pity in her voice. I wasn't talking to a lonely old woman who was craving attention. I wasn't talking to someone who'd lost her mind. Once she was weaned off her atomic cocktail of pills my mother's mind was clear and as sharp as a blade right to the end. She had thought out what she wanted. She had teased out all the moral and religious arguments and squared them in her mind. As she saw it, she'd lived her life and she was doing nothing now but waiting to die. All that could happen in whatever time she had left was that she would become a burden on other people. She was too proud to want that.

I talked her out of it. To my eternal regret, I persuaded her to flush the tablets down the toilet. As ever, I was thinking about myself. 'What's the coroner going to say?' I said. 'He's going to say, "Where were you, George?" and I'm going to say, "I was there with her. I was the one who made her the tea." Mercy-killing is illegal in this country.'

She changed her mind because she couldn't bear the thought of me going to jail. I know every mother loves her son but the love my mother had for me was indescribable. If I could go back and live that day again, I'd do what she wanted me to do and take my chances in front of a jury.

She wanted to die with dignity on a day of her choosing and I owed her that much at least. Instead, I talked her out of it, and she was to die the kind of death she always feared she would, doubled up in pain and with her son missing in action.

I have made my mind up to follow the example she set me. There will be a day when I decide that I've done everything I want to do in life and that next week doesn't look like being too good. I'll have arthritis in my fingers and won't be able to hold a golf club. Or my memory will be shot to ribbons. I won't make the mistake of asking the people I love to help me. But I will find a peaceful corner of the world for myself and make the quiet, dignified exit that I denied my mother.

★

166

I came home from England in the summer of 1993 without a job or a plan. I didn't know where I was going. No reason to get up in the morning. For two years my life had been meaningful because I was doing what I did best but emotionally and financially my future was zero.

Then, out of the blue, I got a phone call from my old friend Ron Mayes in San Francisco. Ron wondered if I knew anyone who'd be interested in becoming director of rugby for the United States Rugby Union. I told him I'd rack my brains and get back to him.

I phoned him back an hour later. 'I know somebody,' I told him.

'Who?'

'Me!'

'Jesus! You'd be interested? The thing is, we can't really afford to pay you, George. How could you do it?'

'I have an idea,' I said. 'I'll put it down on paper and I'll get back to you.'

I sat down and wrote out my own job specification. The USARFU was broke but I would find a sponsor in America to pay my salary. I'd spend twenty-six weeks of the year in the US, teaching people how to coach rugby. Ron thought it was a great idea.

Naturally, I told Ingrid nothing about it.

There's a big difference between being a team coach and a coach educator. They're different skills. To be a coach educator you need good literary and verbal skills. Some educators cannot coach a team and some of the most successful team coaches are rendered inarticulate when standing in front of a group and attempting to explain their ideas coherently. However, the one thing every coach educator needs is a textbook to work from.

It's a fair enough indicator of where my mind was at that, as my departure date grew nearer, I was more worried about having no coaching manual prepared than I was about how Ingrid would take the news that her husband now lived on the other side of the world for six months of the year.

I couldn't find a suitable published manual, so I decided to write a textbook myself. I phoned a guy in the IRFU who was involved in coach education and asked if I could take him out to lunch. 'Look,' I told him across the table, 'I've never done this before. Can you help me?'

By the time the remnants of our lunch were cleared away, I was no wiser. In less than an hour, he made rugby sound like rocket science and gently told me that this game was all too complex for me to understand. The inference was clear: only professionals like him had the ability to write coaching manuals. I came away depressed. I thought about ringing Ron and calling off the deal.

Instead, I phoned Eddie. We met in the Coffee Dock Grill in Jury's Hotel. I told him I had to write a textbook but I did not know how. 'I can't do it,' I said.

'What are you talking about?' he said. 'Of course you can do this.'

'I can?'

He shook his head, and then pulled an envelope out of his inside pocket. Eddie is a minimalist. Everything I needed to know, he wrote on the back of the envelope. 'You have it all in your head, George,' he said. 'Chapter one – Defence. You know all about defence, don't you? Three-up, four-up defences, man-on-man, drift? Chapter two – Offence. You know all about skip one, skip two, loop. Chapter three – The Scrum-half Pass. Technical abilities required for the scrum-half. Chapter four – The Scrum . . .'

When he was finished he handed me the envelope. 'George,' he said, 'you *know* all this. Stop being so hard on yourself.'

I walked out of Jury's, ready to take on the world, and within weeks was on my way to the USA. I was excited about being a proselytizer for the greatest game in the world. I was about to awaken a sleeping giant.

First things first; I had to find a sponsor. In the autumn after the 1987 World Cup in Australia I had been invited back to America to coach for two weeks in Providence, Rhode Island. That was that point where my life intersected with Bob Hoder. He ran an equipment and sportswear company called Rugby Imports and paid for me to come over for two weeks to coach Providence RFC, of which he was the president and major benefactor. I coached the club in the evenings and local universities in the afternoons. The most prestigious university in Rhode Island is the Ivy League school, Brown, and I lodged at the house of the coach, Jay Fluck. I returned often to that beautiful corner of New England to work with both men and their teams in the intervening years. Fluck and Hoder were to become my dearest friends in North America.

I put my ideas for a coaching programme to Bob Hoder and he agreed to put up $40,000, which wasn't going to stretch to providing a salary for me but would just about cover my expenses for twelve months. Bob also provided me with an office and a car. (Public transport is not one of America's strong points.) I told Ron we had lift-off and we set up the dates for coaching clinics across America. I was off and running, poor but happy, and entirely forgetful of my responsibilities in Dublin.

Jay Fluck offered me a bed in his home for as long as I needed but I had to set up some long-term living arrangements. Jay was in real estate and found a small apartment for me on the trendy east side of the city in the university district. The quality address belied the facilities. It was a single room in the basement of a large house. Happily there was a shower and a toilet, but little else. There was no fridge and no cooker and it was so small that it could accommodate a bed or a sofa, but not both. To give himself room to swing his cat the previous occupant had made his bed on top of a six-foot-high platform at one end of the room. I did the same thing. I bought a television. At night I'd clamber up onto my bed and watch my sixty-seven channels. I never enjoyed a full night's sleep. I was too conscious of plummeting six feet to the floor if I turned to my right or scalding myself on the ancient central heating pipes that ran along the wall on my left.

My weight ballooned. With no cooking facilities in my little dungeon, I ended up on first-name terms with the counter staff in all the local fast-food outlets. The man who turned down the franchise for McDonald's out of culinary snobbery now had it as his primary food source. I ate so many Big Macs, I became one. In two years, I gained four and a half stones of the shape I am today.

Every Friday morning I boarded a plane to one of the fifty states. I spent my weekends teaching rugby to wannabe coaches in California, Kentucky, New Mexico, Kansas, Texas and more. In five years, I covered forty-four states. From Monday to Thursday I worked in Providence, setting up the following weekend. It was exhausting but unbelievably rewarding.

While I was tripping gaily back and forth across the time zones my marriage was dying on its feet. Before then, though I was seldom home, there was at least some faint impression of me in Ingrid and the children's lives. When I was coaching in the UK at least I had been home every week, however fleetingly, but America was different because the absences were much longer. To get the coaching programme up and running, I spent thirty-seven weeks of the first year away from home. Though I was working and my self-esteem was returning, I was earning a pittance that was not even covering my own living costs. Unlike the emigrants of old, there were no remittances home. I just did my own thing and let Ingrid worry about feeding and clothing our children.

Of course, my debts hadn't gone away. I still owed tens of thousands of pounds when I ran away to America. It bothered me a lot less than it should have.

In financial terms, I might as well have been unemployed in America. I couldn't exist on expenses. Inevitably, I found a credit-card company to pick up the slack. American Express had gotten wise to me in Ireland. In the States, they didn't know me from Adam. They gave me a card with an unlimited credit ceiling. Although I'd gone to America to start afresh, it took me just twelve months of irresponsibility to start up whole new debt problems on the other side of the world. I racked up a bill of $25,000.

What saved me was that I was, to all intents and purposes, of no fixed abode. I moved around so much in those first two years that the company's only way of tracking me was when I used the card. Then I suspect a siren went off in an office somewhere in Manhattan: George Hook is at the Holiday Inn in Delaware. I'd get a phone call from some sombre-toned customer-care representative, offering to cut a deal. 'We'll accept $15,000,' he'd say, and I'd say, 'It doesn't matter a shit what you cut it to. The fact is that at this moment in time I can't give it to you.'

They eventually got tired of chasing me and sold the debt on. Now, instead of avoiding American Express, I was being chased around America by various debt-collection agencies that had their own ingenious ways of tracking me down. Every so often the phone would ring: 'Hey, George. This is Mick Foley here in Kansas City. You're a hard man to track down, pal. I'm just calling about this credit-card debt of yours. I can cut you a great deal. We're prepared to accept ten.'

I'd tell my new pal Mick what I'd told the American Express customer-care people. Soon, Mick would realize that he was wasting his time and sell the debt on to somebody else for maybe twelve grand. And on and on it went.

I don't write this with a sense of smug amusement at having conned one of the biggest financial institutions in the world. I was behaving recklessly. I had slipped into a parallel dimension where I thought nobody could touch me. When I was threatened with legal action, I didn't flinch. Twenty-five years of living on the cliff edge of bankruptcy had inured me to the fear of it.

Despite everything, I was happy. Dun Laoghaire pier was just a faintly remembered nightmare. When you read biographies of entertainers like Al Jolson, you learn that there are people for whom performing acts like a narcotic. In my first few months in America that's what I discovered about myself. I should have known it from my debating days: I was born to perform. Teaching was like a shot of pure adrenaline to me: I was showing Americans, who'd only ever watched the international game on television, how to scrum, how to ruck, how to line out. I was showing them individual skills, kicking, running, passing, evasion. Eddie was right: I knew my stuff. There wasn't a single question anyone threw at me that I couldn't answer. And I was good. I'd fly into Pittsburgh on a Friday afternoon and leave forty-eight hours later with a hundred people telling me what a great job I'd done.

In a few short months I went from feeling worthless to knowing I was respected and appreciated. It didn't matter to me that the grout holding my marriage together had all been chipped away. It didn't matter that if I flew to Dublin I wouldn't have my bus fare home from the airport. For the first time in thirty years, I was doing a job that I was good at. It was as if I'd been readmitted to the human race.

I spent two years teaching the Americans my level-one coaching programme. Things began to look up. The International Rugby Board gave us money. Bob Hoder continued to support a programme from which he got little commercial return but he was one of the pioneers of rugby in the country and his sheer enthusiasm for the game meant that he never counted the cost of the money or hours that he gave to its development.

After two years, US rugby could afford to start paying me a salary. I had now, again with Eddie's help, drawn up the level-two programme and the following year level three would commence. The job had become too big for just one man. Not only had manuals to be written but also I needed at least another educator to take over some of the additional programmes, especially those for elite coaches.

Eddie O'Sullivan had had great success at Blackrock and was now coaching Galwegians. He had also replaced me as Connacht coach. The Old Testament era of amateurism was over. They wanted him as their first full-time professional coach. The problem – hard as it is to imagine now – was that they wanted him cheaply. He was offered only a twelve-month contract. They wanted him to quit his permanent, pensionable job as a schoolteacher for a guarantee of a year's work.

He conducted most of his negotiations with Bobby Deacy, the treasurer of the IRFU, and Billy Glynn, the chairman of the Connacht selectors, over the phone from my study in Foxrock.

Every now and again, he'd step out of the room, looking more and more upset. It was clear they were playing hardball with him. The choice was to accept what he was being offered or resign.

'You have another card to play,' I told him.

'What card?'

'Well, if all else fails, I can guarantee you a job in America. I need an assistant.'

I wasn't doing it out of friendship. I knew Eddie's worth, even if Bobby and Billy did not. My offer changed the whole tenor of the debate. Eddie phoned them back and told them what he wanted. He said they could take it or leave it. They called his bluff. They let him walk away. He resigned as coach to both Connacht and Galwegians and, in a brilliant stroke, Billy got Warren Gatland from Waikato to replace him. There was an irony that Eddie and I had both been replaced by All Black hookers.

Eddie quit his job at the convent school and prepared to spend twenty-six weeks of his year travelling around America with me. I put together a package for him that included two salaries – one as my assistant and one as assistant coach to the national team, the US Eagles. It meant he was earning more than me but I knew I was going to get value for money. In rugby I was never anything other than an amateur who was getting paid for it. Eddie was the first professional I ever met in the sport. He was professional in every aspect of what he did long before professionalism was introduced. That was just his mindset.

We were based in the USARFU offices in Colorado Springs. We shared an apartment nearby. For the remainder of our time together in America, we lived together, although it was intermittent because of Eddie's commitment to the national team and the fact that we also were there for just part of the year.

There is an indefinable emotional bond between men that women don't necessarily understand, a non-sexual feeling of intimacy that men can share with one another but never with someone of the opposite sex. Eddie and I had that. We were more than good friends. We were Siamese twins joined at the psyche. What made our relationship work was that we recognized and compensated for one another's weaknesses – professionally, socially, and in so many other ways.

Even our personalities dovetailed perfectly. I was the garrulous flesh-presser, Eddie the taciturn, sensible one. To see us pass through airport immigration was to see our two characters in distillate form. I would breeze up to the booth and greet the guy behind the desk like I saw him every week. Immigration formalities would be brief. However, Eddie would approach the desk with the bearing of an illegal immigrant. Invariably it was a longer session.

At work, the roles were reversed. Eddie was the confident, decisive one. He loved solving the kind of problems that sent me to bed in the middle of the day hiding under a pillow. He answered the phone with a curt 'Yes?', like he almost hoped it was trouble. Countless times he'd stand behind me if I had a difficult call to make and say, 'Do it now, George.'

'No, I'll do it tomorrow,' I'd say.

'No, do it now,' he'd say and hand me the phone.

In rugby terms, we were also the perfect fit. I was a better analyst than Eddie. I was a better judge of players. I could look at a number 7 and know whether he was up to the job quicker than Eddie could. He was an immeasurably better technician. If I told him that my inside centre couldn't pass off his left hand and that the back line couldn't score inside the opposition 22, he'd go away and come back with a system that improved the player's ability to pass and allowed the back line to score.

That had happened in my last match as Connacht coach. Eddie was at Blackrock and I was doing the job by myself. My last game was against Munster in 'Fortress Limerick', not a place one would choose to finish on a high note. On the Thursday night before the game I asked Eddie to help at the training session in St Mary's College.

'What's the problem?' he said. Like I said, he loved problems.

'We're all right up front,' I said, 'but we're just not going to score any tries.'

Eddie said he'd fix it. 'We have the technology,' was his catch phrase, which I think he cogged from the opening credits of *The*

Six Million Dollar Man. What he meant was that we understood this game so much better than anyone else that we could do anything. He took over the attacking segment of the session and it flowed with a new purpose. The following Saturday I sat in the stand for the final time as coach to Connacht and had my worst-ever day at the office. We did reasonably well in the first half but in the second we fell apart and Munster put fifty points on us. It was the heaviest defeat in my career at Connacht. Despite the scale of the loss, right wing Michael Devine scored three tries. Rarely does a team that concedes fifty points score three tries. It is even rarer for an individual to do so in those circumstances. That was the genius of Eddie.

Our weekends in America were invariably spent in a motel after a flight from Colorado. We were an odd couple. We were John Candy and Steve Martin trying to get home for Thanksgiving. If Eddie had to fly from Colorado to Pittsburgh, he'd phone up United and book a ticket. I had my own Planes, Trains and Automobiles way of getting there. I'd fly from A to B via C, D and E, if it meant racking up a few more frequent-flier miles. Eddie christened me Zorro of the Skies because of my penchant for criss-crossing the continent. He always reckoned I would fly from Dublin to Galway via Anchorage, Alaska, just to get some extra miles on my card and travel first class en route.

We rarely flew together, anyway. Eddie stuck with United because a lot of his work with the Eagles took him to the Far East. I flew with US Airways, where my miles invariably got me an upgrade to first class. We went our own separate ways in the departures terminal and met up again at the other end, though I'd usually arrive about half a day after he did. A typical example was when we were running a course in Seattle in the American north-west. The straight line between Seattle and Colorado is about two and a half hours' flying time. Eddie took the 6.30 p.m. flight and was tucked up in bed by 11. I spent five and a half hours in the US Airways business lounge, and then caught the midnight red-eye special to Pittsburgh, Pennsylvania, a five-hour trek, from coast to coast. Allowing for the time difference, it was about eight o'clock the following morning when I arrived in Pittsburgh. I had breakfast there, caught a connection back across seven states to Colorado and arrived into the office in the middle of the afternoon, where Eddie, clean-shaven and fully rested, asked how many miles I had chalked up.

We were alike in so many ways and different in so many others. I was more catholic in my reading tastes. I inherited my father's love of biographies and books on the great wars. Eddie read books about explorers and mountain climbers, which he'd read all night. America is the best country in the world in which to be an insomniac. He'd sit in bed with these books about expeditions to the Poles or to the top of Everest in one hand and the TV remote in the other and he'd alternate between reading and surfing the sixty-seven channels. This would go on for most of the night. Luckily, I could sleep in the middle of the London Underground.

Eddie rarely put a foot wrong. Spending six months of every year away from his wife and their young children must have exerted an even greater strain on his good marriage than it did on my bad one. Ingrid and I had been married longer and my children were older, so it should have been easier for me to hold it together. The difference was that Eddie took his marriage as seriously as he did every other part of his life. He and Noreen were solid. The fact was we were in America for different reasons. He was building a career for himself so that he and Noreen might enjoy a better life. I was hiding from the mess I'd made of mine. I never realized that every day I was away was making it worse. When I rang home my conversations with Ingrid just didn't work.

One of the consequences of my living in America was that I knew very little about the last couple of years of my mother's life. It just never occurred to me that she had a finite number of days left and that every day I spent away was one less opportunity to spend time with her. After the incident with the tablets, I told her I'd make more of an effort to see her. Sadly, the words were more important to me than the intention. It was just one of thousands of promises I made and didn't keep.

She fell ill while I was away. She had stomach cancer. Like my father, she kept her suffering to herself for months before she troubled anyone about it. She was home on her own, vomiting, suffering unimaginable pain, while her beloved son was jetting around America, teaching people how to play rugby.

Then the pain got too much for her. She phoned Arthur and he took her to Beaumont hospital. They looked her over and sent her home. Over the next few weeks she had tests and they diagnosed the disease. There was no hope. Barry O'Brien, another rugby friend who was the administrator of the Royal College of Surgeons, phoned me in America to break the news. 'You should come home, George,' he said. 'Do it while she's still in reasonably good shape because the next time you see her it may be too late.'

I flew home and spent a couple of days with her. She'd moved into a nursing home close to the hospital and she hated it. It was her nightmare come true: spending her last few months among old and senile ladies, her mind still alert and waiting for her body to give out. Now her son, who'd talked her out of writing her own ending a few years earlier, had deigned to give her a few hours out of his own precious life.

I was in the ward the night before I flew back to America and this wave of grief overcame me. I knew I might not see her alive again. I kissed her forehead and I said, 'Mam, I'll come and see you in the morning for breakfast.'

I had an early check-in for my flight back to America. I phoned Aer Lingus and explained that my mother was ill. They said not to worry about it. They'd have my boarding pass ready and keep the gate open for me for as long as they could.

I went to see her again on the way to the airport and sat with her while she ate breakfast. Then I walked to the door, turned back and looked at her lying in the bed. I said, 'Goodbye, Mam,' and she said, 'Goodbye, Son.'

I was in a state of high tension by the time I arrived at the airport. As it happened, the flight was delayed. I decided to pick up a few dollars, just to have money in my pocket when I got the other side. I went to the little Bank of Ireland kiosk at the far end of the duty-free shop. I asked the cashier for a hundred pounds' worth of US dollars and I wrote out a cheque for £100 drawn on my account in Montrose. She asked me if I had a banker's card. I said I didn't but I said she should be able to get my details on the computer.

'I can't do that from here,' she said.

'OK,' I said, 'ring the branch in departures and they'll clear it.'

'I can't do that either.'

'OK, forget it,' I said, and took back my cheque. 'It wasn't important anyway.'

I boarded the plane and sat in my seat. As the crew was going through the final formalities before air-locking the door, the cashier came running onto the plane. She looked up and down the aisles before picking me out, then said, 'You never gave me back the dollars.'

'What are you talking about?' I said. 'You never gave me the dollars to begin with. You said you couldn't accept the cheque.'

'Oh, yeah,' she said and disappeared. Five minutes later, she arrived back and said, in a voice that carried the entire length of the aircraft, 'You did take the money. We have you on video.'

I lost it. I shouted, 'I want to be searched. I want my bags searched. I want someone to go through my pockets,' at which point she started backing away. A member of the ground crew in a fluorescent yellow jacket boarded the plane. 'You can continue this argument here or outside,' he said, 'but this plane is taking off now, whether you two are on it or not.'

The cashier got off without a word of apology. As the plane taxied for take-off, I burst into tears. It was like a release of pressure. It felt like I had years of tears to cry. Once we were airborne, an air hostess came down to me and offered me a cup of tea. I told her she was very kind.

'Listen,' she said, 'would you mind just searching your bag, just in case you took it by mistake.'

'That's the worst thing,' I said. 'You think I have the money.' I sounded like a little boy.

I arrived in America in a terrible state.

★

About six weeks later, I got a phone call to say that my mother was on the way out. I've heard a lot of stories about people who are dying who have held on to say a last goodbye to someone coming from a long distance. They always have a special resonance for me.

My mother was in Beaumont hospital and she hadn't stirred for a week. She was unconscious. I arrived in a taxi straight from the airport. I sat beside her bed and I said, 'Hello, Mam,' and she said, 'Hello, Son.' I asked her how she was. 'Not very well,' she said, 'but I'm glad you're here.'

I sat there for a few hours, thinking about old times and all the things I might have done differently, slumped like a drunk in my grief. I went home. The call came during the night to say that she'd died.

Like my father, to save us the price of a funeral, my mother deeded her body to UCD. We had Mass in Blackrock College. I saw Arthur at the funeral. I admire him so much for what he did for her in her final years. He did the dirty work. He took her to the hospital. He visited her in the nursing home when I had more important things to do. He was more of a son to her in the end than I ever was.

The funeral ended and that was that. Another person had slipped from my life, leaving me with nothing but regrets.

8. Last chance

As a provincial rugby coach with Connacht, and a club coach with high fliers London Irish, I was on good terms with most of the journalists who covered the rugby beat, especially Karl Johnson of the Irish Press group, who was a dear friend. In April 1995, Karl suggested to Mick Carwood, sports editor of the *Sunday Press*, that he hire me to write the occasional column. Over the years journalists had interviewed me countless times. My contribution was invariably a bit better than the 'sick as a parrot' or 'over the moon' responses of many sportsmen so Karl knew that I could express myself about rugby and had the technical knowledge to back up my opinions.

Karl's intervention would change my life, although my first foray into journalism was far from auspicious. My second column was about how Donal Spring was flexing his muscles as the new coach to Leinster. He threatened to sue. But Mick liked my writing. That summer the Rugby World Cup was to take place in South Africa. He phoned me and asked if I'd like to cover it.

'I'd love to,' I said.

'There's one problem,' he said. 'You're not a member of the NUJ. Technically, a member of the union should have first refusal. But I want you, George.'

'What can we do about it?'

'I can't be seen to be *sending* you to South Africa, George. But if you were to travel there under your own steam . . .'

'I think I know what you're saying.'

'Go away and price the trip. Then we'll work out how many articles you'll be filing. We'll pay you enough for each one to make sure you more than cover yourself.'

It seemed fair enough to me. I wasn't going to get rich but I was going to get to see the World Cup for free. At this point, despite my impecunious circumstances, I had no vision of working in the media. All my efforts were still concentrated on the job in the US.

I rang Eugene McGee Travel to price the trip. It was £4,355, including flights, transfers and hotel accommodation for the entire month of the tournament. I said I'd take it. A couple of weeks before I left, I phoned Eugene McGee and asked how much extra it would cost me to fly to South Africa business class. It was another £1,200. I figured I was getting a free trip to the World Cup, so I might as well treat myself. I decided to travel in style. Now it was costing me £5,555 but I was getting all but £1,200 of it back. It was buttons for four weeks in one of the most beautiful countries in the world, watching the game I loved.

I was due to arrive in Johannesburg two days before Ireland played New Zealand – with Jonah Lomu – in their opening pool match. Karl had been in South Africa for a week, reporting on the build-up to the tournament. He promised to meet me at the airport.

My flight touched down in Johannesburg. I went through passport control and collected my luggage from the carousel. I walked through the arrivals gate to find Karl waiting for me, looking like someone had died.

'What is it?' I said.

'I don't know how to say this to you, George, but the paper's been closed down.'

The staff of the Press group's newspapers had gone on strike demanding the reinstatement of a colleague, financial journalist Colm Rapple, who had written an article for the *Irish Times* criticizing the management of the loss-making group. Management responded to the strike by shutting the three titles down. Six hundred people had lost their jobs.

Now I was in South Africa with a bill from Eugene McGee for £5,555 and no job. The closure was all over the news back home and I assumed that Ingrid would see it as another of my screw-ups. The only good news was that I was accredited as a journalist for the tournament and would have the best seats in the house.

Ireland played New Zealand in Johannesburg. I had nothing to do. I just sat around the hotel lobby all week, listening to other journalists sympathizing with me. We moved on to Bloemfontein for the second pool game against Japan. Again, no work. The third game was a must-win match against Wales in Ellis Park.

John D. O'Brien, my rival for the affection of Ryle Nugent's mother Barbara thirty years earlier, was a senior producer of television sport for RTÉ and was in South Africa, overseeing the station's coverage. John came to me one day in the hotel and asked if I was interested in some work. I said I was. 'There's only thirty quid in it for you now,' he said.

Thirty pounds was nothing compared to the £5,555 – and rising – that I had spent, but the important thing was to feel that I was doing something.

'We want to do a live piece, with you as an expert analyst, by the poolside on the morning of the Wales game. You'll be talking to Fred Cogley. We'll have Bill O'Herlihy, Brent Pope and Mick Doyle back in the studio.'

'OK.'

'You're not going to have a lot of time. Ninety seconds is all you're going to get. So make your points clearly and succinctly.'

I worked harder for that thirty quid than I'd ever worked before. I went back to my room and I wrote up some notes. I knew that the Leaving Certificate results were out on the day of the game so I decided to base what I had to say on an exam theme. I wrote that the honours students like Brendan Mullin would be expected to do well. It was the performance of the pass students that would decide whether Ireland got through this examination with flying colours. It might have sounded twee but I spent hours reciting my script over and over again to the mirror in my room. I paced back and forth and recomposed it in my head. I timed myself. I reread it. I cut out every extraneous word.

On the morning of the match, I did my piece in eighty-nine seconds. Back in the studio, Bill O'Herlihy said, 'That guy is some communicator.' I walked with a zing in my step for days when I heard that.

★

After Ireland's elimination in the quarter finals of the World Cup I went back to the USA to continue working and watched the semi finals of the tournament on TV in Kansas City, where I was running a coaching course. At this point I thought my brief media career was over. RTÉ had an established panel and the Independent group had a phalanx of rugby writers including David Walsh and Mick Doyle. I simply put it behind me and carried on as before.

If I could live my sixty-four years again, there are a hundred decisions and more that I'd unmake. For starters, instead of agreeing to become adjutant general in the Campbell empire, I'd bombard RTÉ with letters demanding a screen test. When I was a student in the early 1960s, I was interviewed about student rugby on Radio Éireann's *Sports Stadium*, which used to go out on Friday nights. It was one of those rare times in my life when I didn't need people to tell me that I was good. I knew it. I should have asked RTÉ for a job, but I didn't have the courage. During the darkest days of my business career, my friends would tell me that my fortune was in my voice, if I could just think of a way of selling it.

I had first appeared on television during the World Cup in 1987. After the USA had been eliminated in the pool stages I returned to Dublin. A few days later I got a call from Jim Sherwin, who was the editor of RTÉ's coverage of the tournament. He asked if I'd appear as a panellist alongside Ciaran Fitzgerald for the semi-final between Wales and New Zealand.

Because of the time difference between Ireland and Australia, RTÉ would be showing an 'as live' delayed transmission of the match. That made me twice as nervous. I spent days preparing for my few minutes of glory, learning hundreds of statistics off by rote, dreaming up dozens of sound bites that I'd never get an opportunity to use.

I learned that day how unforgiving television is as a medium. Fitzy was an old hand at it, having captained Ireland, but even he could mess up under the white heat of the studio lights. We knew New Zealand had annihilated Wales 49–6. Before the match kicked off, he said that New Zealand were worthy finalists, giving the result away.

I was terrified, but I managed to avoid making any mistakes and I got to use one of my sound bites. In my wrap, I said that watching New Zealand play rugby was like listening to Sir Yehudi Menuhin play the violin – perfection.

In those days, RTÉ was extremely conservative. In their choice of panellists, they tended to err on the side of caution, preferring moderate, inoffensive personalities who would offer such anodyne analysis as, 'The head says France, the heart says Ireland – I'm going with my heart on this one.'

I think I had too many rough edges for them. I didn't fit the prototype of what an analyst should look and sound like.

I wasn't asked back.

When New Zealand came to Dublin in 1989, in the week before the international I was asked, as a coach to Connacht, to do a two-minute piece to camera on the back pitch at Lansdowne Road. Later that season another producer, Niall Cogley, did another cameo with me before the Wales game. The next bit of work I got from RTÉ was when John D. O'Brien took pity on me in South Africa in 1995 and I did my eighty-nine seconds by the pool. But I don't think John ever really fancied me as a pundit.

Niall Cogley remembered my cameos during the 1989/90 season and my ninety seconds of glory in South Africa. All the time I had spent preparing for those short and seemingly innocuous interviews paid off when Niall asked me to be the lone panellist for the Ireland v. Italy friendly in Lansdowne Road in January 1997. Ten years after my debut, I got my second chance as a television analyst. Though it was a great opportunity, it was not the stuff of which fortunes are made. At that time RTÉ broadcast five rugby games a year, one autumn international (if any) and four championship games. Every four years there was the month-long involvement with the World Cup. Bill O'Herlihy was consistently in the chairman's seat but the panel alternated. A new guy like me, even if I were to break in, could expect two appearances a year. Still, it was a chance to do something for which I believed I had a talent.

To me television had always looked easy. I watched Gay Byrne and thought what he did was a cinch. I was to discover that his

1. With Ingrid in 1970, a year after we married.

2. With our first baby, Michelle, January 1973.

3. With Michelle and our new baby, George, Christmas 1975.

4. Baby number 3 on the way, July 1980.

5. Our family completed: Alison, George and Michelle, Christmas 1981.

6. My parents in Rome in the late 1960s – their first holiday together since I was born.

7. My parents with George in August 1976.

8. Three generations of Hook men. George's First Communion, May 1983.

9. The family grown up: Ingrid and
Michelle at Michelle's graduation
in 1994.

10. With Alison at her debs' dance
in 1998.

11. With George in 2001.

12. With my fellow pundit, New Zealander Brent Pope.
(*RTÉ Guide*)

13. Doing what I was always meant to do. (*Newstalk 106*)

14. Michelle's wedding in Italy in September 2002.
Also included is Ingrid's mother, Louise.

15. With the proud grandmother and great-grandmother.
Our first grandchild, Jakob's, christening in October 2003.

skill was in making it *look* easy. RTÉ didn't offer me a single day's training. No one ever sat me down, pulled a tape from a shelf and talked me through the methodology of television punditry. Preparation has always been my strong point and if I spent hours preparing for two-minute cameos then it was days for a complete afternoon show.

I phoned Captain Jack Phelan, who was the doyen of production managers in the Irish film industry and a neighbour in Foxrock. He was also a television commercial maker and he allowed me to pick his brain. He told me how to sit, where to put my hands, what to do with my eyes. It's good etiquette, he explained, always to look at the person who's speaking, even if he's not speaking to you, so it looks like you're interested in what he has to say. I learned where not to place myself in relation to the camera. I learned that the best place for me is about ten paces to the left of the fixed camera, in the seat nearest to the presenter.

I realized that the overwhelming majority of people who watch rugby don't understand it; it's a technical game, with layer upon layer of rules, so complex that even the players struggle with them. People watching at home don't want to know about the tight head's foot position in the scrum or why the scrum-half struggles when he's kicking with his left foot. Television is about entertainment and viewers want someone to talk to them in a language they understand, which is what made Bill McLaren so great.

I set out with a clear idea of what I wanted to do. For years RTÉ had had some of the best soccer coverage on the box with a winning combination of two authoritative and opinionated panellists – Eamon Dunphy and Johnny Giles – and a chairman, Bill O'Herlihy, who knew how to get the best out of them. At that point, nobody at the station had thought of trying to do the same thing with rugby.

For my spot on the panel for Ireland v. Italy, Niall suggested I come to Montrose about lunchtime as the game was a low-key event and *Saturday Sport* had a full schedule of other sports to cover. The station would not be giving the game the full treatment. Niall expected me at about noon. I arrived closer to 8 a.m. The sports department was nonplussed and not sure what to do with this lunatic who needed six hours to prepare.

I sat in the corner and got ready for this minor international with all the intensity of a presenter preparing for the Oscar ceremonies. As the day progressed the weather worsened across the UK and Ireland and one by one the events listed for coverage that afternoon were cancelled. By 2 p.m. the programme consisted of Ireland against Italy – and me!

John D. O'Brien came into the studio where the presenter, Michael Lyster, and I were awaiting the cue to go on air. He smiled and said to me, 'George, can you talk for four hours?'

'John,' I said, 'that won't be a problem.'

For a neophyte analyst all that extra time could make or break a career. All the extra preparation paid off. It was my big moment and I was ready. I predicted Italy to win – and they did. I had selected pieces of analysis to show where Ireland was weak and, luckily for me, it was almost as if I knew what was going to happen. Everything turned out exactly as I had forecast.

After the game I launched into a tirade. Nowadays that might be no surprise, but in 1997 the audience had never seen me before and were unprepared for my style of analysis.

'The soldiers got off the beaches at Dunkirk,' I thundered, 'but these players are not about to get off in a hurry.'

My father always believed that everybody was lucky, it was just that some people never grasped the opportunity. I had failed miserably to recognize the opportunities in racecourse catering, Big Macs or property. However, when bad weather gave me a chance to strut my stuff and fulfil my childhood dream, I was ready. Five times I had appeared on RTÉ television in a rugby capacity, five times it produced no tangible reward. Finally, things began to change.

A month later, I was asked to join Jim Glennon and Tony Ward on the panel chaired by Bill O'Herlihy for the Wales game in Cardiff. I was rash enough not only to predict that Ireland would win but that Denis Hickie would score on his debut. I was right on both counts. (Sadly, the level of prescience exhibited on these two early appearances has not continued.)

I also learned a valuable lesson from Bill O'Herlihy. At half-time I was waxing eloquently about Eric Miller and commented that one of his great strengths was his cardiovascular endurance. Putting on his best impression of a simple Corkman, O'Herlihy asked 'For those of us who do not know, George, can you explain what you mean by cardiovascular endurance?'

I was deflated and a bit shamefaced as I explained that Miller was very fit. Filled with my new-found importance as a television pundit, I had been showing off my vast knowledge of the subject. But, as O'Herlihy subtly reminded me, not everybody who watches sport on television is an expert. It is the role of the analyst to explain, not to demonstrate his cleverness.

Four weeks later I was on again for Ireland's game against Scotland at Murrayfield in the final game of the season. That morning, as I was doing my usual frantic five hours of preparation in the sports department of RTÉ before I went on air, Ingrid phoned to say there was a man looking for me. 'Here's his number,' she said. 'I can't pronounce his first name.'

I phoned the number. The man on the other end was Adhamhnan O'Sullivan, sports editor of the *Sunday Independent*. He wanted me to do a piece for the paper after the match.

'But I'm on television,' I said.

'It's only about five hundred words and we can wait for it until you come off air. What we'll do is we'll get one of our guys to ring you. You talk to him and he'll ghost it for you.'

'No, no. If my name is going on it, I want to write it.'

The line fell silent. 'Are you serious? You can do that?'

I laughed out loud. 'I went to school, didn't I?'

That afternoon when the match was over, I walked down to the sports department, took five sheets of foolscap and a pen and wrote out my five hundred words. I counted them manually, then phoned the *Sunday Independent* and called it down the line to a copy-taker, in the age-old tradition. I bought the paper the next morning and got a great thrill from seeing my by-lined piece, and an even bigger one when a cheque arrived for twenty-five pounds. (I got a special kick from that cheque since, as fate would have it Adhamhnan was the brother of Donal, the meat supplier I'd had to give my slicer to all those years earlier.)

Adhamhnan phoned me a couple of weeks later and told me if I had any other ideas he would be happy to take them from me at the usual fee. I was excited about this new turn my life had taken but twenty-five pounds per article from the *Sunday Independent* would hardly keep me alive. Nevertheless, I figured, I needed a computer and invested £1,500 for a laptop and the software to send my copy down the phone line. Then I bought a CD-ROM to teach myself how to type. I became a hunt-and-peck typist, but it was still a lot quicker than reading it down a phone line. I had spent more on the machinery than I was likely to earn in a couple of years, but I felt like a real journalist. By the end of the 1997 rugby season I had half a dozen articles accepted by the *Sunday Independent* and three fairly successful television appearances. Total income about £300.

Now it was time to head back to the USA for the summer, the peak period for coaching courses. Before I left, there was a surprise party for Niall Cogley in O'Shea's pub in Rathmines. Tim O'Connor, RTÉ's head of television sport, came over to me and congratulated me on my work. 'You have given our coverage a new dimension,' he said. I left the pub, pretty certain that there would be more work for me in television.

I returned in October after the usual lengthy stay in the USA and Tony Whelan, the producer of *Sunday Sport*, gave me the chance to do rugby on the show hosted by Tracey Piggott and Peter Collins. It went out late and had a small audience but I was learning a new trade and delighted to be paid for it.

The problem with television is that it counts contributions in seconds, irrespective of the importance of the topic. My slot lasted four minutes, which made me work hard to say what I wanted to say, to make an impact and get out on time. I used to walk up and down the corridor for about an hour before the green light, working on my phrases and honing them for impact. Peter and Tracey knew I was under time pressure and helped enormously by avoiding the limelight themselves and asking short questions to give me the maximum amount of camera time.

I never thought the job would last very long so I tended to take risks, a trait that has stayed with me to this day. I never deliberately courted controversy but I never shirked making a call. My finest hour came in November when we were about three weeks into the season. It was the Sunday before Ireland played New Zealand at Lansdowne Road. Peter's final question was the usual request for a forecast.

'Ireland will lose by fifty points,' I told the astonished presenter, who promptly went to the next item to cover his confusion and, I suspect, embarrassment at allowing a nut in the studio. Six days later, Ireland was beaten by forty-eight points.

Ireland played three games before Christmas and four in the following Five Nations. I was very disappointed not to get called as a television panellist for any of them, although I continued my Sunday-night appearances. However, I was continuing to write for the Sunday paper. This was uneventful apart from when Ireland played Italy in Bologna on 20 December and I was stuck in Nashville, Tennessee. The *Sunday Indo* wanted a column on the game and there was no way I was going to miss the deadline. I rang Eddie O'Sullivan at home in Moylough where he was watching the game on TV. He gave me a running commentary, complete with analysis, over the phone. I wrote the piece in the Nashville Holiday Inn and my burgeoning career was safe.

In May 1998, just before I headed off to the States for the coaching season, I rang Tim O'Connor and asked if I could come and see him. I was ushered into the great man's office and I opened the conversation by diffidently reminding him of his kind remarks to me in the pub more than a year before. I asked him, if I was so useful why was I not used as a panellist any more.

'George,' he said, 'we are making changes to our presentation of rugby. Glenn Killane will be taking over and he will be in touch with you.'

Killane called a couple of days later and outlined the plan. 'We are attempting to replicate the success of the soccer panel by establishing a consistent team,' he said. 'We've decided that Tom McGurk will take over from Bill O'Herlihy, because Bill's soccer commitments are getting bigger, and we're hoping that you and Brent Pope will be our regulars.' I was gobsmacked. I told him to count me in. Glenn told me he would be in touch and put the phone down, leaving me wondering if Christmas had come early. I don't think I came down to earth until the Aer Lingus 747 hit the tarmac at JFK.

Some of my worst moves in a lifetime of bad decisions have been my choice of enemies. In 1986, when I'd been invited to speak at the coaching conference in Kansas, a bunch of us ended up in a bar one night. It was the first time I had ever seen women rugby players. There was a group of them there, one of whom was a gorgeous Latina. I went over and started chatting her up, with the old Irishman abroad routine that had dispatched my virginity in Northampton and netted Ingrid in Lytham. After ten minutes I got a tap on the shoulder. I spun round. 'Lay off Jack Clark's girl,' somebody said. 'Who the fuck is Jack Clark?' I said, and carried on talking.

Jack Clark was a former star of the US Eagles, a 6'5", blond-haired, square-jawed, onetime American footballer whom everyone seemed to regard as some kind of god. Jack was in Kansas as an attendee and was also highly regarded as a motivational speaker. Physically and mentally, he was a formidable presence. He invariably intimidated people and was not afraid to exercise power when he had it. He meant nothing to me and I saw no reason to show him any deference in or out of the coaching arena. People who were good on their feet were in short supply in US rugby in those days, and in Kansas Jack saw some competition for the first time in this unknown from Ireland. The Latin American girl was our first confrontation and there was no love lost between us thereafter. Ten years later that dislike was to have a crucial consequence for my career in North America.

Jack eventually became manager and coach of the US Eagles. He brought first-class marketing skills to the position and raised a great deal of money for the national team that gave it some credibility. What his team needed was technical coaching input and when I persuaded Jack to take Eddie O'Sullivan on board as assistant, the performances improved to match the money expended.

One of the extraordinary things about Eddie is how he gets respect without ever courting popularity. He went to Blackrock, one of the most notoriously difficult clubs to work in, where you had guys clutching Schools Cup medals from the thirties telling him what to do, and he treated them with disdain. Yet when he left they'd have walked on broken glass to get him to stay. Jack Clark had found another Irishman that he could not cow but this time he both needed and liked the 'Paddy'. He called Eddie 'Sully'. It was never obvious whether 'Sully' felt the same way about him.

During 1998, Jack was looking for a new contract, before his existing one had run its course. The next World Cup was still almost a year away. The tournament should have been the yardstick by which he was judged.

Ron Mayes was chairman of the technical committee of the USARFU and my immediate boss. The technical committee was responsible for all coaching matters, so the national coach's contract would be in its remit to review. Ron asked me to look over the proposed contract for Jack. I took one look at it and couldn't believe they were even entertaining the suggestions. He wanted a new payment schedule that included bonuses based on money raised for the national team. American rugby was unique in that the union didn't control the finances of the national team. The team was autonomous. It set its own budget and raised its own money. The team was in effect franchised out to the coach.

I did some projections. The English team had just done a deal with Sky for an astronomical amount of money. What if rugby took off in the US? What if Sky Sports wanted to extend their current contract with the USA for $100 million instead of the $10 million they were currently paying for a decade of unlimited coverage? Jack stood to become richer than the union. 'You can't have that,' I said. 'Plus, as far as I can see, there is no accountability in this contract. He has to be held responsible if the team fails to live up to expectations.'

Ron agreed, as did the management committee of the national technical group at a meeting in San Francisco. Our report to the USARFU suggested a renegotiation of the deal. After that meeting, I returned to Ireland for my winter break.

The response to our report was that USARFU dissolved the technical committee and I was sacked without compensation as national technical director. There are no employment appeal tribunals in the USA.

As I read my letter of dismissal in Dublin, I got some comfort from the thought that they'd struggle to fill the post. There was nobody in the USA qualified to do the job and candidates from abroad would hardly be prepared to put their lives on hold as I had done for little or no financial reward.

Ron, a man of the utmost honesty and integrity, who coached the Eagles and had devoted his life to rugby as an amateur, decided to plead his case in front of the board of the USARFU in Colorado Springs. He was humiliated. In one of those outrageous incidents that happen in amateur bodies, Ron was left sitting in the corridor while the board played God with his future. As he sat there, hurt and humiliated by the treatment meted out to him by an organization to which he had given decades of unpaid service, he spied Eddie wandering up the corridor towards him.

'What are you doing here?' Ron asked him.

'I'm here for the meeting,' Eddie said.

The upshot of that meeting was that Ron was politely shown off the premises. A new technical committee was appointed, Jack got his contract and Eddie O'Sullivan got my job. Before they had sacked me they had phoned him at home in Galway, asking if he would be interested in my job. Eddie said yes. So they had had no fears when it came to getting rid of me.

I was upset, angry and disappointed. After all, I was the one who'd brought Eddie to America in the first place. When Billy

Glynn and Bobby Deacy in Connacht were playing poker with his life, I slipped him an ace. As I saw it then, he had slipped the stiletto between my shoulder blades.

I was back home permanently. A decision I would never have made, had it not been made for me. I often think I would still be there, ploughing a lonely furrow for US rugby, had it not been for my unwillingness to compromise on what I saw as a matter of principle over Clark's contract. Although I did not see it at the time, my dismissal was crucial to my future success. Now I had to concentrate on my marriage and my burgeoning career in the media.

A few weeks later there was a knock at the door. I couldn't believe it when I saw Eddie standing there. 'Have you a problem with me?' he said.

'Fucking sure I have a problem with you,' I said.

'Well,' he said, 'talk about it.'

This was typical Eddie, confronting his problems head-on. I brought him into the kitchen and put on the kettle. 'They couldn't have pulled off what they did without you,' I told him. 'They couldn't have sacked me unless you were prepared to take my job.'

'George,' he said, 'what else could I do? I've a wife and two children now. This is my job. They'd have sacked me too. What did you expect me to do – commit hara kiri on a point of principle?'

That's exactly what I expected him to do. It's what I would have done. No one loved Pyrrhic victories more than I did. But then, as if a switch had been flicked in my head, I suddenly saw where he was coming from. We were different animals. In my own eyes, I was the great Corinthian. But Eddie was a professional. He made a career decision: he was on a ladder climbing upwards and he simply stepped up onto the next rung. It didn't make me a noble person and him a conniving one. It was just how it was. Once I got that, the animosity I had been feeling just melted away.

In the reasonable light of day, I think we'd both say we were good for one another. In rugby terms, we helped each other. As friends, we did the same. I remember once during my first couple of years in America needing £10,000 to settle one of the many debts that trailed me in the years after I let the business go. I was having a pint with Eddie in the Eagle House in Terenure. We were chatting away and I felt terrible because I knew I was going to put the squeeze on him. He wasn't a businessman. This was his savings I was asking him for. Eventually, I spat it out. 'Eddie, I need ten grand.'

'Fine,' he said. 'When do you want it?'

It was extraordinary. He knew my reputation where money was concerned. He didn't ask me what it was for. He didn't ask when he'd see it again.

Our relationship can never be the same again, but not because of what happened in Colorado. Our friendship would have over-come that in time. It's just that someone who's paid to criticize the performance of the national team cannot be on friendly terms with the national coach. It wouldn't be right for either of us, but it still saddens me. I miss his company. Like most good friend-ships, it involved many interlocking fingers. Ingrid and Noreen O'Sullivan were friends. I was at his mother's funeral and attended the surprise celebration organized by his friends in Moylough when he became coach of Ireland. But we move in different worlds now.

When I returned to Dublin in the autumn of 1998 Ingrid and I might as well have been divorced for all the time we had spent together in the previous few years. To all intents and purposes I had lived in America and she possibly thought that I might never return. When I was home, the atmosphere was cold and uncom-fortable. I never really understood that it might be difficult for someone to relate to a partner who ghosted in and out of her life.

There were never really arguments. I wasn't home long enough to get involved in one. Not communicating was our form of fighting. On those rare occasions that I was home, I'd read a newspaper or watch television, while Ingrid sat in another room, poring over work that she had brought home. There was nothing to talk about. No daily trivia to compare or laugh over. Every day was a reminder of the terrible mistake she had made in marrying me.

When I was away, I went to great lengths to avoid having to talk to her. If I had to give her a message that she wasn't going to like, I'd phone our neighbours Gay and Maura Walsh and say, 'Listen, the phone is engaged, one of the kids must be on it. Would you mind popping in to tell Ingrid I won't be home this weekend?'

There must have been times when the children saw her cry. There must have been times – when I left her short of money, when I abandoned her in the middle of a holiday, when I said something terrible to her over the phone – that she broke down in tears. Her friends must have seen her cry. Her work colleagues must have seen her cry. I was too wrapped up in the shambles of my life even to think about the misery I was making of hers. In spending so much time away I was unwittingly preparing the grounds for a formal separation.

One time, we did speak for long enough to have an argument. I was home for a short break. There was a black mood between us and the atmosphere in the house was becoming more and more impossible to bear for both of us. We parted on even worse terms than usual. I rang home when I got back to Colorado in an effort to improve the situation and make some sort of an apology, but instead I made matters worse. I simply had no idea how to communicate my feeling of regret and instead launched into a volley of self-justification. I finished by saying some nasty things and hung up abruptly. I knew that even by my standards I had gone too far and I made an effort to retrieve the situation by telephoning Ingrid's mother, Louise. I then compounded the error by reacting badly when Louise said, not unnaturally, she could not interfere. I went off on another tirade, blaming my wife for everything, before once more hanging up in a rage. One by one, I was slamming all the doors shut.

Then the Black Dog arrived in full force. I walked out of the apartment, left the office behind and boarded a plane for Houston, Texas. The oil capital of America had happy memories for me.

On previous visits I had always stayed with John Connolly and his family. John was a first-generation Irish New Yorker who had always been very generous to me and knew more than most about my difficult family life. I envied the easy relationship he had with his wife, Stacey, and the happy home life that seemed to have eluded me. I suppose deep in my psyche I saw Houston and Connolly as somewhere I might seek refuge and discover the secret of happiness. I never called John, never told anyone where I was, and instead checked into the Marriott Hotel at Houston airport. I spent a week there, never once leaving the hotel. I would make occasional nocturnal visits to the restaurant but I spent most of the time in my room, with my head buried under the covers, crying, staring into space, and feeling sorry for myself.

During that period nobody knew where I was, although the peripatetic nature of my job meant that the USARFU office would not expect me in every day. The only call of any substance I made was to Jack Ormond, my doctor back in Dublin. I told him I was losing it. 'I can't cope,' I said. 'What am I going to do?'

I was crying down the phone. Novels sometimes describe the hero's chest being racked with sobs. This was what my crying felt like. My chest ached as I told Jack of the destruction I had wrought in my life, but principally my marriage.

'I think it is over with Ingrid, Jack. Can you talk to her for me? Ask her what can I do. Tell her I am prepared to do anything to make things right.'

You can imagine how unimpressed she was, getting a phone call from someone she knew as a friend of her husband's, telling her that George really loved her and wanted to put things right, but could not make the call himself. Jack did not let me down. He tried his very best but he was fighting a losing battle.

What had I become?

Jack rang me back. 'It's not great,' he said. 'It might have been a mistake, my ringing.'

The fog eventually lifted. I should have gone straight home but I couldn't face it. I had a strong feeling that the next time I saw

Ingrid it would be over. I flew back to Colorado and escaped back to work.

But that was then and this was 1998. Now I was home for good.

It was awful. Ingrid put my meals in front of me without a word and she snubbed any effort I made to initiate conversation.

The extraordinary thing is that I felt hard done by.

After three days, on a Saturday evening when the children were out, it all came to the boil.

'What's wrong with you?' I asked.

'What's wrong?' she said. 'What's wrong is that it's over. I'm going to see a solicitor on Monday morning. You should look for somewhere else to live. Perhaps you may wish to live full time in the USA.'

Her views were expressed matter-of-factly and without emotion. I knew that this was no spur-of-the-moment decision. She had thought everything out and was ready to go through with it to the end. For the first time ever in our marriage, I showed my emotions. I started to cry. She looked at me coldly. 'You can't be serious,' she said. 'You don't want this marriage any more than I do.'

'I do,' I said. 'I do.'

She sat up on the kitchen table. I'll never forget that. She never would have done that normally. Her body language was different. It was laden with resignation. I leaned up against the oven, hypnotized by the sight of her legs swinging back and forth. There were tears pouring down my cheeks. 'But I love you,' I said to her.

'You don't love me,' she sad. 'You couldn't love me. You can't put someone through twenty-five years of shit and then tell them that you love them.'

'But I do, Ingrid. Look, I'll do anything. I'll go to St John of God's for assessment. Attend marriage guidance counselling, see whomever you wish. I will do whatever it takes to make things right.'

The thought of losing her terrified me. It wasn't the thought of being on my own. I just regarded her love for me as an article of faith. For all my dysfunctional nature as a human being, this was still the same woman I had seen across the floor at the Lytham St Anne's Squash Club dance, the same woman to whom I proposed marriage on the second date. I could never feel for any woman what I felt for her.

'I want you to go to see a doctor,' she said.

'Anything.'

'A doctor of my choosing.'

'OK.'

'On Monday.'

'I'll do it. I promise.'

'If you are not there, it is over. No more talk.'

On Monday, Ingrid took me to see her GP at the Park Clinic in Cornelscourt. Doctor Murphy had never set eyes on me before. He looked at Ingrid and then at me. 'What is the problem?' he said.

This was the most important hour of my life. I looked at and talked to the doctor, but he was merely a conduit between Ingrid and me. Every word I uttered was meant for her. I spelled out to him how much I loved her, what a shit I'd been and how I was prepared to change. 'There's no limit to how far I'm prepared to go to save this marriage,' I said. 'I'll suffer any humiliation or indignity.'

Ingrid had picked a good guy. Stephen Murphy was a GP, not a psychologist or marriage counsellor, but had a good reputation in the mediation business. They both sat and listened while I emptied myself. When I'd no more words left, he turned and looked at Ingrid. 'What do you think?' he said.

'I don't believe him,' she said. 'I've heard it all before.'

'So what are you going to do?' he asked her.

She thought about it. I thought her answer would never come. 'I'm prepared to give him one more chance,' she said. '*One* chance, and that's it.'

'And what do *you* want from *him*,' he said.

'I want a husband. I want him to talk to me. I want no more lies. I want him to contribute.'

There had been many last chances over the years but none like this one. We had had bust-ups, recriminations and arguments, but Ingrid had never made plans to see a solicitor before. This time it really did feel like my last chance.

On top of my marital woes, after I returned to Ireland after the US fiasco, I felt the ennui associated with being an unemployed man in his fifties. I got up in the morning, put on my tracksuit, stacked the breakfast dishes into the dishwasher (stacking and emptying the dishwasher was the one household job Ingrid assigned to me when we returned from the doctor that day), drove to the shops to buy the *Irish Times* and the *Daily Telegraph*, then lolled around in my tracksuit for the day until it was time to collect Alison from school.

In many regards, I was like a recovering alcoholic, meeting each day as it came, with Ingrid looking at me, always expecting me to fall off the wagon. I was on my best behaviour but experience had taught her that it would not last. There still wasn't much in the way of conversation between us. Though Cold War hostilities had dissipated, the atmosphere was still guarded.

Without me asking, Adhamhnan had increased my rate to fifty pounds per article and RTÉ paid me £150 every time I appeared on television. It didn't amount to much in terms of our overall financial stability, but in 1998, for the first time in my married life, I was making a contribution. Ingrid wouldn't know the difference between a ruck and a maul – she despised rugby because she associated it with the unhappy years of our marriage – but she could switch on RTÉ during the Five Nations or pick up the *Sunday Independent* and know, for the first time in a long time, what I was doing. I was earning less in a year than the average kitchen porter, but I was home for dinner every night and I was around at weekends.

As my profile increased I started to get more writing, more space and prominence. Five hundred words became seven hundred became a thousand, and my by-line began inching its way up over the fold. I did not have a contract. (To this day wage negotiations are conducted in the same way. Every January we meet for a coffee and Adhamhnan pulls a crumpled piece of paper out of his pocket with a number written on it. It is my rate per article for the coming year. We shake hands and another year begins. Happily it is now more than fifty pounds.)

To be doing something creative, to be earning, to no longer be living in terror of the ringing phone, made me feel normal again. In a landmark moment in my slow return to the human race, I registered with the Revenue Commissioners. I declared my earnings for the purposes of paying tax and PRSI. I felt a weight lifting for the first time since I'd left Burroughs Machines in 1967 and that was important for my self-esteem, my marriage and my relationship with my children.

True to his word, Glenn Killane, newly installed as rugby editor at RTÉ, called a meeting before the 1999 Five Nations Championship. The new team was as he outlined to me before I had gone to the USA. With Brent Pope and me as the analysts, and Tom McGurk as the anchor, Glenn got the formula right. From the very beginning, the chemistry between us felt good. Popey is the quintessential New Zealander, concise to the point of bluntness, never saying marmalade if he can get away with saying jam. He is extraordinarily generous in observing the realpolitik of our relationship. Because I'm loud and outspoken, I'm difficult to work alongside in a television context, but he never tries to match my volume. He is the sane and sound foil to my lunacy and he knows that it's our disparate personalities that make the relationship work.

Tom is the quintessential television professional, who can engage us in animated discussion while simultaneously taking instructions from a producer through an earpiece and watching the clock to make sure we don't run into the time allotted for ad breaks. Whereas I'm an inveterate researcher, he's more of a seat-of-his-pants kind of guy. Ten seconds before we go on air, he'll ask me who's playing at tight head for Ireland. I've never worked out whether he does this deliberately to create a spiky air in the studio but he knows it upsets my passion for order and routine. The one thing I'm convinced he does to get me worked up is he cuts across my sentences. If I have a point I'm particularly keen to make, he'll cut in with a non sequitur, I'll get upset and it generates a tension that is the dynamic behind the relationship.

What made it work from day one was that we weren't friends. The popular caricature is of three clubby types who, underneath it all, think the world of each other, and who, when the camera stops rolling, repair to the Berkeley Court for cigars, cognac and more friendly raillery. It's not the case. We don't socialize together, our wives and girlfriends don't meet for coffee and we've never seen the inside of one another's houses.

I find Tom a very difficult person to like and he won't be too surprised to read that. I don't think Popey and I would ever have sought each other out as friends either. All we have in common is that on about thirty weekends a year, for two or three hours, our three very substantial egos are crammed into a very small television studio and, in that testosterone-filled air, anything could happen.

I've wanted to punch Tom in the face a number of times live on air. During the World Cup in 1999, I almost did. Glenn phoned me to ask if I could suggest an Australian we could use as a guest pundit for Ireland's first-round match against Australia in Dublin. I said I knew the very man – Alan Jones happened to be in town, raising funds for Navan Rugby Club. We'd been friendly ever since he lent me his reserve pack to train with twelve years earlier in Sydney before the US Eagles' World Cup match. I told Glenn I'd phone him myself and Alan said he'd love to come on the show.

On the day of the match, I arranged for Alan to meet the other two men he'd be sharing a studio with over lunch in Jury's in Ballsbridge. Popey didn't need to be told that Alan was one of the greatest rugby coaches the world had ever known, had served as private secretary to the prime minister of Australia and was now a media giant. Tom as usual upped the ante with his new guest. He treated Alan offhandedly, which was not something Australia's most successful radio broadcaster and rugby legend was used to.

Even before our starters arrived, there was a palpable edge between them.

We walked the short distance to Lansdowne Road. When the cameras started rolling, Tom asked Alan for his appraisal of Ireland. Alan was quite critical of the team and in particular of Warren Gatland, who'd succeeded Brian Ashton as coach the previous year. He said Ireland didn't have a prayer. Tom turned to me and said, 'What about that, George?' inviting me to rebuff what this supercilious Aussie was saying. But I agreed with every word. I'd been saying much the same things about Gatland since he was appointed.

'Well,' I said, 'I agree.'

Tom cut across me, as usual. 'If *you're* not going to answer the question properly, I'll move on to Popey.'

For a couple of seconds I forgot myself. I wanted to punch his lights out. In the clip, you can see me lean forward to get out of the chair. Then I remembered I was on television.

Four years later, during the World Cup in Australia we almost came to blows in the corridor over another difference of opinion. It made headlines in Ireland on Sunday but the newspaper, in its search for a scoop, failed to understand the dynamic of television. Tom's job is to get his guests to perform. The success of the programme is a testament to his skill. He is, as he constantly says, 'only the conductor to the pianists on the panel'.

As a rugby writer all my training was taking place on the hoof. I had to learn things that most of the press corps had picked up as young men. My first assignment abroad for Leinster's visit to Bordeaux was traumatic. As usual, after the game, I had to send my copy down a phone line into the Independent Newspapers computer. There was no phone link for me at the stadium but I managed to get it across by borrowing a connection from a French journalist. Later, the office wanted me to rewrite the piece for the final edition, so I caught a taxi back to the hotel – a small, typically French, family-run place – disappeared into my room and punched out a thousand words. I plugged the laptop into the phone point in the wall but I couldn't get a line. It was five minutes from deadline.

I rushed downstairs to reception and explained my problem in breathless, broken English, and the receptionist gave me a key to another room. I sprinted back upstairs and into the new room and scoured the walls for the phone point. I couldn't find it. Then I lost the plot. I trashed the place in true rock-star style, looking for somewhere to plug in my laptop. I turned over the bed, tipped over a table, knocked over chairs.

I gave up. I ran back downstairs, clutching my computer under my arm, virtually vaulted the reception desk, yanked the connection out of the back of the fax machine and used the line to transfer my copy, which, a sub-editor pointed out, was late.

It was as though my entire working life had been a training course for these moments of great stress. There was a lot more to come.

Trying to write a column for a Sunday newspaper and work on television on a Saturday afternoon was – and remains – an enormous challenge. At times it has had me close to cardiac arrest. To make the first edition, the sports desk requires my copy no later than 5.30 p.m. Invariably, the television coverage continues until at least 6 p.m. A three o'clock kick-off means that the game does not end until 4.45, giving me forty-five minutes to type a thousand words, format the grammar and punctuation and at the same time deliver an assessment of a game and individuals that will be read by thousands of critical readers over breakfast.

In our television studio overlooking the South Terrace in Lansdowne Road, my laptop is on the floor beside my chair, off camera. When the match ends and the cameras return to the studio for the discussion with Popey, Tom and me, the lid remains down. However, when we go to a commercial break or a player interview, I grab it and frantically punch out words and ideas. I keep typing right up to the moment the floor manager counts in the next studio segment.

I am helped by a number of factors. I am a quick and accurate typist and my coaching experience has given me the ability to make an assessment that I can stand over. There is little difference between giving an assessment to a selection committee or to a television audience after a game. Coaches of my generation, who did not have the benefit of countless hours of video, learned to make decisions based on memory. However, you never lose the fear of getting it hopelessly wrong and waking up on Sunday morning to discover that everybody else saw it differently.

The terror of missing that 5.30 p.m. deadline has never gone away, but all those years spent fending off a nervous breakdown were good preparation for Saturday afternoons in Lansdowne Road. Despite all the improvements in mobile phone technology, 50,000 people all switching their mobiles on at the same time when the game ends sometimes causes a temporary glitch and sometimes the comforting brrr, brrr of the computer connection does not happen when it is most needed.

Still, only once has my mobile connection failed, forcing me to use the nearest phone line to the studio, which is in the press box at top of the West Stand. In a panic I grabbed the laptop and sprinted around the end of the ground, through the after-match revellers, up the concrete steps behind the stand and arrived with my chest heaving amongst the old pros who watched in amusement as I jammed my connection into the wall.

Like my parents, I have deeded my body for medical research. When that time arrives, the cardiology department might like to have a look at my heart.

The first issue I ever stuck my neck out on was Ronan O'Gara. I remember watching him play for Cork Constitution against Lansdowne in the All Ireland League in 1998 and writing; 'Ronan O'Gara attacks the advantage line like no fly-half since Ollie Campbell.'

He hadn't even graduated to the Munster squad at that point. I knew his background from my previous life as national technical director in the USA. He was born in San Diego, where his father, Fergal, had worked as a biochemist at the university. They moved to Cork when Ronan was a toddler and, when he was playing for

Constitution but not yet on the Munster team, Eddie and I had tried to persuade him to come back to America and play for the country of his birth.

When Ronan graduated to the national stage I thought he was a class act, and better than David Humphreys, who had the Ireland number 10 shirt, though I did O'Gara no favours at all by shouting my mouth off about it on television. Although one of my critics may have had a point when he said, 'Hook has never seen O'Gara play a bad match or Humphreys play a good one.'

In 2003, Ireland made heavy work of beating Italy in a Six Nations match in Rome. Philip Matthews awarded Humphreys man of the match. When the coverage switched back to the studio, I suffered a rush of blood to the head. 'Who were the Swedish Muppets in the theatre box who gave the man of the match award to Humphreys?' I said. In my excitement I confused the *Muppet Show* characters Statler and Waldorf and the Swedish chef.

Immediately, the switchboard lit up with calls of complaint, most of them delivered in thick Northern accents. With one sentence I had achieved Wolfe Tone's dream of uniting Catholic, Protestant and Dissenter in Ulster. And on the Monday two Swedes rang the station complaining of a slight on the Scandinavian nation. I could not win.

Similarly, from early in John Hayes' career I suggested that he was a poor scrummager. If championing O'Gara cost me friends in Ulster then criticizing Hayes did likewise for me in Munster. As I watched the big man struggle in the scrum for the Lions in New Zealand, I felt a sense of satisfaction at being right which was tempered by my regret that one of Ireland's players was not good enough.

Backing one's judgement is a crucial part of being an analyst. There is no time to study the video or compare notes with colleagues. The television studio under the lights is a lonely place when tough calls have to be made. Yet it is what I am paid for and what the audience expects, even though they may vehemently disagree.

★

Warren Gatland took over as coach to Ireland for the game in Paris in March 1998. By the autumn of 1999, when the Rugby World Cup was hosted in Ireland, I had begun to question his fitness to coach the national team. At that time I was the lone voice of criticism until Ireland lost the World Cup play-off to Argentina in Lens. It was easy for other people to jump on the bandwagon after that disaster and the subsequent mess in Twickenham.

I always believed that Gatland's pig-headedness in sticking by players when they clearly weren't the best men for the job would be his undoing. I also had a real concern about his ability as an organizer of a national team which rarely comes together, as opposed to a club side that trains and plays on a weekly basis. The skills for one job are very different from the other.

It came as no great surprise to me that Gatland was subsequently successful at Wasps, where, as a club manager, he had offensive coaches, defensive coaches, kicking coaches, video coaches and any number of people to handle logistics. The system allowed him to use his talents to the fullest.

Keith Wood's career epitomized how I felt about Gatland as a coach. The hooker played some of the worst rugby of his career under Gatland and that was no coincidence. Wood's great talent became a liability: he'd pop up in the full-back position; he would take over at fly-half or try his hand at a drop goal. His work as a hooker and captain suffered as a result. He was never a top-drawer thrower of the ball to the lineout but it was his calling of the throw that was his biggest weakness. And as a captain he was so conscious of leading his men from the front that he allowed tactical considerations to slip his mind. Gatland never seemed to want to address it.

If you look at tapes of Keith Wood playing for Ireland under Gatland and later under Eddie, or for the Lions under Jim Telfer, Ian McGeechan and Graham Henry, it is like looking at two different players.

The defeat to Argentina should have spelled the end for Gatland. It was a game that laid bare all his limitations as a coach. Ireland's back play was appalling, the defensive system hadn't been thought out and all Ireland had to offer as they chased the game in the closing minutes were twelve-man lineouts.

Instead of sacking him after Lens, as it should have done, the IRFU foisted Eddie on him as an assistant. The IRFU played their hand cleverly with regard to Eddie. Noel Murphy and Eddie Coleman had him marked down as a future Ireland coach from his time as coach to the Irish under-21 side. When we were in America, they'd sometimes call to chew the fat with me and invariably they'd ask how Eddie was. They'd say, 'Tell him we're thinking about him,' and clearly they were.

Eddie's contract as coach of the US Eagles ended after the World Cup that autumn, where, as another measure of his brilliance as a coach, the USA were the only team to score a try against Australia in the entire tournament.

Gatland wasn't stupid. The subtext of getting Eddie as assistant was that the next time he messed up, the IRFU already had his replacement lined up. This is where Eddie's extraordinary focus came in. While Gatland probably regarded him as a viper in his bosom, Eddie never stepped outside his remit as a number two. He was unfailingly loyal to him. But the more Eddie saw of Gatland up close, the more he must have known that, sooner or later, he'd foul up again.

Eddie's first match as Gatland's assistant was in February 2000, almost four months after Lens. Ireland were dismembered at Twickenham. England scored six tries and put fifty points on Ireland, their complete domination summed up in one period of play in the first half, when they went through seventeen phases without giving up possession. Gatland should have been made to walk the plank after that débâcle. I lambasted him for Ireland's performance. When we came off the air Niall Cogley, always a voice of reason, said, 'Should you really have said that?'

I didn't know which particular line he was referring to. 'You pay me to give an opinion,' I said. 'If you don't like my opinions, you can get somebody else,' and I meant it.

In my column in the following morning's *Sunday Independent*, I paraphrased Oliver Cromwell in his famous address to the rump parliament, 'Depart I say; and let us have done with you. In the name of God, go.'

Ireland then promptly won their next three games including, victory in Paris for the first time in seventeen years, with a hat trick from Brian O'Driscoll. I attributed the success to the assistant, which not only did nothing to improve my relations with the coach, but also was not a universally held opinion.

The players treated me like a pariah, though it's reasonable to assume that at least some of them agreed with me, since there was no revolt among them when Gatland was inevitably dumped. Around the time of some of my most vociferous articles, Popey and I were walking towards Lansdowne Road for a Six Nations match when the Ireland team bus pulled up alongside us, just outside the Berkeley Court Hotel. One by one, the players and backroom staff filed off the bus and into the hotel, turning their heads away as they passed Popey and me on the footpath. Though I had given some of them very generous praise, I didn't exist. That's the bovine passivity of the young sports professional. It was no accident that the two players who did say hello had careers that reached back to the amateur era, when players weren't frightened to stand out on their own. Peter Clohessy and Mick Galwey nodded at me and said, 'Howiya, George?' It took character to do that. (The other player who never took what I said about him personally was Conor O'Shea. I was fiercely critical of his performances for Ireland at full-back, yet he took it on the chin, and today we share the unlikeliest of friendships, which speaks volumes for the man.)

In 2001 Gatland all but delivered a Grand Slam for Ireland. The Championship had been interrupted by an outbreak of foot-and-mouth disease and, after opening their account with victories over Wales, Italy and France, Ireland were still not a good bet to complete a clean sweep when it resumed in the autumn, as mighty England were still on the horizon. Then, surprisingly, they went to Murrayfield and lay down supinely to Scotland. What that match did was to convince the IRFU, who had never forgiven him for Lens, that as long as Gatland was in charge there was always a disaster round the next corner. A fortnight later, Ireland beat England at Lansdowne Road, denying Clive Woodward the Grand Slam, but by then minds at 62 Lansdowne Road had been made up.

Gatland's contract was up for renewal at the end of the year and the media and public, entranced by the victories over France and England, assumed that he was a shoo-in for another three years. Being the unofficial voice of the anti-Gatland movement was no fun at that point. I appeared to be a crank on a mission with an unwillingness to change my mind. However, the affair for me was about everything I held dear as an analyst. My father's childhood injunction was in my head – 'Hold your ground in an argument.'

Colm Murray interviewed me for the *Six One News* and asked pointedly what I thought of Gatland's chances of surviving as Ireland coach. 'None,' I replied succinctly. Later that week, I felt ambushed on the Pat Kenny radio show when he and Des Cahill worked a pincer movement on me, suggesting I had got it wrong.

'There is no call from public opinion for Gatland to go,' said my old mate Dessie.

I fought back.

'He does not work for the public Des, he works for the IRFU.'

Within weeks Gatland was gone and Eddie O'Sullivan was installed as coach.

The popular wisdom at the time was that Eddie had in some way shafted Gatland. What happened was that the IRFU called him in for an interview, told him there was going to be a vacancy and, if he was interested in it, he'd better tell them why he was the best man for the job. Eddie as is his wont, told them. I suspect in no uncertain terms.

I would have liked to have been a fly on the wall for the contract negotiations. Eddie's belief that you are what you negotiate and not what you are worth would have made him a doughty opponent in the discussions on salary and conditions. God, how I envy him!

Eddie's nickname is 'the Dagger', which originated, apparently, from the sharp, thrusting runs he used to make in his days as a winger. Then it was misappropriated to imply that he liked to stab people in the back. It couldn't be further from the truth. Of course Eddie wanted the job, but he never tried to make himself look better than Gatland in front of the players, he never spoke ill of him behind his hand to the press and he never bitched about him to the IRFU. He did the best job he could as his number two and let the chips fall where they might.

And when they fell, as ever, Eddie just happened to be the winner.

9. Happy ever after . . .

It amazes me, the enjoyment I get these days from the simplest pleasures. On Sunday afternoons Ingrid and I do the weekly super-market shop together. In Superquinn in Blackrock they have a system where you can scan your own shopping, and I feel an intense sense of pride as I run the gun over every barcode in turn, and then pack everything into the minimum number of bags. Every Sunday we do that is another brick in our rebuilt marriage.

I can't claim to have undergone some miraculous conversion into being the perfect husband after Ingrid gave me my final chance. I didn't wake up on the morning after that traumatic Monday when we visited her GP knowing the secret to a successful marriage. It was a day-by-day battle. It still is. As I'm writing these words, I'm staring across the kitchen at a pile of dirty dishes on the draining board. Before I crawl into bed tonight, I'll scrape down the plates and empty the dregs from the cups, put them in the dishwasher and switch it on. It's nothing. And yet it's every-thing because it's symbolic. Stacking the dishwasher represents my commitment to our marriage.

Have I done it every single night since then?

No. There are times when I've procrastinated and she's had to do it.

Have I lied to her since then?

Of course I have.

But just little fibs. I've not been a model, but I've tried. I'm still trying.

So this is the way it is in our house. I come home at about 7.30 p.m. after my radio programme and eat dinner with Ingrid. For thirty-six years, no matter how tired, stressed or busy she was, Ingrid has cooked for her family. Invariably I was missing. Now I am a regular attendee, although the number present has dropped from five to two. She goes into the living room to watch television, usually something on the Discovery or Science Channel, while I fart around in my office. At nine o'clock, she'll put her head round the door and tell me the television's all mine. She goes up to exercise, which she does religiously. I'll watch television, invariably an old movie or a drama such as *Frost* or *Maigret*, until late. Then I go to bed.

Even now, as we rediscover the love we had in 1969, it's not a conventional marriage.

If you gave me a blank sheet of paper and asked me to list all of the things that we have in common, you'd find me, an hour later, still staring into space. Ingrid has sophisticated musical tastes and likes classical music; I like big bands, Dean Martin and Elvis Presley. Sport is my great passion but it does nothing at all for Ingrid. She loves crossword puzzles; I can't do them.

Most people find marriage difficult. With us it's not that he leaves the cap off the toothpaste or that she hangs her knickers up in the bathroom, but that we're struggling on every single level because of this lack of commonality. We have nothing we could describe as mutual except one thing – that we love each other.

We hold hands. We rarely held hands before 1998, and for most of our marriage tactile expressions of affection were not welcomed by Ingrid. How could they be? How could you bear to live with an asshole who makes your life a misery, then have him put his arm round your shoulder and say, 'How are you, sweetie?'

Learning to be a husband is almost as much fun as being a rugby pundit. I tend to stay in Limerick on Saturday night after a game but leave at 6.30 a.m. the following day and get back in time to bring her Sunday-morning tea in bed. Now we have begun to go to Munster rugby games together. Well, not quite go to the games together – she still hates rugby with a passion – but to Limerick for the weekend where she amuses herself for the afternoon and then we have dinner together that evening. It is invariably a weekend of chat and laughter as I discover more about the woman I married and rediscover all the qualities that drew me to her in the first place. When I look at her, she's as beautiful to me as she was the first night I saw her. And the fact that she's still with me at the back end of the awful marriage I put her through proves that she loves me. I love her, but I am still so emotionally challenged I find it easier to type those three words than I do to say them.

I can never take back all the hurts and the slights and the damage I did to her spirits through thirty years of utter indifference to our marriage. But the fact that she's forgiven and forgotten is indicative of how she feels about the commitment she made to me. Ingrid has the toughness of her Austrian and German forebears, this Teutonic resolve to stick it out.

That's the adhesive that held our marriage together.

Every so often I'm visited by ghosts from the past. In 2001, I got a letter from the Revenue Commissioners, inviting me in for a chat and asking me to bring details of every bank account I'd held over the past twenty-five years, and also every bank account held by Mrs Hook over the same period. The signature of D. A. McCartaigh, the senior revenue official who led the charge against the banks over the DIRT fraud, was at the bottom. My blood ran cold. I phoned the number on the letter and confirmed the time and date they suggested for our appointment.

I rang some of my friends, who suggested I go in empty-handed, but with solicitors and accountants and advisors, and plead amnesia to all the difficult questions. Happily there is still a presumption of innocence in this country so I decided to dispense with all the experts and trust in the shield of honesty, even though I wondered how the Inspector would react to the legions of bank accounts and the myriad cross-transfers of cheques.

I turned up on time complete with sweaty palms and loose intestine. My appointment was with Mr McCartaigh himself. Like Mr Sampson of Her Majesty's Customs and Excise all those years earlier, he had a younger man with him to take notes. He grilled me for five sweaty hours, without a break. It was like a police interrogation. He asked me to pinpoint where I was on specific dates.

Towards the end of the interview, he pushed a cheque across the table to me. 'What about that?' he said.

It was like seeing an apparition.

The cheque was for £702.50, written by Kyran McLaughlin, for the benefit of G. Hook, and cashed in Guinness and Mahon, which had become embroiled in the payments-to-politicians scandal. 'Back the truck up,' I said, getting tired and testy now. 'Guinness and Mahon used to be a bank. I hadn't a dime in there. I wasn't an investor. I was a borrower. A bad client. They sued me on a number of occasions.'

'Can you tell me about the cheque?' he said.

'Yes, I can.'

Out of all the many thousands of cheques I'd lodged in my lifetime, I had cause to remember this one.

'Has anyone ever threatened to break your legs?' I said.

'I beg your pardon?'

'Two guys called to my door one night. I owed a vegetable man money. They threatened me. Kyran wrote me that cheque to save my kneecaps.'

It was a suitably dramatic ending to the interview and I was free to go. 'I don't say this to too many people,' McCartaigh said as I opened the door to leave, 'but the file on George Hook is closed.'

I walked out into the cool evening air and resolved never to go back there again. I'm careful about my tax affairs now to the point of paranoia.

I have loved the notoriety attached to being a critic. I've been an argumentative person all my life and I was too old to change, just because I was on television. At the beginning, people regarded me as controversial, but I never, ever, said anything just for effect or advanced an argument that I didn't really believe.

In many respects my recognition grew with Munster's success in the Heineken Cup. Before 1999, I was known only to that small constituency that was interested in rugby. As Munster defied the odds, year after year, to make it to the latter stages of the Cup, I went mainstream along with the team. Munster made it to two finals, in 2000 and 2002. I backed them to fail just about every step of the way.

I did it, not to make a name for myself, as some people had it, but because when I looked at them and then at their opponents, defeat seemed the only logical outcome. But what Munster did – and what they continue to do – is to confound rational assessment. Going into the final quarter against Saracens in 2000, you wouldn't have found anyone who'd have staked that month's mortgage payment on Keith Wood scoring a last-minute try and Ronan O'Gara converting it to win it by a point. There are a zillion people out there who'll tell you they always believed that Munster would beat Gloucester, to squeeze into the knockout phase of the tournament in 2003. But no one really did, not even the players, if they were being honest.

They should lose every big match they play, such are their shortcomings. Through all their period of success, they never had a back line. In the modern era, a full-back is to rugby what a striker is to soccer. They've had reasonable full-backs but never great ones. They never had pace where it counted, on the wings. You can win matches by stuffing the ball up your jumper and mauling but it won't win you European titles, especially with a pack that's liable to be bossed around.

Successive Munster teams were better than the sum of their parts.

People who have a passing interest in rugby, who turn on the television for the big Saturday-afternoon matches, prefer Munster to Ireland. For all the success Eddie has enjoyed – the Triple Crown, the victories over Australia and South Africa – Munster make better television because there's romance involved. Ireland under Eddie isn't romantic. They're experts, the sporting equivalent of engineers and accountants and lawyers: well prepared, technically correct, clinical.

In fifty years' time you won't have men telling their grandchildren that they were at Lansdowne Road the day Ronan O'Gara kicked all the points to silence South African coach, Jake White. But people will sit children on their knees and talk about this

Munster team. Theirs is a strange kind of legend because it can gain nothing in the telling. They have given us storylines that can't be improved on by exaggeration. It isn't just that they won matches that they should have lost; it's the manner in which they won them. Alf Tupper, Rock Fist Rogan and all the cartoon heroes from my boyhood never achieved anything as far-fetched as the victory over Gloucester in 2004. They needed to win by twenty-seven points and, to complicate matters, twenty of them had to come from tries; they won by twenty-seven points and scored the four tries they needed.

Tom McGurk asked me to explain it afterwards. 'Fatima, Knock, Lourdes and Thomond Park,' I said. 'The lame will come here and walk.'

I'd never seen anything like it in fifty years watching rugby. It defied belief. No one could have predicted it would happen. What rational person would have believed they could go to Bordeaux and beat Toulouse in sweltering, 80-degree heat? Who would have forecast that they could go to Paris to face the might of Stade Français and win?

I'm not Nostradamus. I'm not paid to read tea-leaves. I'm paid to analyse and do so with my head, as opposed to my heart. I was consistently wrong when I said Munster would lose, but I was wrong for the right reasons. I believed the logic of my analysis was never less than sound. And bar-room experts don't have to make the call before the match in the living colour of television.

I was comprehensively right about Munster when I said they weren't good enough to win the European Cup. For all the close calls, I was fundamentally correct. There was no year that they could claim to have been the best team in the competition. Ronan O'Gara missed a late penalty that cost them the 2000 final by a point but the real reason they lost was because their pack got pushed around by Northampton. They lost the 2002 final because Leicester had a better side.

But if the European Cup was awarded to the most deserving team, then it would be no contest: the competition owes Munster a debt that is unquantifiable. They've done more than anyone to push rugby centre stage in Ireland, so that it rivals soccer, Gaelic football and hurling in the public imagination.

People in Limerick and Cork are hopelessly one-eyed when it comes to rugby, seeing only their team. Happily, they also have the most wonderful sense of humour. I realized I'd become their bête noire one afternoon in Thomond Park. Munster had won again in spite of me. Tom, Popey and I were sitting on a gantry built on six-foot-high scaffolding poles, doing our after-match wrap in front of the camera. Thomond usually cleared out quickly and we'd do our wrap to a background of silence. This time, we must have had close to a thousand supporters swarming round at the foot of the gantry, drowning out our voices with choruses of, 'Georgie, we love you.'

Tom briefly thought there was going to be a riot and wondered if we should send for reinforcements, but it was all good-natured.

A curious thing started to happen at matches. People would stay in the two bars in the ground – the Bohemians and the Shannon clubhouses – until Popey and I had made our pre-match predictions. Then the terraces would fill out and, from where we were sitting, we could hear the word pass round the ground like ripples on a pond that Hooky had backed the opposition and there was universal relief. They reckoned I was such a bad analyst of the game that the day I bet on Munster would be the day they lost.

Munster supporters are the most extraordinarily generous and warm-hearted I've ever known. Even at the height of my notoriety, not one single Munster fan spoke a word to me that crossed the line between banter and abuse. Even if they didn't like what I said, they got a kick out of the way I said it.

At the beginning, people didn't even know I was from Cork. Forty years after I left Jew Town, my accent was positively Dublin Four. When the word spread that I was a Munster man myself it breathed new life into the slagging.

Ingrid came with me to Limerick for the Heineken Cup quarter final against Stade Français in April 2004. We decided to make a weekend of it, flying down to Shannon and staying at the Castletroy Park Hotel. On the drive from Shannon airport into

Limerick, I tuned the radio to Limerick 95 FM. I nearly ran the hired car off the road when I heard the lead item on the three o'clock news. 'George Hook,' the newsreader said in a grave tone, 'is expected to arrive in Limerick some time this afternoon.'

We laughed all weekend long.

I am proud that I've always made the hard calls. I always told the truth, however inconvenient. One of the most difficult was when my old club St Mary's College beat Lansdowne in the All Ireland League final of 2000, refereed by Alan Lewis. Popey was coach to Mary's, who played their part with Lewis in making it possibly the worst final in history. I was fiercely critical of my friend on television and was not any more charitable to the referee.

Popey took the criticism on the chin, although it could not have been easy for him. To compound the problem, I decided to play nine holes of golf at Milltown on the Sunday and, as luck would have it, Alan Lewis and I were sharing a tee time. 'Louey' was great, as he always is, even after the Italian match when I suggested in my analysis that 'he done more damage to Italy than Mussolini'.

Not everybody takes criticism quite so stoically. In a *Sunday Independent* article I was particularly vitriolic about a member of the Irish squad. He didn't take it very well. The following Tuesday night, the phone rang. It was the object of my criticism. 'You fucking bastard,' he said.

'What's your problem?' I said.

'The shite you wrote about me. Listen, I'm not going to do anything to you now, because I've a career. But when it's over, I'm going to take you down a dark alley and I'm going to beat the bejaysus out of you.'

Of the many scary people I wouldn't like to join in a dark alley, a professional rugby player would be top of the list. I'm sure he regrets what he said now but I've no doubt that at that moment in time he was deadly serious.

The next day I rang my solicitor, Brian McLoughlin, and told him what had happened.

'Are you scared?' he said.

'Of course I am.'

'Do you think he meant it?'

'I do.'

'Well,' he said, 'you have two alternatives then. One, you can go to the Gardaí and tell them you've been threatened. The other is you could tell someone in the IRFU.'

I knew that either option would ruin the player's career. I thought that was an unfair price to pay for what was likely nothing more than a rush of blood to the head. Anyway, I figured he still had another four or five years rugby in him, plenty of time to forget about taking me down that laneway.

Chance continued to play an extraordinary role in my life. In 2001 Jim Glennon, the former Ireland second row and an old friend, asked me to speak at a conference on sports marketing in Croke Park at ridiculously short notice. As I remember it, he called on a Monday and the conference was on the Wednesday. 'There's no money in it for you either,' he said.

'It doesn't really suit me,' I said.

'George, I'm calling in an IOU. As a friend. I need you.'

How could I say no?

I spoke without a note in front of me, though I put hours of preparation into what I was going to say. A couple of weeks later I got a call from Daire O'Brien, who said he worked for Setanta Media and wanted to take me out to lunch. At that point I didn't know whether he was buying or selling, but we arranged to meet in Fitzwilliam Lawn Tennis Club. Daire explained that Setanta had a stake in Newstalk, a consortium aiming to launch Dublin's first ever talk radio station, and they wanted me to present an evening drive-time current-affairs show.

What's interesting is that my name had originally been mentioned at one of their early brainstorming conferences but dismissed out of hand, because they figured that my range of interests was too narrow to carry off a current-affairs show. Then Leonard Ryan and Frank Cronin, the two top executives in Setanta, saw me speak in Croke Park and changed their minds. That's why I always say that, while I might have made an unmitigated mess of the better part of my life, I worked hard for the breaks that came later on. I could have delivered a half-hearted speech that day, but that wasn't in my nature, so another door opened.

My contract was dependent on the success of two pilot programmes they asked me to record. The first was scheduled for 10 a.m. one Monday morning in a recording studio on Merrion Square. Typically, I was in the Davenport Hotel from 5.30 a.m., steeling myself for it.

I did three dummy interviews, the first with Gay Mitchell TD, about whether the use of cannabis should be permitted for pain relief; the second with Liam Cosgrave Jr, about the origins and history of Fine Gael; and I closed with a chat to Declan Conroy, a PR consultant for Aer Lingus, on the general state of the airline industry.

It was an eclectic mix. And it was unspeakably awful.

A week later we did another dry run that was even worse. I was having second thoughts about whether I was cut out for it and I knew Newstalk were too. Daire asked me to do a third pilot. I refused. 'You've got two there,' I said. 'That's what I can do. I'm not going to get any better.'

What I should have remembered from my time in RTÉ is that the people behind the camera are far more important than the people in front of it. Similarly in radio, it's the people in the control box who make you a broadcaster. Newstalk producer Garrett Harte was only 30 but he understood radio like somebody who had never seen television. He knew the medium inside out. After my second pilot, he went to the station management and said he wanted to work with me. He was confident he could make something of me.

Right from the start I had a good feeling about him, eventually even agreeing to do a third pilot. The role of a producer is crucial. Throughout interviews he is listening and alert for any difficulty, such as when the mind goes blank and you cannot remember the name of the guest. 'Well, Mr . . .'. The producer is in with 'Jones' and there is a seamless sentence. He watches for possible slander, tees up the commercial break and sometimes gives you an old-fashioned rollicking in the middle of a badly handled interview. A radio studio is a lonely place, you can't see your audience or hear their reaction; the voice in your ear is the only link with the outside world. And working with Garrett went well. This time out, I felt like a pro.

Afterwards, we went for a sandwich and a bowl of soup in Fitzwilliam. 'Be honest with me,' I said. 'Can I do this?'

'Absolutely,' he said.

There was a wonderful chemistry between us.

'If they still want me to do it,' I said, 'I want to work with you.'

'Well,' he said, 'I want to work with you.'

The following day Newstalk offered me a contract. Untypically, given my relationship with the *Independent*, I had broached the subject of money, but was assured that all of the presenters, including David McWilliams who had the morning drive-time show, were being paid the same salary, with a system of bonuses based on audience figures to be worked out later.

Newstalk 106 was due to start broadcasting in the spring of 2002, but like all start-up operations it was a shambles. At the start of the year, it still didn't have a home. Finally, it acquired premises on Mount Street in Dublin, just next to the Pepper Canister Church. For the first few weeks, nothing worked. The building was like an anthill, teeming with carpenters and painters and electricians. It smelled of varnish and emulsion but there was no great sense of progress being made. The gossip at the water cooler was whether there was going to be a station at all.

Paul Kavanagh, the chief executive, had an impressive CV. His background, though, was in saving bankrupt radio stations. His first instinct was to keep costs low, to do things as cheaply as possible, which was the wrong mentality for a start-up operation. Corners were cut. The result was that we missed our original start date.

He needed a trouble-shooter so he brought over a station manager from England to get things up and running. Pete Lunn was Oxford educated, he talked the talk, and we were all a bit in thrall to him. He had worked on *Newsnight* and – how typically Irish of us – we figured that, because he'd worked for the BBC, he had to know more than we did. As far as Newstalk 106 went, his word was law.

For my show to be a success, we had to take listeners from Eamon Dunphy's *The Last Word* on Today FM and from Rachael English on RTÉ's *Five–Seven Live*. The original plan for *The Right Hook* was to broadcast in that same 5 p.m. to 7 p.m. slot, but the station decided to start at 4.30 to get the jump on the opposition. I now had a producer and a researcher, the embryo of a team. We were finally due to go on air on 9 April 2002, a Tuesday.

On Friday afternoon, four days before our first broadcast, a man walked into the studio and handed me a piece of paper. I'd never seen him before and I couldn't pick him out of a line-up today. 'That's your schedule for Tuesday,' he said.

I read what he'd handed me and I flipped my top. 'Get Lunn down here now,' I said.

Newstalk had this idea, which never worked, of news every twenty minutes. According to the schedule, I opened the show at 4.30 p.m. Ten minutes in, we went to news, sport and weather. Then there was news analysis. Then there was traffic news. There were ads. There were all these godawful jingles to identify the station. Out of two and a half hours of programming, only about thirty minutes of it would be mine. My voice was just the grouting holding all these little pieces together. I was furious.

Pete Lunn arrived in what passed as an office but was really a storage area.

'I don't want to start being difficult just before we go on air,' I said, 'but I'm not doing this. It's not what I signed up for.'

'Hold on,' he said. 'This is the way John Humphrys does it. Are you trying to tell me that the BBC doesn't know how to do news?'

'They probably do, but I'm not working for the BBC, and I'm

not interested in this. There's nothing in it for me. I'm sorry, but I'm not doing it,' and I walked out.

I was serious, but I knew I had a problem. The news of my walkout was sure to hit the papers that weekend. I went to the Mespil Hotel, had a cup of coffee and tried to get my head straight. I phoned Declan Conroy, who had just left Aer Lingus and was now working as an independent public relations consultant, and he came and met me.

'I've just walked out on this new radio station three days before it's due to go on air,' I said to him. 'How do I handle this?'

Declan suggested issuing some kind of press statement, as a sort of pre-emptive strike. 'Get your story out there before they do,' he said.

I didn't, though, deciding instead to sit on it for the weekend. On Sunday afternoon Garrett called to say that Pete Lunn had agreed a return to our original schedule. This early clash started a non-relationship between Pete and me that continued until the day he left the station. I went back to work on Monday morning, with just a day and a half to prepare for the first broadcast of *The Right Hook*.

We made a lot of mistakes in the early days. It happens when you're working with young people with lots of enthusiasm but no experience. We had the names of world leaders mispronounced in news reports. We had a lorry 'shooting its load' all over the M50 in a traffic report.

As with television, I had a good idea of where I wanted to go right from the start. I've never asked what the story is; it's always, 'Who are we going to get to talk about it?' It doesn't matter if World War III has broken out – all that's important to us is who's talking about it and what they're saying. I found it very difficult to communicate that to young people with Masters degrees in journalism and an earnest view of the world. I was the only Newstalk employee, from the chairman of the board to the cleaners, who had grown up with radio. Everyone else had grown up with television. From the start, I had the sound of the programme in my head. I still had all these voices – Eamon Andrews, Raymond Glendenning, Alistair Cooke – in my ear.

I veered away from the worthy. I have this theory that people in the Republic aren't interested in the North. It takes up far more column inches in the newspapers and far more airtime on radio and television than it deserves. Even on those occasions when a story requires covering, and we have Gerry Adams or Martin McGuinness on the show, I can hear the clicks of radios everywhere being switched off.

Instead, I was drawn to the interesting. One of the most fascinating features we ever did on the show was an interview with George Monbiot from the *Guardian*, who had written an article about the homogenization of the fruit industry. Supermarket demand for shiny, perfectly round apples meant that most of the 1,500 different varieties of apple were becoming extinct.

I was lucky to have the support of a producer who understood what I was trying to do. Pete, who had this obsession with what he called radio grammer, would have liked to knock the edges off me, buff me up and have me sounding like someone off BBC Radio Four. But to Garrett, my eccentricity was my calling card. He knew my strengths. He knew I had a sense of humour and that I was liable to do off-the-wall things. He also knew my modus operandi. I never worked from a list of previously prepared questions. My research team would put a brief in front of me that concentrated on information from which I could draw conclusions rather than a template of questions to ask. In 90 per cent of interviews, my first question was either, 'What's this all about?' or some variation of it. What I discovered about myself was that – strangely for someone who talks so much – I was a good listener. I didn't have to bring a pen into the studio because I never had to write down my next question. It was always on the tip of my tongue.

Garrett was unbelievably prescient. For the first year or so, I was fixated on Eamon Dunphy, knowing that my success would be judged on how many listeners I prised away from *The Last Word*, but Garrett sensed that Dunphy was losing interest as the programme appeared to be using more and more pre-recorded material and to have more guest presenters. 'Don't worry about him,' he'd tell me. 'He's not going to last.'

He was right. By Christmas of 2003, Dunphy was gone.

Amazingly, I found myself, in my early sixties, happy in the career I should have been doing all along. I had a newspaper column, a radio show and a slot on television. Life was something close to bliss.

Yet still the Black Dog was an occasional visitor.

In November 2002, the day before Ireland were due to play Australia in Dublin, I was in RTÉ for a production meeting. Mike Ford had been appointed as Ireland's new defensive coach and there was some discussion about how we were going to cover this development on the programme. It had already been agreed that I was going to do a two-minute pre-recorded segment in which I talked about his new defensive formation using video clips Remember, at this time the new system resembled space-age technology and not many people understood it. There are always creative tensions when you're dealing with media egos, but, on this occasion, whether through tension or tiredness or passion, I felt the crucial change in Ireland's system was not being highlighted.

When the meeting broke up, I went back to the sports department and had a go at Popey. It got heated and there was shouting, and it turned into a ferocious bust-up between us. Popey, always the calmer one, felt that I had gone over the top. Then we went into another meeting, which involved the same line-up as before but without the technical people. Hostilities continued in the same vein and I burst into tears. I cried like a baby in front of all these people – Popey, Tom McGurk, Niall Cogley, John D. O'Brien. The meeting soon ended. Niall said he wanted to see me in his office.

He sat me down and handed me a tissue. 'What's wrong, George?' he said. Then I really broke down. I was in bits. I didn't say anything for twenty minutes, just cried. Somewhere in between all these sobs, I said I had to pre-record my piece for the next day.

'Forget about it,' he said. 'You can't work tomorrow either, George. Not in this state.'

'I'm fine,' I said. 'I'll go home and get some sleep.'

'I'm not letting you go home.'

Niall was due to drive to Galway that lunchtime for a business meeting that was far more important, I'm sure, than offering comfort to a 61-year-old man blubbering like a schoolgirl. At that moment, though, he didn't care about his meeting. 'Let's go and get some air,' he said.

We left the television building, walked around the radio centre, through the car park, past the *Fair City* set and through the side gate onto Nutley Lane. We walked round the block, Niall talking to me all the way in a sympathetic tone. 'I think you should see a doctor,' he said.

'No,' I said.

'George, you need to. Who's your GP?'

I told him it was Jack Ormond. Jack knew all about the Dog.

'Come on,' he said. 'We have to ring him.'

I called Jack on my mobile phone. He was at home in Rathgar. 'Jack,' I said, 'it's George. I'm a bit down today.'

'Where are you?' he said.

'In the car park in RTÉ.'

'Put him on to me,' Niall Cogley said.

I handed the phone to Niall. When he hung up, he said he was taking me to Rathgar. Niall put me into his car and drove me to Cowper Road. Jack took us into the living room and Niall told him some of what had happened. It wasn't necessary for Jack to get out his stethoscope to know I was hyperventilating. 'Don't worry, he's not going to top himself,' he told Niall, who I suspect was afraid to let me out of his sight in case I flung myself in the canal.

'Well, that's a relief,' he said. 'What about work tomorrow?'

I cut in. 'I'm OK.'

Jack looked at Niall. 'If he says he's OK, then he's OK.'

We got up to leave. 'How much do we owe you?' Niall asked.

'No fee,' Jack said.

226

'Honestly, RTÉ will pay it.'

'It's fine,' Jack said.

Niall dipped into his pocket and pulled out two tickets for the match the following day, his own tickets. 'I hope you'll accept these as a gift from me,' he said, and then drove me back to RTÉ. 'Good luck tomorrow,' he said, as he walked me to my car.

That is just one reason I regard Niall as extraordinary. On that day he showed his concern for me as a human being more than as a colleague and I can never repay him for his compassion.

I got up the following morning with no sign of the Dog. I went into RTÉ early and I did my two-minute pre-record, using video footage to explain exactly how Ford's new defensive system worked. I still regard it as the best two minutes of television I've ever done.

In the first few months of Newstalk's existence, I got the impression that I was on a short leash until somebody better came along, especially since, as is my wont, I had not signed the contract. The station's star was David McWilliams. He was a bright, good-looking young economist and a polished performer. But then the JNLR listenership figures were published and it turned out that, while I wasn't exactly shooting the lights out, I had almost as many listeners as all our other daytime presenters combined.

Companies leak like sieves. It was around that time that I found out about the deal negotiated with McWilliams. I'd been told that we were all paid the same, but that wasn't the case. He was earning close to twice my salary, was on a two-year contract instead of a twelve-month one and had his bonus structure in place although the other presenters were told it was still under consideration.

It was my own fault. I'd never been a good negotiator, being generally embarrassed to talk about money. I never had a figure in my head but I was happy to hear I was being paid the same as everybody else. Now, I was livid.

My contract was up for renewal. I was offered a marginally improved one but I was still way behind McWilliams. I sat down to negotiate in the strong position of knowing that without *The*

Right Hook there was no Newstalk 106. The station was haemor-rhaging money – chairman Denis O'Brien had to invest more and more to cover the losses – and it was smart to keep me for as little money as possible.

I opened the discussion with the company's agent by telling him that I was very happy at Newstalk and that I wanted to stay. Then I asked, 'Is it the position that all of the presenters in Newstalk are paid the same salary?'

'Yes,' he said.

'I will give you my answer tomorrow.'

The following day, I walked into the office, told him I'd thought about what he said and I was quitting the show on 17 March, when my contract was up. I could see he was shocked.

'Why?' he said.

I told him that, despite what he had told me, I knew that not all the presenters at Newstalk were getting the same salary and I didn't like the tactic he had used with me. 'The fact that, in all your business management manuals, it's called good negotiating, is irrelevant.'

'OK,' he said. 'What can I do about it?'

I told him what I thought of his offer.

He made me a new offer. It was one euro a year more than what I knew McWilliams was being paid. We shook on it.

In April 2003, for the first time since I joined Campbell Catering in 1968, I no longer had to worry about money. It's only since that day that I've had credit cards that are in credit. That Christmas I wrote out cheques for Michelle, Alison and George. I'll never forget the scepticism on Michelle's face. 'Are you saying these are actually going to be met?' she said. For the first time in more than thirty years, I could laugh at that question.

One of the greatest pleasures for me in following Ireland over the past few years has been watching Eddie become one of the best coaches in the world. I was pilloried when I said he had that potential four years ago, but right now I can't think of many who are better. Put him with a line of backs and they come alive.

What makes rugby such a difficult game to coach is that in order to go forward, you have to go backwards. David Beckham can hit a long ball upfield for Wayne Rooney to score. Dan Marino can throw the ball forty metres to a wide receiver to score. In rugby, when you receive the ball, there are always fifteen defenders between you and the line. So to coach back play is an incredibly technical skill. It's about angle, alignment and space, and he is *the* master technician.

Though he's regarded by many as primarily a backs coach, put him up against any forwards coach, lineout coach, rolling-maul coach, and there's nothing he needs to learn. He has this way about him – when he talks to players, you can see the lights switch on.

When he was appointed Ireland coach in 2001, I went to watch his first training session with the team at the University of Limerick. Technically, it was closed to the media, but Eddie said he had no problem with my being there. It was pure Broadway. There was an electricity about it. Mike McGurn, his fitness advisor, had a programme, a stopwatch and a battery-operated horn. Everything was choreographed. There was a dynamism about it that was missing under Gatland. You could see the players looking at each other, as if to say, 'This is it.'

What has disappointed me, though, is that Eddie has never acknowledged the role I played in his career.

Would he be the coach he is today had our paths never crossed? Undoubtedly.

But whenever an opportunity has arisen to acknowledge the part I played in helping his career along, he's always shrugged it off with a flippant remark. In 2004, I was asked for my thoughts about him for *Buried Alive*, a television show that offered famous guests an opportunity to view their own obituary. I told the story of the day we met in the Great Southern Hotel in Eyre Square and how I knew instantly that this was a very special guy. When the camera was back on Eddie, he said something along the lines of, 'George didn't know very much but he could always recognize a guy who did.'

It was said with a smile, but I thought he diminished me in people's eyes.

A short time later, when he appeared on *The Late Late Show*, his only reference to me and the five years we spent together in America was the number of times I was pulled over for speeding, which was quite a few. I bit my lip after *Buried Alive*, but to see him encapsulate my entire contribution in America into one story about me driving at a hundred miles per hour on the highways annoyed me beyond belief.

Maybe he has his reasons for wishing to airbrush me from his story. But I gave him his first big break at Connacht. I took him to America with me when the Connacht branch had him over a barrel. I thought what he did was beneath him and I sent a message to his agent to say so.

Things are going to get worse before they get better for Irish rugby. The coach and his players will face greater scrutiny than ever before. Governments have proven that the media can be threatened and controlled. Access for interviews can be denied, inside information can be given to compliant journalists and comment can be ridiculed to diminish the critic. But I am certain that Tom, George and Brent will continue to tell it like it is.

I'm glad that there are still things that make me angry. After all the hours of analysis I've offered on television over the last seven years, the moment that I'm best remembered for came to me in a fit of anger during an ad break.

In March 2004, Ireland beat Italy in the Six Nations and Brian O'Driscoll spent the entire post-match interview sucking on the teat of a bottle of some energy drink or other he was being paid to promote. After every answer, he pushed the bottle to his lips, so that the camera caught the name on the label. It was the pretence of it that got me as much as anything. It made a mockery of the interview.

What made it even more tasteless was that O'Driscoll could be the greatest Irish player of all time. There's only Jack Kyle and Mike Gibson who are in the same league as him and I am fast coming to the conclusion that he's better than either of them, which makes me even sadder to see him acting as a shill for a soft-drink company.

Where rugby is concerned, I'm a barely reconstructed amateur. Sometimes I despair of where professionalism is leading us. I appreciate that players have a short run at the top and that they have to earn what they can while they can. Maybe I'm an idealist, but I've always believed that to be the captain of the Irish team is something special. I think a huge number of people who watched the interview saw it like I did, as crass commercialism.

A week later, Ireland beat Scotland to secure the Triple Crown and I couldn't believe it when he did it again. I was appalled. Tom, Popey and I always have bottles of water to hand, but they have to be kept out of view as, unlike O'Driscoll, we can't be seen to be endorsing a product. When we went to the commercial break, I had a brainwave. I tore the label off my bottle, borrowed some sticky tape from the studio electrician and stuck it back, with the reverse side facing outwards. Then I wrote on it in large capitals, 'Hook's Hooch,' and got ready to drink from it the next time the camera was pointed at me.

I looked at Tom. He was terrified. I could hear the cogs in his brain turning. He was wondering, 'Are we going to get the sack here?' The same thought crossed my mind. I decided to do it anyway. I figured, what a way to go.

Epilogue

The actor Peter Finch won an Oscar for *Network*, in which he played a newscaster who promised to die on air. Ideally, that's how I'd like to go. If I'm going to die some way short of my three score and ten, I'd like to bow out like Tommy Cooper did that night at Her Majesty's Theatre – live on air, maybe at full-time during a Six Nations broadcast, preferably after I've offered my analysis of the match and before Popey has given his.

If it doesn't happen that way, I'm going to have to contemplate retirement one day and, though I feel my career has only really just begun, that day isn't very far away. I have a date in my head. Ingrid will retire on 30 September 2008, and, if all those years of anxiety and gut-wrenching stress don't claim their forfeit before then, that will be my number too.

I don't want Ingrid sitting around at home for the last years of her marriage like she did for the first twenty-five. I'll pack in everything (well, almost everything) at that time – television, radio, newspapers – and I'll do it happily, knowing I made something of myself in the end. That it happened at a time of my life when I was approaching my dotage doesn't matter. Happiness, I've discovered, is measured not in years but in the intensity of the experience. My great hero Winston Churchill died knowing that it's what you do that's important, not how long you do it for. The only aspect of the timing that saddens me is that my mother and father didn't live to see me make a success of something.

I knew from the time I was a boy of seven, standing in the Mardyke, with my Heinz beans can on a stick, that I was cut out to be a broadcaster. A long time ago, back when we were still friends, Pat Campbell lent me his tape-recording machine, a big, old-fashioned contraption on which the tape ran between two large spools. I sat down with it one afternoon and recorded an entire sports show I'd written, featuring 'Eamon Andrews' on boxing, 'Raymond Glendenning' on horseracing and 'John Arlott' on cricket. I mimicked all their voices and individual broadcasting styles. When I played it back for a few friends, they were convinced they were listening to a real programme. I knew then that I had flair, though I never had the courage to do something about it.

But had my break come twenty years earlier, there are no guarantees that I'd have been able to do it. I wouldn't have had the life experience that has perhaps made me a more rounded person. If one wanted to set up a training course for a current-affairs broadcaster, to teach him compassion and empathy for the common man and his problems, then I can't think of any better way to prepare him than the life I lived after leaving Burroughs Machines. I know what it feels like to have no money, to be stuck in gridlock, to be depressed to the point that you don't want to see tomorrow. We're all familiar with the expression, 'a lived-in face'. I have a lived-in body. I can honestly say I've been there and done that.

And something else I've realized: all those years that I spent hiding from people weren't entirely wasted. When I wasn't racking up the mileage driving around the city, I was invariably sitting in a corner of some hotel with my nose stuck in a newspaper or a book. All that reading I did left me with a hard drive of knowledge in my head, so that I can engage my radio guests in intelligent conversation about the Marshall Plan or the foundation of the states of India and Pakistan, without reading a single note.

I've never been one to get bound up in what-ifs. Had I taken the McDonald's franchise, I'm sure I'd have become the first man in history to make a loss out of selling Big Macs. If I'd stuck it out with Campbell Catering, today I'd own 25 per cent of a company worth millions, but there's no way of knowing the ways in which success could have changed me. I might have got carried away with the money I was earning, started drinking, or run off with a woman half my age.

What I can say for certain is that when success finally arrived, I was psychologically ready for it.

While other men of my age are looking back over the span of their lives, pleased with what they've done and looking forward to retirement, I still have so much to do. Every contributory pension scheme and life insurance policy I ever had, I cashed in when times were hard. Recently, I started a new pension plan. Not many 63-year-olds do that. For the first time, I'm planning for my future.

I want to travel for the sake of travel, not escape. I want to go to America and tell Ingrid that I'm in America, not Killarney. Better still, I want Ingrid to come with me.

Sharing is a new experience for me. In marriage, I was a taker, never a giver. Now I look at the first thirty years of our married life as a training course. I graduated six years ago, with a bare pass. I'm still far from being a Grade-A student, but I'm improving. I'm madly in love with my wife and she's madly in love with me. The extraordinary thing is her forgiveness – that after all the miserable years to which I subjected her, she still wants to know me.

It's only now that the last vestiges of the low self-esteem and the sense of uselessness that I felt during most of my adult life have disappeared. I've discovered that all along I had courage; that there was a reason to be confident.

What makes life all the more enjoyable for me is that people are genuinely happy for me. People who used see my name appear in *Stubbs Gazette* and wonder why an amiable, outwardly self-assured man like me was making such a mess of his life now tell me that they're happy to see that I turned it round.

I'm asked quite often to speak at rugby-club dinners and, when I do, I make a point of never charging a penny, because rugby saved my life. When I stand up to address a room full of people, especially the ones we all blithely dismiss as 'blazers', I tell myself that, but for people like these, I wouldn't be alive today. Now it's payback time.

There is no pretence when I say that I feel like the luckiest man alive. When I see Brian O'Driscoll or Roy Keane or Pat Kenny signing autographs, I can understand it, but I still can't think why anybody would want my signature. Even so, I get something like a narcotic rush from giving it to people. At Thomond Park it takes me for ever to walk the 400 yards from the gantry to the exit. On Sunday mornings in Superquinn, Ingrid is invariably two aisles ahead of me while I've stopped to talk to some stranger who has said hello.

I can't understand why Greta Garbo wanted to be alone. I make no bones about it: I love the attention; even if people are telling me they thought I was wrong about something. It means they watch me, read me or listen to me.

My phone number is still in the book. On the night of the US election in 2004, I gave out my mobile number on the radio, in case anyone else who was glued to the count wanted to discuss the results as they came in.

'Are you mad?' Garrett screamed in my earpiece.

The phone didn't stop ringing all night. Unlike the old days, I answered it.

Acknowledgements

This book has been a painful labour of love. I have had to confront many of the demons of my past in an attempt to tell the whole story of George Hook. It could not have happened without the help and support of many people. Some were intimately involved in the production while others, by their friendship and backing, kept me afloat long enough to be in a position to have a life to write about. All of them have my grateful thanks.

When Michael McLoughlin of Penguin Ireland approached me about writing a book I must admit my reaction was one of total surprise that the publisher who had produced the distinctive paperbacks of my youth wanted my name on the cover of one of its books. Michael was not explicit about the kind of book he wanted, yet his confidence in my ability was crucial to a first-time author's decision to write 100,000 words when my previous forays into print had rarely exceeded 1,200. He had a belief that I could write a book to Penguin's exacting standards. I hope that his faith has been repaid.

Paul Kimmage once said that the secret of writing a book was to get a big advance and a tough editor. The first is a matter for my accountant, but Patricia Deevy of Penguin Ireland certainly had all the qualities required to edit this book. From the first day she kept me on an even keel and brooked no delays to the schedule. I am more grateful to Patricia than she knows.

The great change to my lifestyle has been the joy I get from my work. But radio during the week, rugby at the weekends and writing for the *Sunday Independent* has left me little free time. To write a book to the deadline demanded by Penguin Ireland looked an impossible task, until I discussed the problem with Paul Howard. His infectious enthusiasm for the project and his willingness to help was the single most important event in the genesis of this book. We spent hours in my kitchen as I talked into his recorder, sustained by chocolate Goldgrain biscuits and coffee. Paul brought the biscuits and I made the coffee! Paul faithfully transcribed hours of my memories, which saved me time and provided a template for me to tell my story. Paul never acted merely as a transcriber but constantly double-checked facts, times and dates. It has been a privilege to work with Paul, whose work ethic has me in awe and whose respect I hope I have earned.

My good friend Simon O'Leary knows me better than most and was a pillar of strength in the dark days. He offered to read the manuscript and his suggestions were always accurate and apt. He shares with Patricia and Paul the credit for the finished product.

The Presentation Brothers in Cork gave me the education to find my niche in life and Brother Athanasious, now retired in Cobh, was a wonderful example of the dedication of those men of the cloth. He gave me my first introduction to the wonders of rugby, Shakespeare and Caesar. I hope he enjoys the read.

On countless occasions Barry O'Brien of the Royal College of Surgeons was on hand to help me. All too often I let him down but he never held it against me and generously continued to be a vital support when all seemed lost.

The late Gerry Boyd features prominently in this book and his son Ian remains intimately involved with my family. He is solicitor to Ingrid and the children and he has inherited all his father's integrity and good humour. My family are in good hands.

Hopefully this book will be read in far-off America, where for almost a decade I attempted to rehabilitate my life. Jeff Hollings, Ron Mayes, Jay Fluck, Jim Mathias, John Connolly and Bob Hoder were, even by the standards of generosity associated with that country, truly outstanding. I will never forget them.

Famously, Groucho Marx refused to join any club that would have him as a member, which encouraged the belief that clubs were elitist. It ignored the friendships they fostered irrespective of class or creed. The members of Milltown Golf Club, Fitzwilliam Lawn Tennis Club and many rugby clubs treated me equally during periods of triumph and disaster. For that they have my admiration and gratitude.

Reputedly, behind every husband there is a surprised mother-in-law. I suspect that none can be more surprised than Ingrid's mother, Louise.

I want to acknowledge the support given to me by my wife Ingrid and children Michelle, George and Alison. Finally, they may have a husband and father.

The late Mick Doyle believed that an index to a book was a bad idea as people would merely flick through it to find their names and never buy if they were not listed. I have omitted far more people than I have mentioned simply because I have been lucky enough to have so many helping hands along the way. To everybody who helped me, please accept this as my thanks.

Index